IN QUEST OF BEAUTY

IN QUEST OF

BEAUTY

BY

Dom WILLIBRORD VERKADE, o.s.b.

Author of: "Yesterdays of An Artist-Monk"

Angelico Press

In Quest of Beauty is an authorized translation
of *Der Antrieb ins Volkommene*, by Dom Willibrord
Verkade, O.S.B. The original in German was published
in 1931 by Herder & Co., Freiburg in Breisgau.

This Angelico Press edition is a reprint of the work
originally published in 1935 by P.J. Kenedy & Sons.
Angelico Press, 2023

For information, address:
Angelico Press, Ltd.
169 Monitor St.
Brooklyn, NY 11222
www.angelicopress.com

ppb: 979-8-88677-054-4
cloth: 979-8-88677-055-1

Cover design by
Julian Kwasniewski

FOREWORD

THE fountain from which monasticism derives its never-failing charm rises in a hidden spring. Over the life of the monk there has been spread a veil of mystery such that the world has been led to wonder and ask: Whence comes the secret power of monachism, to hold multitudes in its thralldom and make it an unfailing source of astonishment to those outside the cloister? Monasticism does hold a secret, just as Christianity holds a secret. In fact, the secret of one is the secret of the other: it is the working of divine grace in chosen souls. And no matter how often and in what divers ways, whether by friends or enemies, the secret is publicly set forth, it remains a secret still and loses none of its esoteric power. When this secret is made personal and embodied in the life of an individual monk, especially one around whom the romance of artistic association and achievement has been woven, we are captivated by the story, as we are captivated by the *Apologia* of a Newman, or the *Confessions* of a St. Augustine. No two life-stories are identical; even the workings of divine grace show a wide diversification as they blend with the changing hues painted upon or woven into the life-pattern of a man.

In his volume published under the title, *Yesterdays of an Artist-Monk,* Dom Verkade revealed how he had wended his way to the door of the monastic enclosure. Beginning

[v]

with his life, first as an Oblate, then as a novice and finally as a monk and priest, he now gives us, with candor and evident honesty, the narrative of his spiritual progress, with all its difficulties and occasional set-backs to the point where he finds himself, in the twilight of life, able to grasp the whole as a marvellous instance of human struggle and divine goodness.

On occasions, the searing of the soul which goes along with the worthiness attained only by the abandonment of father and mother and of every worldly attachment reveals itself. Nor does he hide it. Christian perfection is not gained in a day. It admits of no compromise: "He who is not with Me, is against Me." The monastic life itself presented difficulties, so much so that he remarks, "Happy is he who has a ready-made interest such as mine was." For it is not easy for man to be interested in God alone. Yet this is the vocation of the monk, and the real meaning of his name. As artist, laboring in many countries; as monk, bound to the choral office and the enclosure; as priest, offering the Holy Sacrifice, he had and has a manifold interest and an experience as variegated as it is wide. His meetings with his family, with old friends, his work, studying, and painting, all mingle delicately with the real story he is telling, the story of the monastic life; not in theory, but as, under the rule of St. Benedict, it worked out with one who found it sincere, earnest, and truly evangelical, but nevertheless hard, stony, and sometimes apparently barren. Verkade leaves us with no delusions about the life of a monk; we soon see that monachism has no secret other

FOREWORD

than the actual living of the life which it professes in its rule, and that this contains a rare secret indeed, one which is not discovered by the reading of a book, but by the actual deeds of a busy religious life. The man in the world can gather consolation from such a life; for he finds the same struggle in himself and hopes for the same victory in the end. All holiness has kinship; one Lord and one God is over all.

I am happy to write this word of introduction to this setting forth of the monastic life. Certainly it will help to turn the sorrow of worldly despair into a hopeful joy; for in the inner kingdom of Christ, the plaintive note yields to the joyful song of him who has left all to follow the Master.

FRANCIS AUGUSTINE WALSH, O.S.B.

St. Anselm's Priory,
Washington, D.C.

CONTENTS

[ix]

IN QUEST OF BEAUTY

❦

CHAPTER ONE

OBLATE VERKADE

Over thirty years have passed since that momentous day when as a young man, full of budding life, I first sought admittance into the cloister of St. Martin at Beuron. The youth of twenty-five is now a white-haired monk, taking his place very near the head of the long procession of Fathers and Clerics as it files solemnly into church for the daily chanted Hours. To the wonder of all his old boon companions and fellow-artists, "Long Jan" of the Hattemer days and the "*Nabi obeliscale*" of Paris has persevered in his monastic calling, finding happiness and fruitful activity with the passage of the years in this state so strangely contrasting with his former one. The world is full of miracles!

And now I would write about those happy, fruitful years; for many who have read the account of my experiences up to my entrance into the cloister will be wondering just how far my rosy dreams were realised. Then too, I wish to do something to show my fervent gratitude for so many blessings received during this period of my life, which, though sometimes stormy, sometimes bringing many changes and disappointments, was on the whole so full of interesting activity upon a tranquil background that my heart thrills with joyful thanksgiving as I look back upon it.

So I applied for admission into the Beuron community; but the Archabbot, after listening to my plea, sent me down to the novice master's room for a further examination into my qualities. I remember knocking at his door and receiving no response; then after waiting some minutes in a state of breathless agitation, I perceived at the far end of the corridor a tall spare monk approaching, his head hidden in his hood and his hands folded beneath his scapular. It was Father Benedict Radziwill, of the noble house of that name, then novice master at Beuron. He told me to come into his room; I entered, and at once burst out: " Father Abbot sent me to you to ask what I must do in order to become a good novice." " Yes, so I have been told," was his reply. " I was with the Abbot a moment ago. And so you wish to enter our monastery? This is a happy surprise! " Then he asked me a number of questions about my nationality, my family and the life in Holland, my artistic career, my religious habits. But soon he perceived, from my account of my stay with the Franciscans at Fiesole, that I was already familiar with the requirements of monastic life, and broke off his questioning. However he told me that my clothing-day would have to be postponed quite some time, as I was still deficient in my knowledge of Latin, so necessary for one whose life is to revolve around the daily liturgical prayer of the Church.

Next day, Father Benedict came to my room to take away

my worldly valuables. It was customary, he said, for one
to give up these things on first entering the monastery. I
smiled, for all I had was a few hundred marks, some trifling
trinkets, and (to his surprise) no watch. True I had owned
one up to a short time previously, but had gotten used to
doing without it ever since depositing it *chez ma tante* — at
a Paris pawnbroker's. Eventually I got it back again, but
later when in Rome I gave it away for good, during the
Carnevale of 1893. My friend Ballin and I were merrily taking part in the innocent frolic of the streets, and some mas-
queraders led us to a dance-hall. Ballin soon got tired of this
sport and left, but I kept on hopping with the rest. Soon a
pretty *signorina* who was dancing with me, noticed me
glancing at my watch and exclaimed delightedly: " *Molto
bello:* how fine! Please let me see it," adding with true Italian naïveté: " Here, let me have it." Taking it off the chain
I handed it over to her: " Here you are," I said; and as the
dance ended just then, picked up my hat and went out,
leaving her still standing there and looking after me in
blank amazement. I seemed to feel a strange relief on getting rid of this expensive object. There are timepieces everywhere, I mused; so why carry one about? And indeed I
never felt the want of it afterwards, except when travelling,
and then only on awakening in the early mornings when I
wished to see how much time there was before I should
have to get up.

So I told Father Benedict I no longer had a watch, thus
making a good impression on him, as though I had already
begun the process of getting rid of all worldly possessions.

[3]

I did not like to tell him the watch episode however; though I might as well have, since he himself had had a great reputation as a reckless giver in his former days. They say that when he was still a secular priest, his valet used always to keep his extra clothing and shoes under lock and key, lest he give them to the first beggar coming along.

During the short interval when I was under the direct supervision of the novice master I spent my free time in diligently poring over a Latin grammar. Soon I was placed in the Oblates' school, a department wherein candidates with an artistic bent were trained in the principles of religious art along the lines laid down by Father Desiderius Lenz, well-known pioneer in this field. There were five of us in all, the other four all much younger than myself. We followed a quasi-monastic regimen of life, having our own superior (Father Wolfgang Schnell), and regular hours and duties. Designing and the Latin classics were our chief studies, and soon we were making rapid progress in both subjects, working together in one large room which was our sleeping quarters as well. We wore a black tunic exactly like that of the Beuron lay-brothers, except that we had a sash of cloth and they a leather girdle. I felt quite at home in my new garb, and was happy and proud to be allowed to go about the monastery in this unworldly attire. True, I was still deemed unworthy of the scapular, a garment reserved for the monks and full-fledged novices; but I was determined to prove myself fit for it by ardent study and work. Whenever another oblate or postulant was invested with it I always watched the ceremony with a kind of holy envy.

How lucky they were, at last to be admitted to this sacred state! Younger than myself by many years usually, they outstripped me in knowledge of the classics; and would later always have precedence over me even though I was older and had arrived in Beuron before them. Monastic ranking is always determined by the time elapsed since first taking vows.

So I began to assimilate the technique of Beuronese art, and became a willing disciple of Father Desiderius. His " canon " of measuring and dividing, his method of mathematical construction, appealed to me very much. But still I remained true to my old love, Giotto and his school; and always kept little reproductions of them on my rude table. And, now too, I began in earnest the work of my interior purification. Perhaps my new garb quickened in me the desire to allow nothing that was worldly to be harboured beneath it; at any rate, my zeal for self-reform became unbounded, and most unmercifully did I condemn and try forever to banish all vestiges of my former loose habits. My hatred of evil became so strong that it transferred itself even to the localities where once I had transgressed. I wanted to effect a complete break with all that had been before, and to live a life completely new, as if the past had never existed; and shrunk from no pain nor sacrifice in my attempt to cast off the old skin in which my ideal " new man " still found himself imprisoned. But of course I went too far: a reform so radical and complete must needs be slow and gradual, an organic process, whereas I wanted it to come all at once. Nature soon rebelled, and I began to suffer from severe headaches, and had to leave off some of my rigorous practices. Years later, when some critic of my work called me *un decorateur austere* I laughed, recalling this earlier period as the only one in my life wherein I could have been called austere with literal truth.

During this time too I was a severe trial to those about me. My extreme zeal could not adapt itself to the natural peculiarities of other people, especially to the apparent lack of seriousness in those younger than myself. And perhaps too the fact that I was so recent a convert made me somewhat intolerant; for as I have discovered since, new converts almost invariably distort and exaggerate everything they find in their new surroundings that does not measure up exactly to the ideals they have formed. Fresh from being enlightened and reformed themselves, they want to teach everybody else. My ears still burn with shame when I read the letters I wrote to my mother during this period: what a mixture of undigested principles and immature reflection! I should have remembered Verlaine's wise saying: *Faire bien obscurement son devoir et se taire:* " Do your duty in silence and obscurity," and the fact that " the just are radiant like the sun." Just to see them is enlightenment; their very existence, an inspiration to all. But I gradually learned to be patient and to adapt myself to those about me, especially when I began to see how I was becoming an object of irritation and torment to many truly earnest souls.

After some months of this sort of trial, I received my first assignment in my new role as a Beuronese artist. Father Desiderius who with several of the lay-brothers had been for some time working in Prague decorating the church of St. Gabriel's Abbey, a foundation of Benedictine nuns, needed help; another Oblate and myself together with one of the Fathers were commissioned to go. We left on August 8, and again I was in the " world " after being isolated from it completely for a year and a half. But nothing in it seemed attractive to me any more: I remember being particularly displeased by the loud talking of my fellow travellers. The monastery is above all a place of quiet, and of subdued voices; why people should have to shout and bawl to make themselves understood in conversation I could no longer fathom.

On arriving in Prague we first paid a visit to the Abbey of Emmaus, which had been, thanks to the generosity of Emperor Francis Joseph, the refuge of the Beuron community when driven from their home by the Prussian *Maigesetze* (May Edicts) of 1875, and after having spent their first four years of exile in the little Tyrolean village of Volders. The Abbot of this community was Dom Benedict Sauter, who had been the first novice to be received in Beuron under its founder, Abbot Maurus Wolter. He received us with paternal affection; and after having been given some refreshment we made the rounds of the monastery, inspecting with particular interest the church which had recently been decorated with much beauty and harmony of detail by Fathers Desiderius Lenz, Gabriel Wueger, and Luke Steiner, with the assistance of several lay-brothers. Many of the designs were reproductions of those at Monte Cassino, but some were new, such as the scenes from the

[7]

life of the Blessed Virgin, which have since become very well known.

After a few hours we repaired to St. Gabriel's, which is located near the *Weisser Berg* (White Mountain) in the suburb of Smichow. We received a hearty welcome from Father Desiderius and his co-workers, who were naturally glad to see the arrival of willing helpers; although their work was already well advanced, the ceiling and choir-arch being already finished. After having inspected everything and seeing what had still to be done, we were taken to our quarters, the so-called " Villa." This was a dilapidated, forlorn structure which adjoined the Abbey and had long been unoccupied. In fact it had been slated for demolition until the arrival of the artist-monks! But as the circumstances required our being housed in close proximity to our work, we did not mind; and it did not take long for Brother Xavier (my oblate companion from Beuron) and me to install ourselves in the dingy room assigned to us. Then we went down into the church for Vespers, sung by the nuns behind their grill next to the sanctuary. Though we could not see them, their voices were clearly audible; sweetly, joyously they sang, as from their very souls. It was most edifying and uplifting.

From that day on the beautiful chant of the nuns was our daily inspiration. Unable to interrupt our work during the frequent hours of divine service, we painted while they were singing High Mass or Vespers, or reciting the other parts of the Office. And sometimes, when we were perched high up on our scaffolding, we could just see into their hidden choir. What an impressive picture it was! The black-clad nuns in their brown choir-stalls, with their rosy faces enshrined in white neckcloths, and the rows of red-edged choir-books made an effective colour scheme, while the Lady Abbess sitting in a special chair at the head of the choir, with her daughters surrounding her like maids-in-waiting around their Queen, reminded us of the choir of virgins in the celestial court, singing the praises of the eternal Bridegroom.

One of my most consoling experiences as a religious has been the observation that so many fine and beautiful souls belong quite unreservedly to God. Truly, no one has ever been loved so deeply and completely as His Son; characters that are the very noblest in their aspirations and richest in natural endowments have so consistently and universally dedicated themselves to Him, that it is impossible to think of man's creation or Redemption as having been anything but the greatest success. And how Our Lord seems to rejoice over the chaste beauty of these chosen souls, refreshing Himself with their pure, simple love as man would do in drinking fine old wine!

My first work at St. Gabriel's was the humble task of scouring, smoothing down, or gilding the walls, or sometimes painting little ornamental details. Father Desiderius insisted on having everything done by hand, detesting anything stereotyped and artificial like the device of stencilling. He made his very best workmen do the most rudimentary things, holding to the principle that even the smallest details should bear the stamp of talent and good taste. " The artists of classic Greece," he used to tell us, "made all their ornaments and figures by hand, even those on the smallest vases." And the idea of saving time or money never seemed to enter his head. He once told us that it would be a sure sign that we were producing worth-while art, if the scaffolding commenced to wear out! "When the tyro thinks he has finished, then is the time when real work is just beginning," he used to say.

So I whitewashed and gilded many a wall, and lovingly painted countless ornaments, persuaded that no matter how meticulously I should work I was not wasting time. I was still a youngster, and therefore less conscious of time's passage; and I certainly wanted to learn everything from the ground up under Father Desiderius, whom I esteemed so highly. He in turn was pleased with my fidelity, and soon let me do some of the more important figures.

But now I began to be tortured with severe headaches again, the aftermath of my undue asceticism in Beuron. Constant fatigue assailed me too, and I began to worry about my fitness to enter the novitiate. I was now eligible, but dared not ask to be received as I feared a refusal because of my dubious health. But I gradually developed a firm trust in God, and my patience was rewarded when in the summer of 1896 the Archabbot wrote me saying that it had been decided that a group of postulants were to be taken into the novitiate, and that I was to be one of them. "For," he added somewhat humorously, "you are not getting any younger!"

Soon after this he arrived in Prague himself and sent for

me. All that I recall of this interview was his inquiry as to my financial status; for once a candidate is accepted by the monastery, his assets as well as his liabilities pass over to the corporate body. He assured me that even if I came empty-handed I would be accepted, which gave me great consolation. Then he gave me his paternal blessing, and also permission to go and visit my parents for a final farewell.

I set out for Holland almost at once; and on arriving at my old home, found a most cordial welcome awaiting me. Both my parents as well as the other members of the family had by now become reconciled to my having become a Catholic; but they could not get used to the idea of my becoming a monk. That was going too far, they said; it was a life so contrary to human nature. But their arguments moved me not at all. On the feast of St. Francis, October 4, I decided to tell them all my final decision to stay in Beuron forever as a monk. I chose this day because of the attraction I had always felt since my conversion for *Il Poverello*, recalling especially the difficulties he met with in his attempt to leave the world, and hoping thus for his special intercession in my cause.

The day was a Sunday. I came upon my father alone in his room, engaged in some drawing. " Father, I want to talk with you about a very important matter," I said. " I really want to stay in Beuron for good." He started, and looking sternly at me said: " You know my opinion on that subject. I cannot stop you, for you are of age; but if you think I shall give you so much as a penny you are sadly mistaken." Then I told him what the Abbot had said on this point. He seemed greatly puzzled, and turned to his work with an air of sorrow and perplexity, probably giving me up as a hopeless case.

I left to go to my room upstairs, but on the way met my mother, who had been hovering around anxiously as if she sensed something tragic. "Mother," I blurted out, "you have eight children. Do give one to God!" She burst into tears, murmuring, "God cannot ask that of me, not that!" "But Mother," I pleaded, "I shall be so happy." But she clung to me as though never to let me go. I struggled loose, begging her to let me be alone for awhile, the strain was too great. "I understand," was all she said, as she went quietly away. Then in the privacy of my own room my pent-up emotions released themselves in a torrent of sobs and tears. My love for my parents was very great, and I could not bear the thought of parting from them bearing the stigma of filial ingratitude, yet my resolve to enter Beuron was unshaken. I grew calm after a while, and in the evening went with my parents to a birthday party in honor of my sister-in-law in Zaandam. After the dinner my father delivered, as was his custom in these affairs, a "birthday speech," in which he contrived to present his point of view with regard to my departure. I was glad to see he had softened considerably since the morning; it was to be hoped, he said, that Jan would do nothing foolish, or follow strange, unheard-of paths. The natural thing would be (he continued) for him to stay with his twin-brother, or at least not far away from kith and kin. One's family circle, to which so much is owed, should be preferred to the homes of strangers to whom one

[12]

owes nothing. But there might be extraordinary circumstances allowing exceptions to be made, and after all, he said, he himself desired only the happiness of all his children.

After this my father made a few more attempts to deter me from my course, but when he saw I was a chip off the old block and as determined as himself, he finally capitulated. On looking back now, I realise more than I did then, what it must have cost my parents to allow me to go willingly. True, theirs was not that kind of parental affection which clings to the child as if coming-of-age were some kind of a calamity. But to break away from sacred family traditions, and for reasons that must have seemed obscure and fantastic in the light of inveterate Protestant principles, would have seemed to my parents as the blackest kind of treason were it not for the innate nobility and generosity of their hearts. My mother finally said to me: " Be happy, my dear child. That is my one desire for you, and even if we must be separated, I shall always live your life with you in spirit." My father even gave me money for a final visit to London, after I had hinted that I might never again have the chance to get acquainted with English culture and art.

So I crossed the Channel, and engaged at once with breathless interest in a study of British life, manners, historical and artistic treasures. All intrigued me intensely, though at the end I was not convinced that England was superior to the Continent from an artistic point of view. Her greatness lies, it seems to me, rather in the realm of imperial conquest and organisation by peaceful (if not always ethical) methods. And the sober conservatism of her citizens appealed to me very much, reminding me of what I had read of the *cives* of ancient Rome: the sense of human equality, the spirit of fair play and mutual respect, the abhorrence of all extremes in social and educational life, struck me as being a survival of classic culture which all the world should be grateful for.

Three incidents during my London stay remain still in my memory as being typical of the English character. I was living in Brockly, and used to take the train to the city every morning. One day it was very foggy, and the train had to stop repeatedly for " orders." In my compartment were eight or nine gentlemen, all faultlessly groomed and each one possessed of a carefully rolled-up umbrella and a huge newspaper. But only two or three were reading; the rest sat bolt upright, staring into space and striving mightily to seem indifferent. But finally the strain proved too much for one of them, who was manifestly a Jew. After about the sixth stop of the train he began to gnash his teeth and to lament loudly about the loss of time. Nobody paid him the slightest attention. " As soon as I can change to a subway I'll get out," he growled to the company in general, but no one ventured a reply. Finally we reached a subway station, and the poor man bounced out and banged the door behind him. Immediately the remainder of our group became animated, uniting in their expressions of disgust at a man who showed, so manifestly, his lack of self-control. Afterwards, two of them even went so far as to exchange a few sentences of polite conversation! But soon our company was as stonily silent as before, each one sitting there stiff, correct, dumb, motionless. We reached Charing Cross, and as we all got out I was dumbfounded to see each of my erstwhile companions break into an undignified trot, like so many long-confined greyhounds eager for the chase. Whereupon I, easygoing Hollander that I was, also had my laugh, being in no haste at all!

Another time as I was making my way to the British Museum, a tall, spare man, respectably dressed, brushed past me and without any warning whispered hoarsely into my right ear the words: "*Have you been saved?*" Then he hurried on without as much as another glance in my direction, as I stood there in blank amazement. Perhaps he belonged to the Salvation Army. At any rate, I could not help thinking that his message, uttered in this impressive manner to many an abandoned lonely soul among the crowds of London, may well have done much good. The "bill-poster" preaching one sees so much in England (sponsored chiefly by the Salvation Army) I approve of in principle, but rather than printing Biblical quotations (which ought to be held too sacred for this sort of thing) or the wishy-washy appeals one so frequently sees, I would suggest an advertisement like the following:

What are you, leader or corrupter?
Do you help, or do you pervert others?
Are you a trouble-maker, tale-bearer?
Is your tongue loose, forever wagging?
Are you just a time-server, heartless bureaucrat,

Or any other poor substitute for a MAN?
If so, BEWARE: your time is short,
The RECKONING will come!

Or a short message like this:

Why spoil your life, living like a beast?
Whither has flown your peace of mind?
How can you laugh, when your soul is so sorrowful?

Another illuminating episode happened one day as I was making my way to the South Kensington Museum. A youth who was pushing a cart along the cobble-stoned street, where I was passing, suddenly collapsed and fell headlong into the gutter. At once sympathetic people began to gather. Two young fellows stopped and raised the unconscious form to a sitting posture, rubbing the cold hands to stimulate circulation. A young girl with a face that reminded me of one of Rossetti's portraits came by, pushed her way to the stricken man and stroked his forehead and cheeks with an air of sublime compassion, then hurried on. Several other persons paused only long enough to see there was nothing for them to do, until finally two strapping bobbies arrived with a stretcher and carried the poor man to the nearest first-aid station. The whole thing vividly revealed a side of the English temperament which till then I had no idea of: solicitude for the unfortunate, at once tender and practical, and wholly without that mask of self-conscious reserve worn otherwise so habitually.

I returned at last to my parental home in Holland, and

in all too short a time received a letter from the Archabbot of Beuron, ordering me to return. But not directly to Beuron, for to my keen disappointment, my entrance into the novitiate had been postponed so that I could go back to Prague and help in putting finishing touches to the work there. But I resolved to obey without protest, though I tried to put off my departure as long as possible. This did not please my father, who always disapproved of giving in to mere sentimentality; and though he felt the pain of parting as much as my mother (she it was who kept urging me to stay longer), he told us that what had to be done should be gotten over with, and the sooner the better.

So the day of parting finally dawned. The evening before I had tried to say good-bye to my father who was not well, and I was to leave in the early morning. But he objected; he would see me off, he said. . . . Came the fateful moment when I had to leave my dear parental home perhaps forever. . . . Mother, who had been fluttering about looking after all my wants and trying bravely to keep back the tears, wanted me to eat a last snack before setting out on my long journey. " I cannot, Mother," I said brokenly. She gathered me into her arms, embracing and kissing me tenderly. . . . Father came. Looking at me searchingly, his eyes filled with tears, as he said with lips trembling: " *Dag* (good-bye) my Jan. May all go well with you! " Then he grasped my hand, shaking it violently. Another hasty kiss from mother and I tore myself away, hurrying from the house without once looking back. Mother called something after me, but I could not distinguish what she said. Ten minutes later I was in my train, utterly done up and upset. The sacrifice I was making seemed to suffuse my whole being with a bitter pain; and showed me that I was far more deeply rooted in my family environment than I had before realised.

And ever since this dark moment in my life I have been impressed with the close relationship which farewells always have with the so-called tragedies of life. Indeed, life itself may be said to be one continuous leave-taking. The days and hours come and go, the yearly seasons arrive and take their leave again. Joy and pleasure brighten us with their presence only to fade quickly away. Always something or someone claiming our adieus, until at the last we shall say a final farewell to all. And yet, how often these renunciations lead to higher things, bring us nobler possessions still. An indispensable condition, indeed, for human progress and growth: which by its very nature cannot remain stationary, but must go on, and up, and away from all that went before. " Wherefore shall a man leave father and mother and cleave unto his wife, and they shall be two in one flesh "; and from this renunciation and this union there springs new life. So too, he that leaves father and mother and his brethren, friends, relatives or worldly possessions for the sake of Christ has been promised a hundredfold in return, even in this life, and, afterwards, life eternal. What a thrilling prospect! Life eternal, permanent and unchanging bliss, knowing nought of abandonment, but only possession and fruition in holy love, without fear of parting, leave-taking, separation! Or as Ruysbroek expresses it, the " shining darkness " of the Deity, which in heaven will both sweetly satiate us and yet impel us forward in a blissful quest for treasures ever more sublime.

After several hours of travel I became much calmer and soon began to feel even a kind of quiet joy deep down in my soul. At last, I was free to carry out my cherished desire! With this thought my stomach began to grow clamorous; an excellent institution, I mused, which can make its demands felt under such trying conditions. So I made my way with alacrity to the dining-car; and mindful of the austere fare awaiting me at the convent in Prague, I ordered a beefsteak, rare, with all the trimmings. I ate ravenously, and when finished felt strong, brave, ready for anything. By Jove, thought I, this time I really shall make a go of it; at the worst, only a few months in Prague, where I'll have plenty of painting anyway; and then, to Beuron and the novitiate!

So I was not in the mood to get off my train for sightseeing, though I did stop over in Frankfurt for the night; on reaching Nuremberg next day, I could not resist the temptation to spend an hour in the Germanic Museum there. Early in the morning of the third day I arrived in Prague and went straight to St. Gabriels', where I took Father Desiderius completely by surprise, as he had long since given up all hopes of my return. My procrastination in Holland had led everybody to think I had weakened in my resolve; and Father Desiderius had, weeks before, set a certain date beyond which my arrival could not possibly be hoped for. That day had long since passed, and on it he had pronounced my obituary: "Since he has not come, we must believe that he has lost his vocation and will remain in the world." Which of course did not lessen one bit the joy of all my good brethren and fellow artists on seeing me again. I found them in our dingy old common-room, poring over their Latin as of yore. But a shock went through me as again I faced the dilapidated appointments of these quarters. One rickety chair for each of the five of us, an antique table in the centre of the room; no curtains on the windows, walls painted a dirty red and bare of other adornment, floor cracked and creaky, one miserable little bookshelf near the door. What a contrast between this and my parents' cosy home! "An awful hole," I said to myself. "But if I must camp here, I'll go through with it, in God's name and with His help; and it can't be for very long anyway." So after receiving a hearty welcome from all, and an explanation from Father Desiderius as to the progress of the painting since I had gone ("Oblate Xavier," said he, "has had a terrible tussle with the apse, but it is coming along nicely now."), I retired for a rest, being very tired from my long trip. As I lay upon my hard pallet, placed in a row with those of the other four oblates, I felt like a soldier in his barracks, but this time, please God, a soldier of Christ, under the blessed ægis of Saint Benedict, for the rest of my mortal life.

It is often interesting to find out under what conditions and surroundings artistic works have been produced. Only a small proportion of the masterpieces now adorning the churches, civic buildings, museums and private collections of Europe and America originated in well-fitted studios or richly appointed dwellings. Even the immortal Phidias did his work most likely in the open, just like the ordinary stone-cutters of his day; with nothing but a roof of boughs over his head, and standing upon a narrow scaffolding which scarcely allowed his stepping back and away from his work to see it in perspective. And we know that Michelangelo worked on the ceiling of the Sistine Chapel standing on a crude scaffolding covered with plaster drippings, the paint running from his brush down his hand and arm till he was literally lathered with it. The light must have been miserable, for the chapel has windows only on one side, and these must have been nearly covered by the scaffolding. The stupendous proportions of his Last Judgement probably obliged him to work in a two-story fashion, having to climb down ladders or stairs to get from one portion to another. The intervention of planks and poles probably prevented his viewing the work as a whole until the scaffolding was removed. Only one who is himself an artist can appreciate what the mere physical exertion must have meant to this aged master.

And it would indeed be interesting to know what sort of a den Van Gogh and Gauguin shared at Arles, while they painted so consummately each other's portraits; or under what difficult conditions the former produced his glorious landscapes. Knowing his habits, I can picture him at work, standing in a field, hatless (he always tore off his hat as soon as he began to paint) and unmindful of the burning sun. Gusts of wind threaten every moment to upset his flimsy easel, but he is oblivious of that too. Sometimes in his haste to capture an effect he presses the tube of paint directly into the canvas, then spreading the layer of color over the whole with his brush. He calculates most carefully the effect of each colour, for the sun is shining on his picture, and he knows from experience how different the effect will be when seen under a more subdued light. He keeps on daubing in a kind of agonised ecstasy, even though some urchins gather about and jeer at him. Soon he has finished his sketch, and flies home to complete the painting. Flinging easel and paint-box on a couch he stands his picture on a chair, studying it. " *Sapristi,*" he suddenly exclaims, " what did I do with that confounded brush and paint-box? Ah, here they are! " and forthwith he starts to change, re-touch, always dissatisfied and anxious. Suddenly Gauguin bursts in, looks at the picture, and cries: " Beautiful, magnificent! Don't touch it again, you pig; you're spoiling it! "

Sometimes art is practised, perforce, as a side-line, during snatches of leisure or while travelling. Thus, Goethe wrote from Naples to his friend Seidel in reference to his *Iphigenia:* " I wrote the first sketch during a recruiting trip, and completed it while travelling in Italy. How will it turn out, I wonder? " And so it is that every great book or painting or statue really has a history, and usually no dry prosaic one either.

During these days in Prague my thoughts travelled often back to my artist friends in Paris, now that I was once again associated with a group of collaborators in the production of a work whose perfection was the care of all. Even in Paris I had secretly longed to do something with a church

[22]

but of course it was not possible. Now at last my dream was being realised, and in how simple, how ideal a manner! In the meantime, what had become of Vuillard, Bonnard, Ranson, Sérusier? Maurice Denis had married, settled down, sold a few pictures: that I had heard; but of the others' fate I was in ignorance. So one day I sent Sérusier a long letter, taking care to explain at some length Father Desiderius' concept of art, and at the end inviting him to visit us in Prague. He answered in part: " Your letter was for me truly providential. It was a ray of consolation to a keenly suffering soul. I find the world a continual torment, yet I cannot leave it as you have done; and till your letter came I seemed to lack all power of resistance. In such moments we must look for peace and strength from those who so truly possess them as you do. What you say about art and Father Desiderius coincides exactly with what I have been thinking for a long time. The reconstruction of our basic ideas, in accordance with mathematical measurements and simple figures, is something that needs badly to be done, but a single person cannot do it alone. A group should do it, all collaborating in the making of joint experiments. Our old circle whose members I so pompously called *Nabis* might conceivably have achieved it, but we were all afflicted with too much sentimentalism, too much of that journalistic individualism which has shattered so many fine aspirations in the past."

And now it seemed that all the Nabis had been scattered to the four winds, each seeking his way alone; and consequently Sérusier, who had been the first to get them together in the *Atelier Jullian,* was suffering keenly from his solitude. But he, the *Nabi à la barbe rutilante* actually came to Prague upon my invitation, remaining several weeks and gathering a good deal of fresh inspiration and hope. His first-hand contact with Father Desiderius and our work evoked his heartiest approval, and he left breathing enthusiastic promises to promote our theory, saying that he would try to interest all the Nabis as well as other artists in Paris in the principle of " measuring and dividing."

Another joy that came to me in Prague was the news of the final return to the Catholic Church of the Danish poet, Johannes Joergensen. His spiritual Odyssey had already begun when I first met him in Copenhagen several years before. Tired and disillusioned with his empty quest for happiness in the worship of self and of material nature, he now was longing to return to the Church of his youth. But he lacked the courage to make certain sacrifices; while believing in God once more, he saw Him rather as the terrible Judge than as a loving Father. He seemed to dread too the stifling of his lyric powers, till now springing up from his subconscious self with such joyous, effortless abundance. What he had already gone through in the way of introspection and the setting-up of a system of ethics for himself now seemed to check the free flowing of his genius, and he feared to go any further . . . not realizing yet, of course, that one must " die to live anew ": what we have once attained, made part of us, is not lost but only chastened, mellowed by life's fiery trials.

So friend Ballin and I tried to help him as soon as we

sensed the nature of the crisis he was passing through. We managed to get him to agree to go abroad, thinking that if he would immerse himself in foreign, and especially Catholic, atmosphere his artistic sense would respond at once to the newer and finer impressions. At first he balked, saying he had no money; but Ballin (who always could manage the affairs of others more successfully than his own) held a successful benefit-lottery of paintings contributed by a number of our friends, and so the two of them started out (I having meanwhile departed for Beuron with the intention of remaining there) with Italy as their objective. Stopping first in Berlin and then in Nuremberg, they found themselves at odds: Ballin wanting to make straight for his dream-place of Assisi, and the other determined to taste more deeply of the sweet cup of German romanticism being offered him on every side. So they parted; and Joergensen sauntered on through the attractive countryside just as sweet fancy led him. It was a severe crisis for him, and he is undoubtedly referring to it when he says in one of his books: " the magic of German pantheism made his reeling soul long for the long bright evenings of his homeland, and for the pleasures of his misspent youth."

But he had promised to accept my invitation to visit me in Beuron, and finally one day (June 16, 1894), having first fortified himself for the ordeal with a good-sized *schnapps* at a nearby inn, knocked at the Abbey gates. I had told the guest-master to be on the lookout for him, and so was not surprised when the former told me with mischievous smile: " Your friend is here." Going down to the parlour I noticed at once that he was not himself, which filled me with a wicked glee as I felt it would soon pass over, and then, what fun I would have with him! But his perturbation was not all artificial, as I was soon to find out.

At dinner we sat together at the guest-table in the monastic refectory. My friend was seized with such a fright at seeing the long rows of black-hooded monks along the sides of the room that he could scarcely eat. And after having taken part in the usual post-prandial procession, in which the monks chant the psalm *Miserere* on their way to the church, we escaped to the guests' parlour, where my friend's first words were a kind of agonised cry: " This is simply awful! "

In the afternoon we took a stroll up the valley of the Danube to visit Father Desiderius' masterpiece, the St. Maurus Chapel. I cannot recall having said all that Joergensen quotes me as saying on this walk in his *La Livre de la Route,* but I am quite ready to believe it was all quite radical. After supper we walked about in the peaceful monastery garden, then went into church at the sound of the bell for Compline. Then we retired for the night, for though still very early, about eight thirty in the evening, the chanting of Compline marks the completion of the monk's day, and absolute silence must be observed. Joergensen (as he related to me next day) stood long before the opened window on reaching his room. He could see nothing, as a group of red chestnut trees was just outside. But through their leafy branches floated the soft voices of several villagers, while in the distance was the sound of children still happily at play. He sighed, longing for companionship, his far-away home in the north. Closing the window he prepared for bed, but his eyes fell on a copy of the *Imitation of Christ* which I had lent him. Opening it at random he read the words: "Leave all, and you will find God."

Next day I wakened him before daybreak, as it was Sunday and I wanted him to be ready to attend High Mass. When it was time I took him to a small secluded balcony in the church where he could watch unnoticed. He was visibly impressed, afterwards, but still seemed nervous and unhappy. After dinner he came to me in great agitation, saying that he had not the courage to remain another night, and must leave immediately. And so he did, going on foot to the nearest village on the road to Sigmaringen, Hausen-im-Tal, where he put up for the night. From here he wrote me a characteristic letter, thanking me for the " long, long time " he had been allowed to stay in the monastery, and describing his feelings during the walk to Hausen. He had taken his time, he said, and also a fitting amount of liquid refreshment in the first convenient nook he found. Then he had sated his gaze upon the blue mountains, the green fir-forests, the azure sky. How good it was to be alive, and how worthy of adoration was the Creator of all this beauty in the world! Nor was this exhilaration, he assured me, the effect of the wine, but rather of the sweet incense rising from the meadows, the soft chant of buzzing bees, the murmur of the placid Danube.

Another letter came two days later, thanking me for a book I had given him at our parting, and telling me that after having sated his soul without hindrance for two days in the charms of his surroundings, he had actually summoned up courage to pray the whole of Vespers and Compline in the evening, which made him calm and cheerful, and drove away all thoughts of melancholy. The depths of his soul were no longer blank, there was something solid and comforting there, for which he said, he remained indebted to Beuron and to me.

Continuing his way south he visited Lake Constance with its picturesque towns of Radolfzell and Ueberlingen, thence going on to Zurich and Lucerne. He was both charmed and enervated with all he saw. Beauty seemed to beset him on every side, and yet the deeper nobler longings that were stirring within him gave him no peace. And always there was that sinister desire to surrender to the charms of careless indolence, to give free rein to all the impulses of sense.

One evening, exactly a week after his departure from Beuron, there came the turning point in his great struggle. He was strolling in Lucerne along the banks of the Reuss at nightfall, wrestling with his thoughts. A black thunderstorm loomed up over Mount Pilatus, which seemed to symbolise the tempest gathering in his heart. He longed for peace, for respite from this conflict, when suddenly his ears caught the faint echoing of a strangely familiar song, the *Gloria Patri*. Turning he saw the open portals of a nearby church, the congregation inside worshipping on bended

knee, lighted candles on the altar. As if drawn by an unseen power he entered, knelt, made the sign of the cross,
and was filled with an overflowing joy. At the end of the
service he blessed himself with holy water as did the rest,
went home completely at peace with himself, and slept
soundly until morning.

From that time on he was a changed man. His attraction
for all that was good and noble grew steadily within him,
leading him more and more to seek the security of solitude,
away from the temptations of the world. He went on to
rejoin Ballin at Assisi, stopping en route to visit Rapallo
and Pistoia. In Assisi he would undoubtedly have made
his final peace with God, had it not been for the indiscreet
zeal of my good friend *Padre Felice,* who in his talks with
Joergensen failed to make the proper distinctions between
Catholic dogma and certain popular beliefs and legends.
But despite this set-back he was charmed with Assisi, which,
so redolent with the spirit of the Poverello, made a lasting
impression on him. The sincere piety of both Ballin and
the good Friar, who were his daily companions, showed
him a way into the mystic graces of the Church. On his
return to Copenhagen an experienced Jesuit Father gave
him what he still lacked: a lucid comprehension of the
body of Catholic dogma. So on Quinquagesima Sunday,
in the year 1896, he made his public profession of faith,
receiving back his lost " vision of things unseen," much
like the blind man whose miraculous healing is recounted
in the Gospel of that same Sunday.

It should be noted too that the conversions of Ballin and

Joergensen caused quite a stir in the wide circles in which they were known, and above all in Denmark. Both artist and poet had proved that one can be "cultured" or "modern" and at the same time devout, believing. Later they joined the Third Order of St. Francis, a world-wide association of devoted followers of the Poverello, and have since successfully worked to make the latter — so striking an example of warm-hearted, selfless Christian benevolence — known and imitated in their own rugged land. Joergensen especially has added to the stature of his genius since becoming a Catholic. Formerly his fame had been confined almost exclusively to Denmark, but now he began to be known and appreciated in all Europe and America. His former idols, self and the things of nature, suffered no great loss by being taken from their pedestals; for in all his subsequent works both the greatness of his mind and the beauties of the visible universe shine out clearly in all their native glory. But somehow, though he shows us still the same calm moonlit nights, silvery morning fogs, gorgeous sunsets, though he makes us hear the same sweet whispers of the evening breeze, the hum of insects and song of birds, though he paints for us the charms of violets and anemones with the same master-hand, it all rings differently than before. Doubtless because, as he would say, "the heavens and the earth show forth the glory of God . . . "; and "he that rejoiceth, let him rejoice only in the Lord."

CHAPTER TWO

IN THE NOVITIATE

AccORDING to St. Benedict's Rule, every monk must first
have passed through a full year of thorough testing in what
is called the novitiate, a kind of training camp wherein all
his future duties and sacrifices are explained to him, and he
is given chances to practise their fulfilment. Special emphasis is laid upon the necessity of seeking only God in the
monastic state, and not in any way oneself; while a true
predilection for the liturgical prayers and functions, and
love of obedience and humble self-denial must be shown by
every candidate. So during this year " all the hard and
rugged paths by which we walk to God," as the Rule says,
are carefully set before the novice; daily lectures and constant practical trials affording him ample opportunity for
understanding the manifold implications of the life he
would embrace. If successful in his probation the novice is
allowed at the end of the year to pronounce the three Benedictine vows of Stability, Conversion of Manners, and Obedience. Originally binding for life, these vows now, according to Canon Law, lapse at the end of three years, at which
time the candidate may either return to the world, or renew
his vows, this time forever. Thus each prospective monk has
a period of at least four years in which to consider his step.

Some religious orders in the Catholic Church organize

their several member-houses into a " province " with a common novitiate for this regional group. But it is not so with the Benedictine Order, wherein each full-fledged house is called an " Abbey " or paternal home (from the title " Abbot " or " Father " given to the head of the community) and is a self-contained, independent family unit. Though living in accordance with the same Rule, each Abbey will naturally develop its own traditions and characteristics, like families in the world; and, above all, will seek to rear and train its own spiritual offspring within the " family " precincts in preference to sending them away to some common novitiate removed from these special influences. And whereas certain modern requirements of administration have caused groups of Abbeys to join together in a form of confederation, each one still jealously preserves its traditional autonomy of rule as something essential to its very being.

The novice-master who is appointed by the Abbot to supervise directly the training of the candidates, should be, according to St. Benedict's stipulation, " a senior monk, who is skilled in gaining souls." At Beuron this official has a *zelator* to assist him, whose special task it is to acquaint each candidate with the practical details of the monastic routine and to note any breaches thereof. In addition, he is in charge of the daily manual labour of the novices, which may be either domestic tasks or working in the garden and fields. Ordinarily novices stand in great awe of this minor official, much the same as army recruits fear the top sergeant or sheep their menacing shepherd dog. But later on this fear turns into profound gratitude when once the vows are taken; for then the monk realises how precious this careful solicitude has been to him.

This system of monastic initiation is really constituted throughout upon teachings of the Gospel, interpreted and applied by means of St. Benedict's Rule; which in turn has been supplemented and clarified by a code of constitutions drawn up by each Abbey and having the approval of the Apostolic See. These constitutions are designed to serve the double purpose of providing for special needs of our times and of circumstances which may be peculiar to the Abbey, and at the same time of preserving intact the ancient spirit of the Rule. The same holds true, generally speaking, for other Orders in the Church; which explains why it is that after going through this stringent training, a " typical " Benedictine emerges from a Benedictine novitiate, a Dominican from a Dominican one, a Jesuit from a Jesuit one: an individual transformed and re-modelled, literally, so that he bears a stamp, a demeanour, even sometimes a facial expression peculiarly his own.

And fortunate indeed the religious community blessed with exceptionally good recruits. Often this seems to come as a reward for a specially high standard of regular observance. Strict discipline has, strangely enough, a strong power of attraction for all who are sincerely desirous of embracing the monastic state. In Beuron we have always seemed to have a good number of young candidates, save during the Great War period when all our novices were drafted to serve at the front. Then it was that our " family " noticed that something was sadly lacking, for the presence of youth can keep a monastery in good spirits just as it can the secular family. The fledglings are always a source of inspiration to the older ones, with their spontaneous efforts, their earnestness in conforming to that routine which has become as second nature to the " old-timers." And I have often heard young people — Boy Scouts especially — speak with enthusiasm of the life they observed when visiting Beuron. Once I popped this question to a youthful enthusiast: " But why then don't you join us, if you like so much our way of living? " To which he replied: " Only because I do not want to be so tied down." I could not keep back the rejoinder: " Liberty does not consist in being free to knock about."

It was in March 1897 that on my return from Prague, I was at last admitted to the novitiate. I was assigned a desk in the common-room, and an alcove, bed and washstand in the novices' dormitory. Already I had been wearing the tunic, but now I could wear the neat postulant's scapular with hood attached. I was officially given this habit one day, by the novice-master in a little ceremony in the Abbot's chapel. Next I received in accordance with Beuron custom a complete shaving of head and beard, after which I was conducted to the Archabbot who said laughingly: " Well well, now you *are* a different man! Your beard made you look so unkempt, you know. And now Father Magister (this is the novice-master's title in Beuron) see if you can make a good monk out of him! " Then he gave us his blessing and his ring to kiss, and I was led back to the novitiate quarters. The novices all stared at me as if I were a stranger; but

IN THE NOVITIATE

Father Magister only said: " Congratulate him! " Congratulate whom, and for what? was their first reaction, until they suddenly penetrated my transformation, at which there was great hilarity. I was now called Frater Verkade, to distinguish my new status from that of the former Oblate Johannes; but only for a few days, until my official investiture with the monastic habit by the Archabbot and my reception of a permanent name in religion.

This function, common to all religious orders, denotes the beginning of the canonical year of novitiate; and at Beuron is attended with great solemnity. Our ceremony proceeds as follows:

The postulant prostrates himself on the ground, and is asked by the Abbot: " What seekest thou? " The reply is: " The mercy of God, and fraternal communion with thee." The Abbot bids him rise, saying: " May God grant thee society with the elect." He then briefly describes to the postulant the difficulties of the monastic state. The latter promises to comply with all its demands depending on God's mercy and not upon his own strength. The Abbot then says, " May God perfect what He has begun in thee," girds himself with a linen cloth and proceeds to wash the novice's feet, a beautiful ceremony modelled upon the liturgical one of Maundy Thursday. Two choir-groups meanwhile chant appropriate antiphons. Then each member of the community approaches and kisses the novice's feet, to signify the ideal of brotherly love which should inspire each member of the community. During this the Abbot prays that God may grant to all the tears of love that Mary Magdalen shed as she washed the feet of the Saviour, and that this prayerful act may have a fragrance like to that which came from the precious ointments she used in her act of humble love.

Then the novice is invested with the habit. First the tunic, the Abbot reciting the prayer: "May the Lord clothe thee with the new man, created unto the likeness of God in justice, and in the holiness of truth." Then the leather girdle, with the words: "May justice gird thy loins, whilst thou remember that another is to gird thee, and lead thee whither thou willest not." Finally the scapular is placed over the shoulders of the novice with the words: "Receive thou the yoke of our Lord Jesus Christ and carry His burden, for it is sweet and light." Then follows another prayer in which the Abbot implores God's favor and the grace of perseverance on behalf of the novice, after which the latter is given a new patron saint, whose name he is henceforth to bear; and the ceremony of official reception is concluded. In my case the name of Willibrord was chosen, probably because St. Willibrord had been for centuries the patron of Holland, having been the first bishop of Utrecht (d. 739 A.D.).

Soon after my reception a change of novice-masters was effected, which proved most fortunate for me. Father Benedict Radziwill was sent to our foundation in Portugal to act as Prior, and in his place Archabbot Placid appointed Father Ambrose Kienle, till then librarian and master of the choir; and as he had pronounced artistic leanings, we got along admirably together. He was one of those rare characters in whom fine perception of ideal values is combined with a true universality of interest: a combination which in the end rests, I think, upon æsthetic rather than intellectual gifts. And surely no other master could have been better suited to prepare me for the taking of my vows. Indeed, he succeeded in impressing all the novices with the grand beauty of Benedictine life. Not much of an orator (perhaps because he was too brilliant a singer), he would often seem unable to frame suitable words while addressing us; but this was so clearly the result of his emotional fire that it heightened rather than detracted from the power of his message. Sometimes when addressing us on a solemn feast day he would halt and stammer, as though his subject were bordering on the unutterable, the absolute.

In addition, Father Ambrose was an uncompromising champion of the traditional choral or liturgical singing which Pope Pius X had recently revived in the Church; and his frequently belligerent attitude on this point endeared him even more to his youthful disciples. Youth is ever ready for battle! He was also a great lover of Benedictine history, thereby setting us another high example of monastic perfection, for our Order has always shown a special predilection for historical studies. Nor would he ever allow any of us to be idle for a moment, if he could help it; he spared us no hardships, which he regarded as an essential part of our training. During harvest time he would always set the pace of our work in the fields; and on our frequent walks and climbs he seemed positively indefatigable. True, he would sometimes be heard to murmur: " We are so very, very tired "; but I knew him better than to have compassion on him. Always shall I remain deeply grateful to that high-minded man who for a whole year, preparing me for my profession, gave so munificently from his rich store of experience and knowledge. Some part of him, I love to think, lives on in these pages.

The good recruit has pleasure in standing at attention, presenting arms, saluting, marching on parade. Then he feels he is truly a soldier. So also does the novice love all those little details of regular routine which is the outward framework of conventual life. Whether it be in walking to choir or to meals, bowing to his superiors and fellow monks, observing the restrictions as to talking and laughing, he is made conscious in these and a thousand other ways of the nature of his calling. He is taught, of course, to regard them with an eye of faith, and never to lose sight of St. Benedict's admonition: " Let him (the monk) consider that he is always beheld from heaven by God, and that his actions are everywhere seen by the eye of the Divine Majesty, and are every hour reported to Him by His angels " (Rule, Ch. 7). Thus the danger of mere formalism is provided against; and habits of restraint and reverence are developed which, later on, when long custom tends to dim one's spiritual awareness, aid materially in evoking that realisation of the Divine Presence which is the very *ethos* of the monastic state.

I must confess that I have never attained to that high degree of exterior regularity that distinguished many of my confrères. Perhaps because I could never quite shake off my easy-going Dutch ways and my congenital dislike for formality. But I have never lost my love for all our monastic observances, which, in the springtime of my religious life, was so well implanted in me.

What a heavenly life it was for me in the beginning! The novitiate is indeed a little Paradise, as any monk will tell you. There are tribulations, of course, but only enough to accentuate the many pure joys and consolations which like sunshine can only be appreciated if there are times of fog and darkness. But especially blessed was it in my case, as it meant release from a long and troublesome servitude: the slavery of art, the cares and incessant distractions of the world. My daily nourishment was the choicest of spiritual viands, as well as excellent if homely bodily fare. Twice a week there were long rambles in the deep fir forests that surround Beuron. Every night, sound and refreshing sleep, albeit not long. Above all, there was that serene, unruffled peace which comes with close intimacy with God.

In particular, my mind was absorbed during these blissful days in contemplating the Scriptural truths so beautifully set forth in the daily Liturgy (Holy Mass and the Divine Office) and in the Rule, which I supplemented privately by reading the Bible from beginning to end during my first novitiate year. In addition I would often delve into the *Psallite Sapienter*, Archabbot Maurus' famous commentary on the Psalms, and into the *Lives of the Fathers of the Desert*, a book which exhales a most delicious fragrance of piety in spite of what it may be said to lack from a standpoint of historical criticism. Other books which benefited me greatly were the *Soliloquies* and the *Meditations* of St. Augustine, and St. Gertrude's *Herald of Divine Love*. St. John Climacus' *Ladder of Perfection,* an exceedingly austere treatise, almost proved my undoing: it made me melancholy over my many imperfections, and impelled me to impose upon myself a rigorous penitential fast, the chief result of which consisted in making me so hungry that I would think of nothing else than eating during the whole day! But a wise retreat-master led me back to sanity in time; and another book, Father Beda Weber's *Life of Giovanna della Croce* proved an ideal counterpoise in its attractive picture of the sweetness of spiritual consolations. Books like this that appeal more to the affections than to the will have a decided importance in the formation of a soul, for often the spontaneous zeal thus evoked will lead it to union with God more quickly than planned systems and methods. One may skip over a few steps generally required by the latter, and be guided only by intense and pure longings for the bounties of heaven. Such a soul is like a young sparrow recklessly gorging itself in a tree of luscious cherries, conscious of neither fear nor reproach. The richness and variety of divine grace utterly captivates him, fills him with spontaneous desire that compels as it were the affluence of God to satiate him. Certainly God seems to deal in some such way with the budding novice whom He first intoxicates with rapturous delights. But soon enough, the " sparrow " must be chased away from his too-easily-acquired treasure; and there comes a time when God seems to say to the soul: " Now run along, young fellow, and dig up something for yourself." My novice-master in fact told me something of the sort when he heard of my spiritual intoxication. I became

[40]

IN THE NOVITIATE

" weaned," but not before I had had my fill of sweetness, which still retains its after-taste in my soul, even though I now look upon that period in my life as one of sheer spiritual gluttony. Nor do I wish to recommend my experience for the emulation of anyone else: God has His own way of dealing with each individual soul, and what seems good for one may very well turn out to be poison for another unless He Himself proffers it.

Nor would I convey the impression here that the novitiate is always a kind of cloudless Eden. There were for instance severe physical burdens which, in my case, weighed most heavily at times, such as the frequent turns at manual labor, and always the daily long hours in choir. I was often tired and listless in spite of myself during the latter, and would have trouble in keeping up with the spirited tempo of the recitation. One Sunday evening after a particularly trying " bout " of this kind I took refuge after choir in an empty room just off our novitiate common-room, to regain my breath and compose myself a bit. But Father Magister discovered me, as the other novices were all at their desks dutifully working. He was very indignant, and next day gave me a public scolding at his conference.

Then there were events that made us sad, like the time when one of our number suddenly packed up and left. None of us had any inkling of what was to happen until one day after High Mass, Father Magister explained the absence of our beloved brother thus succinctly: " Frater X has gone from us today. Pray hard for him; it was not easy for him to leave us but it had to be." And then the thought came to me, as I recalled the seemingly good qualifications of this young man: " Merciful heavens, what would happen to me if I had to do *that!* " And for quite some days I was troubled with this thought, until a wise word from Father Magister put an end to my fears.

Joys and sorrows of the novitiate year, how shall I narrate them all! All too quickly came the end of this blessed period, but with a compensation in the joyful announcement that came to me at last: " Frater Willibrord, you will be allowed to make your vows! "

In the monk's life, profession day resembles in its joys and blissful hopes the wedding day of people in the world. And rightly so, for it marks the beginning of a life intimately united with God, inseparably bound up with the interests and service of God and not of self. The soul is then filled with warmest gratitude for having been called to so sacred a union, in spite of having so poorly merited it. An indescribable happiness floods its depths, a joy and peace unmixed with aught of earth sweeps it through and through as though it were already in heaven itself.

The ceremony of profession is one which never fails to impress profoundly all who witness it. Presiding at our function was the venerable Archabbot Placid, now over seventy years of age. He celebrated Pontifical High Mass (it was likewise the Feast of St. Benedict, March 21, 1898), during which, after the *credo* had been sung, the entire community filed out of their choir-stalls to form a semi-circle around the high altar with the aged prelate seated in the center. Then we candidates were conducted *ad altare Dei:* " to the altar of God," much in the same manner as little children who are about to make their First Holy Communion. Unlike them however we were not clothed in white garments to signify the innocence of childhood, but our hearts were truly as pure and bright as new linen bleached in the soft air of spring. . . .

The ceremony was conducted in this wise:

Archabbot (to each candidate separately):

" Wilt thou renounce the world and all its pomps?

" Wilt thou undertake the conversion of thy manners, placing the love of Christ above that of all creatures?

" Wilt thou promise Obedience according to the Rule of our holy father St. Benedict, renouncing thine own will?

" Art thou resolved to persevere in this holy Order to which now thou seekest entry? "

To each question, the candidate answers:

" I do so will, and so desire."

Then follow several beautiful prayers read by the Archabbot, invoking God's blessing upon these several promises; after which each candidate in turn makes his actual profession, reading aloud the special formula required by the Constitutions, and which he has written out with his own hand previously. Mine follows:

" In the Name of our Lord Jesus Christ, amen. In the Year of our Lord 1898, March the twenty-first, I Frater Willibrord, of Zaandam in the diocese of Haarlem, do solemnly promise Stability, the Conversion of my Manners, and Obedience according to the Rule of our holy father St. Benedict

and the Constitutions approved by the Holy See for this venerable monastery of St. Martin in Beuron of the Bouronese Congregation, before God, and His Saints whose relics are here kept, in the presence of the Right Reverend Lord Placid Wolter, Archabbot of the aforesaid monastery, and of all the monks of the same. In testimony whereof I have written with my own hand this petition, on the aforesaid day and date."

Then the candidate placed his document on the altar table; after each had finished this ceremony, the entire group of novices sang with eyes uplifted, arms outstretched, this antiphon (thrice repeated, each time on a higher note):

" Uphold me, O Lord, according to thy word, and I shall live."

Then kneeling, with heads bowed profoundly, they continued:

" And let me not be confounded in mine expectation."

This climax of the profession ceremony, so simple yet so profoundly impressive, has remained one of my most cherished memories, and never fails to bring tears to my eyes when I see it repeated. For it expresses, in majestic tone and cadence, all the holy longings and dedications of a pure soul casting itself into the arms of God, forever. . . . I sigh with a heart that is heavy, thinking of how I have fallen short of the promise of that day. In spite of good will, my weakness and perversity have caused others pain, harm to myself. O Lord, shelter me again beneath the shadow of Thy wings, faithless as I am. Take me and protect me against my very self, and let nothing separate me from Thee again. Let me truly *live,* which is to live in Thee, upon Thee and with Thee; for away from Thee there is but famine in the midst of fancied plenty, waste and squandering in spite of feverish human husbanding. . . .

Then, after some further prayers recited by the Arch-abbot, we were invested with the monastic scapular and cowl, which latter is an ample, flowing mantle with wide long-hanging sleeves. This garment gives the monk a very stately appearance, but rightly so as it is his official garb when chanting God's praises in choir, and when he is finally laid to rest. Incidentally, it has its practical advantages, being an effective protection against the cold and damp which so often invade the monastic church in winter.

Next came the beautiful ceremony wherein we were officially greeted as members of the monastic community. In turn we were taken to the Abbot and to each monk to receive the kiss of peace, and to kiss the hand of each in return, saying: "Pray for me, Father (or Frater)," the latter responding: "May it be to your salvation." During this engaging little function I remember that my face was wreathed in smiles, and I was so full of joy at being now a member of the monastic family that I gave no thought at all to the absence of my own blood relatives.

After this we all lay prostrate on the floor of the sanctuary and were covered with a black cloth, to represent the

" death " to the world, which we were now beholden to seek. Meanwhile the choir sang the glorious Offertory verse:

Desiderium animae ejus tri-buisti ei, Domine; et volun-tate labiorum ejus non frau-dasti eum: posuisti in capite ejus coronam de lapide pre-tioso.	Thou has given him his heart's desire, O Lord; and has not withholden from him the desire of his lips. Thou hast set upon his head a crown of precious stones.

No other words could have expressed more perfectly the holy joy and gratitude that filled my heart. I had yet to merit the crown of victory, but dared hope that some day it would be mine. At the end of the chant, the deacon bade us rise, saying:

> " *Arise, thou who sleepest: arise from death,*
> *And Christ shall give thee light."*

Then the Mass was continued, and we finally were privileged to receive our divine Spouse in person, coming to us in the sacramental form of Holy Communion.

At the festal dinner afterwards, we sat at the Archabbot's own table, though still obliged to wear (for three days constantly) our cowl and hood, in token of our new state. After Vespers in the afternoon a solemn *Te Deum* was sung, during which we newly-professed knelt in the middle of the choir; and thus the festivity was brought to a fitting close.

So at last I was consecrated to God and to His special

service, occupying a rightful place in the ranks of those who perform in the name of Christ's Bride, the Church, the function of praise and thanks that is His due. At the same time I was called upon now to be more truly than before a " branch of the Vine " and to bear fruit in kind. Christ's own life was to be mirrored in my own, to overcome all that was alien in me, to refashion my very being.

What a sublime aspiration! And yet, never must I forget that its realisation is to be *His* work, not mine. . . . Man's voyage through life often resembles that of an ultra-modern ocean liner which in spite of its magnificent construction and careful handling meets with disaster through some uncontrollable elemental force, or some undetected structural flaw. We plot our course, we take account of dangers to be met, and still fail to reach our goal. Even the animals, despite their marvellous instincts, often fail rightly to direct their strivings. The imprisoned bee tries vainly to fly through a window-pane: spent, it finally falls to the floor and dies, while nearby there was all the time that easy passage into the open. A beetle will stop, hesitate, turn aside or retreat entirely often just when it is about to reach its obvious goal. And worms and snails will stubbornly try to cross the open road or street, only to be crushed by passers-by, or smothered in what to them can only be an arid waste. So too we mortals are ineffectual, insufficient unto ourselves, above all when striving for our eternal goal. Splendidly equipped we may be, like a super-liner; or endowed with keen intellectual gifts that for directive purposes seem far to surpass the mysterious instinctive qualities of the animal. And yet, we go astray:

[47]

we founder in the sudden storm, we swerve aside to follow stubbornly some dangerous bypath. How supremely confident we are in our own powers, how seductive the promptings of our Enemy! And when God tries gently to deliver us, to set us back on the right road to freedom, how we protest and struggle!

What is important for us to remember is I think, this fact: Even though we *know* our goal, we do not always *see* it. On great days of our life or in exceptional crises it appears plainly before us, like a landscape illumined by a lightning flash at night, or like a mountain-top suddenly revealing itself from out its veil of fog. At such moments an overpowering emotion seizes us, and mindful of the rough and dangerous paths we have already traversed and still must traverse, we cry out from our soul's depths: " *Adjuva Domine,* help me, O Lord! "

After my profession, more time was allowed for me to paint, as during the novitiate no one is allowed to be absent from the regular Office unless for a very serious reason. Some months before I had been commissioned by Father Archabbot to carry out (with the help of two other novices) a sketch Father Desiderius had made for the vestibule of our refectory. It had been slow work indeed; but now we began to make real progress. Sometimes I wondered, though, whether I was to be allowed to aspire to the priesthood, as no word had yet been vouchsafed me about the study of theology. Perhaps, I thought, I was going to be like Father Desiderius, who was only a subdeacon; and certainly at that time, I felt no pronounced call to the priestly state. So I was quite content: "If I only am allowed to sing the Office and then daub away, everything will be all right," I thought to myself.

But one fine day in October of that year, I was told to enter the clericate, where the newly-professed monks are taught the various branches required by Canon Law for priestly candidates. Vacation time was over, and the group of us was told to assemble in the conference hall to hear the reading of next term's curriculum. Not certain as to whether I was expected to attend, I inquired of Father Prior and received the answer, "No." So I climbed up into my scaffolding in the vestibule and began to paint away, the meeting going on meanwhile. When it was over some of my fellows passed by and announced jovially: "*You* are to enter the course of dogmatic theology!" But I was not conscious of any supreme elation at the news, though I felt relief at being rid of uncertainty as to my future duties. "So I am to study after all," I mused; "Very well: *Deo Gratias!*" and then went on with my painting. . . .

Chapter Three

IN THE CLERICATE

THE clericate is a far different world from that of the novitiate. Having passed through the first stages of probation, one feels more at his ease, and is no longer conscious of being continually under observation. There is no longer an ubiquitous *zelator* from whose appraising glance one would like to hide. Laughter and conversation become less restrained, poise and self-possession return. One is now a full-fledged member of the family, and soon ripens into the maturity of the true monk. Tonsure and Minor Orders are soon to come, and in the distance looms the great dignity of ordination to the holy priesthood. Indeed, it all seems so impressive and grand at first that one's head could easily be turned, and periodic admonitions from the superior are needed to keep youthful enthusiasm within proper bounds.

Our prefect in the clericate was Father Gregory Molitor (who died in 1926), a very learned man and a capable musician. As our group was fairly large and as Father Gregory was at that time busy with the building of a new organ in the church, an assistant was assigned him in the person of Father Fidelis von Stotzingen, who later became Abbot of Maria Laach and afterwards Primate of the Benedictine Order with residence in Rome.

[50]

IN THE CLERICATE

And now at last, I was given a cell of my own. It was not a pretentious one, being only twelve feet square. But at that it was much bigger than many of the cells used by the medieval monks, as for example those still preserved in the Dominican Convent of San Marco in Florence which have been immortalized by Fra Angelico's paintings. And how I learned to love my cell! Nor has that love ever cooled; for though I have occupied perhaps ten different cells during the thirty years of my monastic life, each one is still dear to me, like a most cherished friend. *Cella coelum:* " the cell is heaven," as runs an ancient monastic saying. What makes it such a little paradise?

Doubtless the peace that reigns there, the serenity it seems to exhale especially at night. Its sanctity is jealously guarded by the Rule, so that no outer distractions are allowed to enter. Inside it, one is supremely alone; only God and four silent walls are his observers. In so unprofaned a sanctum one dwells as in a consecrated shrine, its atmosphere redolent of the peaceful courts of heaven. True, it is at times the scene of bitter struggles, when the monk's soul is torn with contending feelings. Bitterness assails him, a half-stifled sob of anguish is audible. But these storms quickly pass, and once again the monk's cell assumes its air of blissful serenity, where all passion and human contention is buried as in a tomb.

The study of theology proved a great stimulus to my spiritual development. Not only did my faith become more profound and more solidly established, but my intellect was enabled gradually to penetrate into regions hitherto closed to me. My early schooling had had only " practical " ends in view, and now it was being broadened and completed in a most happy manner. True, the practice of art is an education in itself, and most great painters are in a sense, philosophers. But usually the artist lacks the ability to reason in a systematic manner; and this cannot be supplied by mere intuition or talent, however abounding.

I was allowed to keep on with my painting the vestibule of the refectory, and when that was finished, I was asked to carry out a pictorial design on the exterior wall over the entrance to the church. Several of us occupied our leisure moments with this for about a year; and although now (1928) the elements have nearly obliterated our painstaking frescoes, I for my part feel that it was not a wasted effort as it gave me wholesome diversion, good experience, and a chance to " let off steam " during this transitional period of my life.

That same year (1899) I was appointed House-inspector, which meant that I had to keep tabs on the conditions of the physical fabric of the monastery. I had as my assistant a very saintly lay-brother, Brother Felix, whose name is still revered among us (he died in 1925). A strong man, apparently requiring hardly any sleep, he had the duty of nursing the sick in addition to his household tasks. The Capuchin saint, Felix of Cantilice, was his patron, and in a most literal sense; for the former's custom of giving thanks to God for anything and everything he imitated to perfection, and the words *Deo gratias* were continually on his lips. His fellow lay-brother dubbed him " our holy father " rather jocosely, on account of the household keys which he always carried about (and frequently made use of for the benefit of his patients), which made him a kind of walking symbol of the powers proper to the See of Peter.

Brother Felix and I began our task with gusto, and before long had sawed up into handy pieces of firewood a whole collection of antique furniture that was cluttering up the attic. Some of the brethren protested vehemently when they heard of this radical proceeding, but to no avail, as I had the Abbot on my side. As a result, we had enough fuel to keep two stoves going the entire winter!

A weakness common to all of us is an unwillingness to part with little keepsakes accumulated from the past. Such treasures as old letters, our first artistic attempts, or other relics which may still serve some useful purpose. But usually it all amounts to only a pack of rubbish which our " heirs and assignees " will promptly get rid of when we die. And God bless them for it. God knows the tortures I have suffered when, chancing upon a pile of dust-laden sketches and cartoons long forgotten, I was forced to live through again all the mental struggles that gave them birth. No wonder that so few of the great masters' original designs have been preserved: they represent all too plainly the wear and tear of creative effort, as worn-out clothing does the stress of life.

By the country roadside or in a forest thicket we sometimes come upon a cast-off pair of shoes, a torn jacket, a shoddy pair of trousers. They always move me with a peculiar mixture of awe and pity, as I try to imagine who

[53]

were their last wearers, and what scenes of strife they have
mutely witnessed. Similar emotions grip me sometimes
when looking over the forlorn relics of the past in a second
hand shop. Though truth to tell, these places have afforded
me many an artistic thrill, in paintings I have discovered in
their dingy recesses. Almost always these crude efforts are
notable for their buoyant *naïveté,* in which respect they
surpass the work of many a master who has been unable to
free himself from inveterate routine. All in all, I have a
profound respect for keepers of second-hand shops, who at
the worst are true lovers of the past, and often save from
destruction priceless things. And I have an affection too for
the itinerant junk-dealer, that curious figure who haunts the
streets of a great city garbed like a scarecrow, and with
apparently nothing but contempt for his more respectable
fellow beings. His peculiar cry always fills me with a sense
of mystery, a feeling that historic glories are being in part
at least retrieved, and preserved for some unknown moment
in the future when they will burst forth again in all their
brilliance.

Our souls too are like these second-hand shops, since they
are always hoarding up old memories and impressions.
Much of this is of course valuable, but much too is a cause
for sorrow or even does us harm. Unaided by divine grace,
it is next to impossible for the soul to rid itself of these
accumulations of rubbish; and perhaps that is why Mother
Church is continually praying (especially in her Advent
liturgy) that we may be enabled to " renovate " ourselves
spiritually; to " purge out the old leaven," or to " put off

[54]

the old man " in exchange for the " new man " of justice and of truth.

In February, 1900, I became ill with influenza, and for two weeks Brother Felix was able to turn the tables on me and make me follow his orders. The Kneipp cold-water cure was then highly thought of in Beuron, and several times a day my good assistant visited the infirmary to give me an icy bath. It was not a very pleasant experience, yet there were compensations. Adjoining our sick-bay was a chapel, so that every morning we patients could hear Holy Mass from our beds, and receive Holy Communion. And then, the kitchen served us its choicest viands, our brethren came often to pay us visits; and every evening the Archabbot or the Prior would come to see how we were progressing, and to impart his paternal benediction. Indeed it is almost a pleasure to be ill in a Benedictine monastery, for then one becomes the center of a universal effort on the part of all to carry out that portion of the Rule which says; " Before everything let care to be taken of the sick, and let them be served in every need as Christ Himself, since He has said: ' Whatever you have done unto the least of these, you have done unto Me.' " And undoubtedly, sickness is to be looked upon as a valuable element in the monk's spiritual formation. Sometimes it serves as relaxing check in his overzealous activities, sometimes perhaps as a warning, a kind of rehearsal for that hour when he must bid farewell to earth. Taken away from everyday life, rendered helpless, miserable, he seems to hear God saying: " Are you ready now, will you be ready when My call does finally come? "

IN QUEST OF BEAUTY

After a fortnight I was able to get up, but was still too weak to go to choir. I remember having to keep to my room during the celebration of the splendid liturgical feast of St. Joseph on March 19, and that of St. Benedict two days later. But outside my window lay a world of magic beauty: trees covered with hoar-frost, and the meadows blanketed in snow. So I tried to do a few little sketches symbolising the meaning of these feasts, aided by the exquisite landscape which so well harmonized with the pure lives of these two great saints of God. Came Holy Week, and I was still very feeble; but I was resolved to attend the grand liturgical functions, and said to my fleshly self: " Brother Adam, I have pampered you for five weeks now, and it was Lent. That is more than you deserve, so now exert yourself and be a good servant to my soul again, for Easter is nigh. I intend to take part in everything no matter how trying it will be, together with my dear brethren in choir." And strangely enough, all went well; and on Easter Sunday I could sing and rejoice as never before.

That same year (1900) I did some *al fresco* painting in the vestibule of the monastery church, and tried to follow the directions of Cennino, Giotto's pupil, in my work; as I had been giving serious study to his *Il Libro della Pittura* (which later on I translated into German). The following year however a much more important task came my way, when I was told to assist in the decoration of the Lady Chapel, a newly completed annex to the Church built for the double purpose of accommodating the greatly increased number of pilgrims to Beuron and of affording a worthier

[56]

IN THE CLERICATE

"home" for our greatly venerated *Mater Dolorosa* statue. As this structure had a fairly large apse and a wide dome, it offered plenty of scope for mural painting. A general design was made by Father Paul Krebs, which however left considerable room for independent work on the part of all of us engaged in the work. And as Father Desiderius, together with three of our most capable lay-brother painters, had recently gone to Monte Cassino to begin work on the crypt there, it was up to us his pupils now to show in enduring form what we had learned.

All beginnings are difficult; and especially so when painting a chapel which has nothing but blank white walls to offer. My friend Serusier suggested that we begin by putting pure colours, such as yellow and red ochre, ultramarine and black, on various sections of the space. This would encourage us to give the tints their proper depth and intensity. For on their pure white background all our colours seemed too heavy and dark, and needed considerable toning down. The reader may test this effect by studying the colours of a painting sometime with the aid of a white handkerchief held up close to its surface. He will thus see how full of colour and shading are the parts that appear to be pure white to the casual eye, and will understand the courage it takes to put on a gray colour where later a pure white is apparently to be seen. Thus, in the dome of our chapel we painted six angels in white garments, bearing in their uplifted hands a large medallion of the Madonna and Child. Luckily I managed to get the right tint of gray in this, although we could not tell for certain, until all the white in the wall of the dome had been covered with the other contrasting colours.

Other problems we had of course, such as finding exactly the correct division of space for the various sections in the design, the proper proportioning of the figures, and a happy composition of the whole. These difficulties are met with I suppose in every form of painting that is at all creative, and increase in proportion to the magnitude of the task in hand. But really creative and enduring work demands still more of the artist. He must be no mere clever technician, nor even just a consummate designer. Really to *create* he must execute what at first he sees only dimly in his mind, whose gradual dawning he observes with wonder and appropriates with fidelity; as meanwhile he is able instantly to know when his work is good or still in need of improvement. Always when engaged in some really important painting I have felt the influence of this mysterious power: now in the form of a sudden impulse as it were to surpass myself, reaching out to catch and fix an image I but vaguely saw; now in an unwonted clarity of vision which enabled me to evaluate the quality of my own work in the light of those fervent obscure longings which imperiously drove me on. True, I am aware that nothing I have painted has reached the summits of artistic genius. Yet what I have created has brought me joy and satisfaction comparable perhaps to that which attends the birth of a babe in a humble peasant cottage. Frequently such an event causes more real happiness than the arrival of a new-born infant in the richest home. And after all, every good mother loves her babe, even though its nose may be imperfect! For it is her own flesh and blood. Happy then the artist who can feel a similar emotion over what his genius has brought forth, and who is no mere trickster, imitator. It is unimportant if what he creates is of but a relative value. After all, as Plato has observed, there are not many *perfectly* beautiful dogs in the world, nor many perfectly ugly ones either. So be consoled, ye whose artistic talents are only mediocre!

Decorating the interior of a church resembles the building of a house, whose walls, once the foundations have been laid, grow up rapidly and soon the roof is there too. Then perhaps a celebration is held, a kind of initial house-warming with singing and gay decorations. But the really strenuous work is still to come: architect, contractor and laborers must keep at their task even though visible progress is hard to find. Nothing " new " or creative remains to be done, and yet there is so much to be finished, rounded off. So it is with painting, and in this second period the most painstaking care must be observed lest something be spoiled. But finally comes the happy day when the owner arrives and inspects the work, finding it completely measuring up to his requirements. " Be off with you," he says to the workmen, " I want to move in now with my family." Nor are the workmen sorry, for long association has made their tasks seem tedious. But they are proud nevertheless of their handiwork, and later will point out the house to friends and say: " What a fine job that was! *We* helped in it, too."

Certainly it was a proud day for us monastic artists when finally it was decided to remove the scaffolding in the Lady

Chapel, for we could find nothing more that remained to be done. Of course, none of us were able to judge the total effect until all the view-obstructing poles and planks were taken away. I was on pins and needles, and peeped in countless times to see what I could. It took the whole day however to clear away the débris, and when only two or three planks remained I stole a look which bitterly disappointed me. The frescoes seemed a failure, and I went back to my cell greatly depressed. But half an hour later I returned to the chapel, and lo! not a single obstruction remained, and the general impression of the dome was truly fine. It appeared to be floating in incalculable heights above us, the vaulting being accentuated on account of the lines of the angelic figures all pointing upward; and the effect of the whole design was so harmonious and true as to surpass my fondest hopes.

With the completion of this task I was forced to devote myself more intensively to the study of theology, as it had been decided to allow me to be ordained to the priesthood the following year. The Orders of subdiaconate and diaconate had been conferred on me in the summer of that year (1901); and tonsure and Minor Orders I had received two years before. But in January, 1902, I began to have trouble with my eyes, and had to visit a specialist in Tuebingen. He ordered me to take a complete rest, eat and sleep well for a whole month, and then come to see him again. I followed his instructions to the letter, and when I visited him again had gained eighteen pounds in weight! He complimented me on this achievement, but counselled extreme care as to the use of my weakened eyes. So for six months I read only by daylight, until I found that my sight was normal again.

It has been my observation that tribulation in some form or other almost invariably comes to the candidate for the priesthood shortly before his ordination day arrives. Generally it is sickness or nervous debility, brought on by the continuous strain of study, which is increased as he nears his goal. The eyesight rarely passes through this ordeal unimpaired; and fortunate indeed is that cleric who, if forced to curtail his reading, gains in the knowledge of himself by reflection. Often our reading is only the result of inquisitive curiosity; and often too, the printed page exercises a tyranny over our minds that is wholly needless. Our modern world especially suffers from an insatiable hunger for news, probably because it is really starving and has little within itself that is solidly nourishing. But the more this craving for news is satisfied, the more dull and blasé our world seems to become. Yet men like St. Jerome and the Venerable Bede, we are told, read almost continually. But what *they* read, and what *we* moderns read today, ah! that is a different matter!

My six months of comparative idleness due to my weakened eyesight created in me a state of great tension, as my physical strength grew apace. But there was no help for it: I had to " put the brakes on," which again was good experience for me because since then I have had to curb my energies, for ænemia has bothered me for over thirty years. Like St. Francis' " Brother Ass " in the *Fioretti,* my body

[61]

refuses to bear too heavy a burden, and rebels whenever I try to load it very much. Which again has been to me a blessing, as it has necessitated the practice of a valuable self-restraint which otherwise I might have never acquired. So I thank God even for my ænemia!

Came the day of our final examinations, and with it the end of " school days," though not of course, of study. With the day of ordination but five weeks away, I was sent to do a job of painting in the parish church of Fachsenfeld, Württemberg. This consisted of preparing the wall of the apse for the laying-on of the actual design later by some of my brethren. It was really nothing but scrub-work, but I enjoyed it none the less; and when later the others came to do the " gentlemens' job " of painting they found the walls thoroughly washed, polished, and sectioned-off.

Among the requirements of a candidate for priestly ordination is the ability to execute faultlessly his future ritual functions. For this purpose an improvised altar had been set up in our chapter-room, on which each one of us took his regular turn at performing the Mass ceremonies. This " play-acting " reminded me of childhood days, when we youngsters often used to mimic the worship of the " Roman Church." But now I did it with a sweet and solemn joy; and soon was able to go through the rather complicated ritual without a mistake, and in not more than a half-hour, which was the time-limit set for Low Mass.

On ordination day (August 20, 1902) we deacons, twelve in number, were conducted into the church clad in amice, alb, stole and cincture, each with a folded chasuble over his

[62]

left arm and carrying in his right hand a lighted candle. The officiating prelate was the famous Bishop Keppler of Rottenburg, then in his prime; and he carried out his part of the function with feeling as well as with impressive dignity. Though the oldest of our group, I ranked last among the twelve; but when the solemn moment came, and I knelt at the great Bishop's feet to receive the Imposition of Hands there was no suggestion of haste, nor of cut-and-dried formalism. As he placed both his hands upon my head he seemed truly to be *giving* of himself, pouring out in this sacramental gesture some of the fire of divine love that burned within his sacerdotal heart. And rightly or wrongly, I thought that he was paying particular attention to each of us candidates, as we appeared before him for the various rites: placing the stole over the right shoulder, investure with the chasuble, anointing the hands with sacred oil, touching the wine-filled chalice and the golden paten with its immaculate white wafer or host. His words of exhortation, which he read from the ceremonial, were deeply moving. His low musical voice was charged with emotion as he prayed that each of us would lead a chaste and unworldly life, and that neither we nor those who had raised us to the priestly dignity would ever be found blameworthy before the Lord.

As he read this prayer I thought of that first ordination of a group which also numbered twelve, one of whom was Judas. Fervently I implored the Divine Mercy to uphold each one of us, that always we might have light to remain faithful to our sublime vocation, " taking heed, lest standing,

[63]

we should fall." After the final anointing, our faces beamed with holy joy, as though " inebriated with the plenty of God's house," we had been made to " drink of the fountain of His pleasure." Twenty-five years later eleven of us celebrated the silver-jubilee of our ordination. The twelfth had gone out into the world again, straying from his chosen path in the wild turmoil of the world. . . .

On the following day (August 21), filled with great emotion, I celebrated my first Holy Mass in our monastic church. Others of the newly-ordained had gone to celebrate theirs in the midst of their families and friends. But nobody came to mine: my people lived too far away, for one thing; and then, they had no idea of how great an occasion this was for me. However they did send me a handsome present. A young business man whom I had become acquainted with in Fachsenfeld had promised to come when I told him of the event. He kept his word, but overslept the morning of my Mass and when he awoke I had long since finished. But I was too supremely happy to notice much the absence of my family and friends. Later on though I came to regret it, and it is still a sorrow to think that my parents have never seen me at the altar. But on this festive day there was naught but heavenly peace and joy in my soul, and all I could wish for was that the night would come, and then the morrow when I could celebrate again. Five days later I sang my first High Mass, ten years to the day since my Baptism and reception into the Catholic Church.

For the priest, to celebrate Holy Mass daily is an ever-recurring banquet, at which he partakes of the " bread of the strong" and the "wine of the elect." This Food is always sweet to the palate of his soul, and wholesome, invigorating. Then too, there he daily converses with his best Friend, who also is his Captain and Leader. His heart is filled with charity at the very fountain of Love. His soul becomes rich and abounding in good things, so that he can give to others of his plenty. His mind is enlightened, clarified; so that he is able to judge justly, to direct the steps of others wisely. His will becomes strengthened in calm peace, so that he is sweetly patient, and ever ready to forgive. His whole being gradually is established and made to feel at home within this sacred Action, which like a strong fortress protects him in temptation, upholds him in hours of trial. Thus slowly, surely, he is led to spiritual perfection, and intimate union with God.

On snowy white linen lies the immaculate Host, the golden Chalice. . . . The Chalice, with its sparkling wine that gleams with a mysterious light, like an Alpine lake encircled by dark forests and yet reflecting the grand mountain peaks that rise up behind. . . . Two gleaming candles feed on flame, and consuming are themselves destroyed. . . . Fires of willing immolation, like the priest of God. . . . Roses, red and white, delicate symbols of love and purity, exhale their delicious fragrance as they too droop and die. . . . And there stands the priest, praying with arms outstretched, as he, himself a holocaust of love, offers to God the spotless Lamb. . . . Taking the Host in his hands, with eyes turned heavenwards he offers thanks, blesses the Bread and says (as Christ speaks with his tongue):

[65]

" Take ye and eat, *for this is My Body.*"

Then lifting up the Chalice, he blesses it and again gives thanks, saying in the name of Christ:

" *This is the Chalice of My Blood.*"

Thus again has Golgotha's grand Mystery been fulfilled, though now in an unbloody manner. And Bethlehem's too, for is it not true that now again " A Child is born to us, and a Son is given to us, with government on His shoulder "?

Truly the priest of God, and with him God's faithful people have been made mighty, being thus empowered to make unto the omnipotent Divinity an offering pleasing in His sight, and worthy of His Name — His only Son, the Word Incarnate. And yet not always is the priest filled with the glowing love and profound veneration his celebration of Mass should inspire. For he is a weak man, and not an angel; yet there are times of grace and light when he too cries out from the depths of his soul:

> *How beautiful are Thy Tabernacles, O Lord of Hosts!*
> *My soul longeth and panteth for the courts of the Lord.*
> *My heart and my flesh have rejoiced in the living God.*
> *For the sparrow hath found herself a house, and the turtle-dove a nest wherein she may lay her young.*
> *Such are Thy Altars, O Lord of Hosts!*
> *My King and my God!* (Psalm 83)

For a while after his ordination, the Beuron monk remains in the Clericate with his quondam companions, but there comes the day when two of the older monks come to him to conduct him to the Fathers' Recreation. That means that he is no longer familiarly to associate with the group of younger candidates, but must henceforth consider himself a part of that circle of full-fledged monks which is presided over by the Abbot himself. Though proud and happy over this advancement, he nevertheless bids farewell to his youthful companions with some sadness in his heart.

Chapter Four

PRIEST, MONK, AND ARTIST

AFTER having been admitted to the ranks of the *patres,* I returned to my first love: art. That is to say, I was now allowed to devote all my time to it, outside of choir and community duties. It is customary for every monk to develop during his leisure hours some special interest, such as historical or theological studies, teaching, pastoral work, art, music, or scientific research. Happy is he who has a " ready-made " interest, such as mine was. However, I now looked at art from a quite different viewpoint, naturally; as I was God's consecrated servant and only as such could I serve art. But I still loved it, still wanted to remain obedient to its inspirations and exacting demands. More than ever now was I conscious of what admirable contributions it has made throughout history, to the cause of the sacred and the sublime, lifting up men's hearts by the beauty, the nobility of its concepts. In particular the work of Father Desiderius struck me as having merited a place of distinction in this way, and I willingly absorbed all that I could under his direction. Gradually I succeeded in achieving a style that conformed to the rigid requirements of the Beuronese School, and that did seem worthy, in spite of its flaws, of adorning a house of God.

At first, I did only individual figures, and a few ornaments, following strictly Father Desiderius' " canon " based on the proportions of the human body. Though this left me precious little room for individuality of expression, it mattered little as I have always been free from the fear, which so often besets the beginner in the Beuron method, of " losing individuality." *That* is something which never can be exterminated, and will always assert itself in time, even if temporarily obscured during the period of initiation into the exacting and rigid requirements of the " canon."

All this was indeed something wholly new to me as an artist, a fact which I did not fail to appreciate; though there were moments I must confess, when a twinge of pain touched me, as when I chanced to view some recent work of one or other of my old Parisian friends. All of them had made progress, especially Denis, Vuillard, and Bonnard. and whenever I saw a Delacroix, a Cézanne, a Gauguin, a Van Gogh, ah! that would hurt! But only for a fleeting moment, as I would instinctively weigh what I had had to give up in the way of " personality," in the balance with the lofty aims of Beuron art.

After all, I thought, how infinitely better it was to produce only a few figures or ornaments for a church, which would fit in with the totality of the liturgical work, than to turn out an apparently endless accumulation of paintings with no higher purpose than to satisfy " personality." Modern art too frequently succumbs to this craze, I reflected; and the result is that it produces mostly trash. A painter moves into a studio, bringing along nothing but his easel, chair, and paint-box: in a couple of years the walls are covered with pictures, big and small, framed and unframed, finished or only sketched. Only a fraction of them salable, and even these too " personal " to be of any real value. " God pity and forgive such artists! " I would say to myself, and then go on with my own work greatly consoled.

At this period I entered into correspondence again with some of my old friends. As is the custom with newly-ordained priests, I had souvenir cards printed for my First Mass and sent them to all my relatives, friends, and acquaintances. A whole bundle of them went to Maurice Denis who was to distribute them among the Nabis. His letter in reply contained his hearty congratulations, and much news of our mutual Paris friends. This included an alarming report about Sérusier, who had ceased entirely to do any work, slept during most of the day, and gave his friends cause to fear for his mental condition. Denis was now urging him to come to Beuron to pay me a visit, to which I added my own cordial invitation, but got no reply. A second letter evoked an interesting and, to me, reassuring answer, part of which I quote:

" My dear Willibrord: Even before hearing from you I have often thought of you and of those whose life you are sharing. I have never seen a group of men so conspicuous for their culture, their ideals, and the *consistency* of their lives. But more than all else, it was their concept of art that has captured and held my soul ever since my visit to Beuron, so that I care nothing any more for all this artistic experimentation that is going on in the world about me. Since that visit I have tried to spread the light among my companions

—but they are all blind. Worse still, they *want* to be blind. . . . Whenever I venture to talk of the function of mathematics in art, according to the ' Canon,' people smile pityingly, as if I were a fool. . . . This is really why I can now do so little work, and why I have withdrawn from all the so-called centres of art. Lately I have decided to spend at least nine months of every year in Brittany, far from all the jarring influences of city life. I shall feel less alone among the kine and trees than I do now in the midst of this turmoil in Paris. . . . Your letter implies the fear that I am spending a lot of time in the *taverns,* as I did in Pont-Aven. No, don't worry about *that:* I am being very careful, and my health is excellent.

" Possibly when spring comes I shall come to talk things over with you in Beuron. I hope to bring Denis along, as it would do him good and I can think of no more desirable companion. It would rejuvenate me too, as my artistic transformation begun in Beuron has been somewhat retarded by the influences around me. All is *naturalism,* from which I am determined to liberate myself, cost what it may, so that I may paint pictures which seem to satisfy the lofty ideal that now inspires me, whether my contemporaries like them or not. . . .

" To get back to earth, I sometimes see X . . . for whom you have done so much good in every way, also Chaumillard who goes on painting, though still in a realistic, impressionistic way. I close my letter in speaking of its main purpose, which is to tell you of my joy on hearing of your first Mass. Now my great desire is some day to serve you at the altar."

I have quoted Sérusier at some length because I think his is a typical case. Almost every artist who has lofty aspirations meets with a similar crisis, a period of sterility and despair when all his powers and ambition seem to have fled. The greater the artist the blacker this depression seems to be, and we know that giants like Leonardo, Michelangelo, Mantegna went through periods of truly terrible desolation. Any one of several causes, or a combination of them, may account for this: a continual dashing of one's hopes, failure to win appreciation, a sudden vision of ideals still grander than one's own, or the continued torments of one's own restless genius. Sometimes it is the more ignoble surrender to sloth, and inability to bear the irksomeness of doing over again what seems to be one's best; sometimes, and most tragical of all, it is the dawning realisation that one's genius cannot take him any higher, that already his powers are in their decline.

Basically, however, this crisis is due I think to that insatiable longing after *perfection,* which every creative spirit possesses in spite of himself. Inexorably this *élan* urges him on towards the attainment of the beautiful, the absolute: to make this visible, audible, tangible so that he and others may embrace and cherish it. Passionately he craves the kiss of the Eternal, that from this union-in-love may spring some concrete replica of transcendent values, cast in the mould of his own creative powers. But now, if such an ascent into the rarified atmosphere of the sublime be made too impetuously, either through underestimating the limits of human possibility or overrating his own creative talent, the artist is liable to get lost. In his rapid ascent he has left all that is familiar far behind; and is unable to find his way down to earth again. Slow, lingering death to his creative genius is the sad result: a terrible death of starvation, or of loneliness — unless some saving hand is extended, *and grasped,* before it is too late. "Leave me alone, please; I would rather die," is all too often the response of such an unfortunate genius to proffered help. Or perhaps he puts an end to his own life before help can reach him.

But if love and friendship do succeed in making contact with him before it is too late, what is to be done? He must be given new hope, new courage, and at the same time, led back to tangible realities. His mind must be diverted from its vision of the transcendent, and made again to see and rejoice in the beauty of created nature. He must be put in touch again with the current of mundane affairs and events, and meanwhile delicately be made to understand that his flight upwards was something of an eccentricity, or perhaps (in plainer language) just arrogance, or even downright laziness in that he scorned the time-honored, but much harder, paths to greatness. Above all, he must be shown again the good that still is in him, the really valuable things that he has done. Thus encouraged and thus weaned away from his fatal brooding, he will gradually find himself, and perhaps yet produce something truly great.

Maurice Denis accepted Sérusier's proposal; and in the spring of the following year (1903) accompanied him into Germany. Stopping first in Nuremberg and Munich, they arrived in Beuron on the day before Palm Sunday, to spend

[73]

Holy Week and Easter with us. Sérusier seemed to have benefited much from the journey, and from Denis' soothing presence. He was quite talkative when we met in the parlour, and soon we were all three chattering away as of yore. Suddenly Denis asked: " What are all the crowds of people doing in the village? We could hardly find a room in the hotel." " They are pilgrims," I replied, innocently enough (for it was true), " come to make their Easter duty: to confess themselves and then go to Holy Communion." My shaft struck home; for Sérusier, whom I knew to have been neglecting his soul for a long time, was visibly agitated and soon slipt out of the room. Denis then remarked: " Our friend has not been so cheerful and talkative on the whole trip as he has here. But yet, there is still something ailing him." I said: " I believe I know what it is. He needs to go to confession! " " *Allez donc:* what makes you say that? " exclaimed Denis. " Well," I replied, " I hardly know why, myself. But I am sure of it, and this time I do not intend to let him escape, as I did four years ago. He must not leave here before his conscience has been set in order." " *À la fin* — perhaps you are right, after all," agreed my friend.

Of course, mine was only a guess, but I was convinced it was the correct one. It would explain much of Sérusier's unhappy and morose demeanour, and I did know that he had been seeking for many years some priest who would fully understand him (as he thought). But like many of the so-called intellectual class, his demands in this respect were far too exacting, as was the standard of holiness that he imagined he had to attain. Human pride is many-sided, and there is, after all, some comfort for our harassed ego even in self-abasement, if we can hold onto the opinion that we are so out of the ordinary and different from other mortals (even in our sins) that only the exceptionally holy and wise spiritual director can help us. Not that I would disapprove of exercising any choice at all in this matter, which would be going to the opposite extreme. But surely it is being overly fastidious to delay for a long time so imperative a duty, and to suffer all the enervating effects of that delay which gradually robs the soul of all true peace and joy, simply and solely for so trifling a reason. And besides the pride behind it, there is perhaps also a bit of cowardice, in this search for a man so saintly and understanding that he will solve all our troubles. We seek, and yet are afraid to find.

Luckily, however, there was just the man to suit my friend's exacting tastes staying with us at the moment, in the person of Father Paul Damman, a monk of Maredsous (the flourishing Belgian abbey near Namur). I managed that Sérusier and he should get together, and they got along so well that on Good Friday the former made his confession. After the ordeal he seemed as one born anew, but wanted to be left alone with himself for a while. I remember his going for a long tramp in the woods while we were singing *Tenebrae,* evidently to allow his new-found peace to penetrate into all the depths of his being, to allow it to take deep root, and thus to grow gradually, surely. . . .

On Easter Sunday both my dear friends attended my Mass and received Holy Communion from my hands. It was a beautiful, joyful day for all three of us, truly a Resurrection feast. We chums had never felt so close to one another before. . . .

Sérusier's contact with Father Paul did much for his artistic regeneration, too. After he had overcome his mistaken notion that only a saint and a prophet could help him, he began at once to lose his exaggerated ideas about art. He abandoned his imaginary world and came back to the real one, and at once was captivated by its beauty. His long-idle fingers began to itch, and as soon as he had returned to Brittany after Easter, he began to paint. His subject was a landscape, suggested by his impressions of the wooded region around Beuron. He surpassed himself in this work: one saw the stately *Tannenbäume* (fir trees) with the rugged cliffs, in the background, and in the foreground, tilled fields, a lay-brother tending his flock, and fruit trees in blossom; all painted with a realism that was startling, yet entrancingly beautiful. This picture was sold very soon, and one fine day Sérusier surprised his friends by appearing unexpectedly in Paris, wearing a new suit of clothes, and in excellent spirits as of old.

The Mr. " X " whom Sérusier said I had once benefited much, was a disciple of Gauguin's whom I had met in Pont-Aven in 1891. Denis had sent him one of my First Mass cards, at which he wrote me a congratulatory letter which affected me deeply. Its every line spoke of distress, both moral and physical. Though this did not astonish me overmuch, as when I knew him he was already leading a frivolous life. So I wrote him an affectionate, fatherly letter; and his reply revealed still more of his pathetic condition, as one completely demoralised and helpless, yet longing for someone to help him to his feet again. What a contrast (he wrote) between our two careers since we had last been together! His had been a staggering descent towards the abyss, mine a climb upwards to shining heights. Now he lay prostrate on the very edge of the precipice. Yet, he had never entirely abandoned trying to save himself. Once he finally got courage enough *d'aborder un prêtre:* " to see the priest." For the first time in thirteen years he had been happy again, and for two months had gone daily to Holy Communion. Then he slipped and fell again. Brittany beckoned to him, and he fled from Paris, " that hell," to find only a " greater hell " in the provinces, where he a lonely stranger had to suffer " all the cruelty decent people know how to inflict."

Of course, he made the mistake many immature artists make, of adopting country life without having that creative store of ideas and experience necessary to fertilise solitude; not to mention the lack of financial means, physical strength, moral stamina. Solitude was thus even more dangerous for my poor friend than the turbulent life of a large city, for he soon became so completely enervated that the smallest matters irked him. He tried to ward off approaching catastrophe by occupying his mind with unwholesome day-dreaming, which he then would describe in weird literary essays. Thus was his last bit of stamina used up, at the period when I made contact with him. But he had fortunately never lost his faith in Divine Providence, of which he had experienced the clearest proofs; and the manner in which he responded to the news of my ordination showed that he regarded the latter as but another clear proof of God's care in his behalf.

There are people who think that "trusting in God" means to sit with folded hands and wait until the meat and potatoes fly into their mouths, as it were. But my afflicted colleague had better sense; he did his share of the work, and thus was not disappointed in the end. He set his spiritual affairs in order, but as I could see from his letters, his temporal situation still constituted a danger for him. " This case demands beefsteak rather than pious advice," I said to myself; and forthwith wrote to my father in Holland, begging him to help the poor artist for my sake. This he did, sending him a considerable sum of money which enabled him to pay his debts and have something left over. Sérusier, too, now came to his aid, and soon he was on the mend again, and painting happily. The following year the two of them paid a visit to Chateauneuf, where X was taken gravely ill. On December 30, fortified by the Sacraments of the Church and fully resigned, he passed away, at the age of thirty-four years.

At this same period I became acquainted with another interesting character, in the person of a young Danish student of philosophy who called at Beuron to bring me greetings from my friend Johannes Jorgensen. He told me he was a recent convert, and was journeying to Italy. I invited him to stop overnight with us, as from his appearance he was in need of sleep, and of a good square meal. " Have you eaten anything today? " I ventured to ask (it was already late in the afternoon). " Yes, this morning a priest in the

' Heuberg' gave me breakfast," he answered. "And you have come from there on foot?" I demanded. "Ah, yes," he confessed; "all the way from Cologne, in fact" (a distance of about two hundred miles). This aroused my admiration as well as pity, and I told him: "Come, we must get you something to eat right away." When he got up I saw his stockings peeping through the toes of his shoes, and said to him: "No, wait here a moment. I'm going to get you some shoes, as I can't take you through the cloisters in those you have on." I hurried out, and obtained from the "Brother Shoemaker" a pair of mended stout-soled brogans from the store we keep always on hand for the poor. These fitted him perfectly. Then I took him to the guests' dining room inside the enclosure, where he refreshed his famished body.

Afterwards he told me his story, which summed up in the fact that he was now on his way to Father Felix, the saintly Franciscan from Assisi, whom he had met in Copenhagen on the occasion of Ballin's wedding (at which Father Felix officiated), and who had so attracted him that he wanted to join the community he belonged to. To this end he had sold all that he possessed, paid his debts, and started out for Assisi. But his money became exhausted when he had arrived only as far as Cologne, so he was forced to continue on foot. Along the way he had asked help at the various rectories, and the few *pfennigs* thus obtained usually had sufficed to buy him a bed and breakfast at some wayside inn. For five days he had been subsisting on the latter meal alone, though on one or two luckier occasions he had been

[79]

able to afford the luxury of a plate of soup at night. But one day he had a bad scare.

As he was nearing the town of Frankfurt-am-Main, he seemed to see, in the distant flat landscape, the Cathedral of Cologne rising up. " Alas, to add to my troubles I am now going mad! " he thought despairingly; and not until he had had something to eat did he realise that this was simply an hallucination due to physical and nervous exhaustion. And so he wandered on, now almost always in the rain. . . . It had been terrible in the Black Forest, so dark and deserted. . . . One night he had been unable to find shelter, and had walked till dawn, which made eighteen hours at one stretch. He would have collapsed then, had not a kind priest taken pity on him and given him shelter for a day.

At this time we had no Guest House in Beuron, and Father Archabbot disapproved of receiving people who were not well known to someone in the community. That constituted a problem, as I had no money to lodge this brave idealist in a hotel. But with the aid of some of my brethren I fixed up a room for him in an inconspicuous corner of the monastery, got him clean linen, and fed him copiously. After three days he was quite recovered, and from the Father Cellarer I procured him enough cash to get as far as Altdorf in Switzerland, where the family of one of our monks agreed to give him shelter. From there he managed somehow to get to Italy and Assisi. The good Franciscans were petrified with astonishment when they learned that he had come all the way from Denmark on foot. This was sufficient proof to them of the sincerity of his intentions, and so he was allowed to enter the novitiate at once. He emerged from this successfully, studied theology and was finally ordained. He now is a much sought-after confessor in one of the famous pilgrimage churches of Italy.

For some time, after my ordination, the Abbot of Monte Cassino (Dom Boniface Krug, formerly of St. Vincent's Abbey, Latrobe, Pennsylvania) had been urging Abbot Placid to send me and one of the oblates to help Father Desiderius, who was now engaged in restoring the crypt at St. Benedict's famous shrine. When I heard of this, it inspired in me mixed feelings. The prospect of seeing beautiful Italy again, and some of its art, was very alluring; but on the other hand, the thought of again working under Father Desiderius' immediate direction was not quite so agreeable. How exacting a task this would likely be, I knew from past experience. But I only told myself: " Do nothing one way or the other. Just let circumstances push you along, and you will not be sorry."

Little as I knew it, a new period in my life was now setting in. For six years I had been immured within the peaceful precincts of our monastic cloister, and had no expectation, still less any desire that a change should come. But my Archabbot, who was so reluctant to send me to Monte Cassino, probably had some presentiment that such a journey would mark the beginning of a career quite opposite to that calm unruffled one within the monastic enclosure that he had envisioned for me. I seemed to have been always quite a favourite with him, probably more because of the extraordinary graces God had vouchsafed me in drawing me first to the Catholic Church and then to the cloister, than because of any particular gifts I may have possessed. But he finally had to give in to the pleadings of Abbot Krug and he allowed me to leave Beuron. He was nevertheless apprehensive, and I shall never forget the little sermon he gave me shortly before my departure. " God has been very good to you, Father Willibrord," he said with sadness in his voice. " You have found happiness so easily; and now to keep it, all you need is to do your duty in quiet obedience. You came here to us, and knew very little. Yet now you are a priest. So now, never try to do anything or be anything extraordinary." These words of a wise old man nearing the long-awaited goal of life should have impressed me with the futility of mere human striving, of the decisive sway God holds over the lives of all, especially of those consecrated to him. But I was still young, and restive as a young colt. Though my grey hairs were beginning to show, I was as ready as ever to tackle anything new, provided of course it was a worthy enterprise. But somehow, the portentous warning of my father-in-Christ struck home: I found myself recalling it again and again. Especially that reference to the paucity of my knowledge when I arrived in Beuron; my poor father had spent so much hard-earned cash to have me learn something!

At all events, I did follow in this, as in all subsequent changes in my life, the axiom " Let circumstances push you." I believe this rather Oriental bit of philosophy fits in well with even the highest religious aspiration, as God's holy Will is usually manifested by exterior visible happenings pointing out the way we are to travel. We of the West value personal striving for a self-determined goal too highly, I believe. We are unwilling to remain passive, and thus often poach on God's preserves. The day will come perhaps when we shall see, in the light of His unerring Truth, how mistaken we were in thus trying to mark out our own path instead of waiting for Him to " push " us onto it. Then we shall realise how thick-headed we were, and how difficult (humanly speaking) it was for Him to lead us safely into Heaven, yet without doing violence to our freedom, without making us the eternal laughing-stock of the angels!

Yet it takes a very sensitive spiritual *antennæ* to achieve the proper balance between action and passivity. Since few of us possess this, I venture the following advice as a kind of substitute: never say " no " too quickly when something intrinsically good is demanded of us, but which happens not to suit us at the moment. After one has well tested himself spiritually, say for two or three years, then may be the time to act more readily and securely on one's own view of things.

Chapter Five

ITALY AND MONTE CASSINO

O<small>N</small> August 20, 1903, the eleventh anniversary of my baptism, Oblate Sarkander and I set out from Beuron for Italy, after having received a solemn blessing from the Archabbot for our journey. We travelled all day through Switzerland, arriving at Milan about ten o'clock at night utterly exhausted, it having been terribly hot all day.

Italy is, as we know, one of the youngest regions of the earth geologically. Stratification is still going on there, as is evidenced by the continuance of volcanic activity and the frequency of earthquakes. And so too, its inhabitants always impress the visitors as being youthful, volatile, primitive. They seem to have retained their pristine vigor, the soundness and strength of their racial characteristics, in spite of the dizzy heights to which their culture has attained. Their political history too has resembled the geological peculiarities of the land, in the terrific upheavals it has witnessed ere national unity was attained. But now serenity and happiness reigns on the Italian peninsula, where once the storms of unfettered human passions wrought havoc in the land; a fact which appears to us as only natural, in a country where salubrious springs, ravishing landscapes, and the perfume of perennial flowers make us forget the smoking horrors of the past. Indeed, human cares of every kind are put to flight in such an atmosphere of peace and warmth and loveliness. Even duty weighs less heavily upon us, and our souls seem to expand, our minds soar to unexpected heights, our hearts thrill to the call of beauty unalloyed that is everywhere about us.

Perhaps this explains why Italians generally do not seem much concerned with intellectual problems. The ordinary citizen's main preoccupation is in thinking about his (and his family's) daily bread. Or better still, he does not think at all. He reads very little, apparently preferring *life* to much knowledge. This has great advantages, as it keeps him instinctively humble, and prevents that kind of megalomania which so often afflicts the voracious reader. Such a person imagines himself to be extremely clever because he has been able to retain a lot of miscellaneous information, extremely alive because of the continual hubbub in his heart, extremely virtuous because he has acquired a variety of prejudices and silly scruples. Your true Italian is seldom found in so morbid a condition; though on the other hand, his disinterestedness in extraneous events and problems sometimes creates the impression that he is superficial.

Among the younger generation in Italy, phenomenal talent in art and music is abounding. One seems to have landed among a regular army of geniuses. But relatively few carry their endowments with them into mature age. In the middle twenties there always seems to be a halt, and I believe this is due to the fact that the sensitive faculties, which begin to slacken with the arrival of physical maturity, do not find the necessary compensation or stimulus in intellectual development. Yet when the latter *is* present, what splendid fruits of genius the gifted Italian brings forth!

Whoever wishes to understand the Italians thoroughly must visit their beautiful country. He will be received with unfailing courtesy, sincere friendliness and a readiness to oblige. This is due in part perhaps to the traditional respect the Italian has for rich people; and the foreigner, of course, always has money to spend. He is able to maintain an appearance of respectability and *dolce far niente* which never fails to awe these naïve southerners.

Yet they really do feel kindly towards the foreigner who comes to admire the natural beauties of their country, and the artistic masterpieces of their great ancestors. And the stranger should meet them with a kindred feeling of confidence, if tempered with a little sagacity. For if the Italian is made to be suspicious, or wounded in his national pride, he will show that he can be cunning too, and mean. If he becomes too obtrusive, as he is likely to, he can be disarmed with a single kind word, or a smile of understanding; but an angry word or frown only arouses his contempt and derision. I remember seeing one day an amusing incident in Rome which illustrates this point. A sizable young lad was running ahead of a sedate Englishman, turning handsprings and somersaults hoping to win a few *soldi* for his pains. But the son of Albion walked stolidly and disapprovingly on, with the result that he was unable to get rid of the boy (whose antics were really most amusing), and for quite a distance was the object of a most unwelcome cynosure of eyes. Had he clapped and shouted " bravo! " throwing a *soldo* or two in the general direction of the enterprising youth, the latter would have called a friendly *" grazie!* (Thanks) " in return, and have been off at once.

In Italy too the artistic past seems to have been preserved better until the present, than anywhere else. The aspect of the towns, the landscape, the very people themselves, all breathe an atmosphere of ancient glories. In London, Paris, or Berlin we find this only in museums, and a rough hand awakens us to crude reality as soon as we have quitted them. But in that charming land beyond the Alps all contributes to allow our blissful dream to remain. True, it may be only an empty dream, an hallucination, but we keep it, we live in it for days, weeks, months even, and return to our drab homes again as if born anew. O blessed, kindly Italy, who so graciously bestows all this bliss upon your alien brethren!

For me, the city of Milan has an especial charm, perhaps because of the heroic sufferings it has undergone to preserve its ancient traditions. It has survived wars, pestilence, famine, and even total destruction, and the spirit of its great patron saint, Ambrose, still seems to hover over its streets and walls benignly, protectingly. Above all in the grand *Duomo,* whose chapel of St. Victor contains a marvellous mosaic of the heroic Doctor of the Church. It was made shortly after his death in the year 397, and delineates most strikingly what were his chief characteristics: the spirit of mystic contemplation, prudence, gravity and sobriety. His countenance seems to radiate both that power of will which made him the terror of his enemies, and that supreme *righteousness* of character which reflects itself so movingly in all his writings. On viewing this masterpiece one finds it easy to believe the accounts of how a single look from him sufficed to bring a sinner to repentance, or awaken a salutary fear of God's retribution in the hearts of frivolous women. We can almost see the faces of his audience wince, as words like these smote upon their ears:

Not to know Christ is the soul's death.
Ignorance of Christ is the greatest ignorance of all.
Let no Christian dare plead ignorance of the Mystery of Christ.
Surely it behooves thee to know well Him who is thy Love.
He who lives without Christ walks in deepest darkness.
He who walks without Christ, walks astray.
He will remain small of stature indeed, who does not join himself unto the greatness of Christ.

To me, the homilies and dissertations of St. Ambrose have always been a source of the greatest spiritual joy. Many of them are to be found in the Breviary, which is the monastic form of daily prayer, and thus gradually grow familiar despite the complexities of thought and language which they sometimes contain.

Milan, too, is the city of Leonardo da Vinci, where the most momentous years of his life were spent. Reminders of this great figure are met with everywhere, although with the exception of his masterful *Last Supper* only one other authentic painting by him is to be found in all Milan. This is a charming portrait of a young princess, preserved in the *Ambrosiana*. But countless pictures painted by his pupils are to be found in the churches and museums, notably those by Solario, Melzi, Boltraffio, Cesare da Sesto, Luini, artists who closely followed the principles of their master. But works from the latter's own hand still remain in a class by themselves, and one of them is worth a dozen paintings by his imitators. He reached out after the sublime, caught it, and imprisoned it on his immortal canvases, even on those he left unfinished, such as his *Adoration of the Magi* in the Uffizi Gallery, and his *St. Jerome* in the Vatican. Perhaps this is why his paintings all seem to have an enigmatic, eerie quality about them, as though charged with the mystery of the Unknowable, of Beauty that is transcendent, ineffable.

Yet they give evidence of his having produced them *consciously,* knowing always what he was about. Coolly deliberate, they are yet full of fire. In no ecstatic dream did they originate; rather, they seem to have slowly matured, as an oak tree grows. The longer their production took, the better seems to have been the final result. Sometimes though a work would grow to such prodigious, breath-taking proportions that the master would weary of it, and leave it unfinished, or tell his pupils to look after its completion. At such times he would absorb himself in other pursuits to distract his mind from the cloying vision of the sublime — saddling one of his spirited horses, he would ride out into the open country. Or perhaps, shutting himself up in his

[89]

study, he would delve deeply into some problem of higher mathematics.

Leonardo's immortal female heads, such as the *Mona Lisa, St. Anne and the Blessed Virgin,* the *Portrait of an Unknown Lady* in the Lichtenstein Gallery, all have something definitely in common. Do they represent the one and most vital experience in his sentimental life? I am inclined to think so, for he certainly possessed all that would make him adorable in the eyes of woman, in the purest and most profound sense; and it is this same phase of womanhood, enigmatic, sphinx-like, while remaining pure and guileless, that he has chosen to immortalise in all his famous female portraits. What to us appears puzzling in them is thus only the expression of what to him was woman's character true and undisguised.

One day I went to the Brera gallery, to view Veronese's large canvas: *The Child Moses being presented to Pharao's Daughter.* I was literally transported with delight, for besides the exquisite beauty of the figures, the masterful selection and blending of colour (in which Leonardo is equalled only by Titian and Palma), and other details which from the standpoint of technique were superb; the Arcadian theme of the whole appealed strongly to that part of my soul which after nine years in the cloister had perforce been considerably neglected. Here was a group of happy people from all walks of mundane life enjoying themselves thoroughly, in an idyllic atmosphere, and obviously without care or worry. True, I had no desire to exchange places with any of them, vaguely feeling that I should be fearfully bored in such a company. But I did admire and perhaps envy just a trifle, the way they seemed to be enjoying innocent worldly pleasures. It was all so simple, naïve, spontaneous.

Another detail of the picture that appealed to me strongly was the figure of a young maiden sitting apart from the crowd and playing on a lute. Her eyes were gazing wistfully up to the heavens as though she too longed for a happiness richer and more satisfying than that to be found in these idyllic mundane surroundings.

But on the whole, visiting famous galleries is much like visiting a morgue. The few really great pictures they contain seem to snuff the life of all the lesser ones, and it is dreary to confront such an array of corpses. Individually and in their proper surroundings these might provide much pleasure and inspiration, but here they seem superfluous and forlorn. Yet each one's author has probably done his best, and deserves our appreciation. But who ever remembers on leaving such a gallery to breathe a prayer for these forgotten ones? Perhaps it would be a good thing if all our museums were to have a kind of chapel, placed near their exits, dedicated to these " Immortals " whom fickle fame has passed unkindly by. My good friend Ballin never forgot his departed artistic heroes, like the poet Baudelaire and the novelist Barbey d'Aurévilly, on whose anniversaries he always had Holy Mass offered. And on his honeymoon he and his young wife paid a visit to the tomb of Paul Verlaine. Before their wedding they had read together the latter's *Sagesse* with much profit, and had thereupon resolved to make a pilgrimage to his grave. Ballin's account of this episode (which he gave me later) is not without its poignant appeal.

It seems they had difficulty in locating the grave, as they had been told he had been buried in the cemetery of Montparnasse, whereas they finally found his tomb in the Verlaine family-plot at Les Batignolles. It was an ugly and unkempt monument, with no decoration or motto save the names, simply inscribed, of the members of the family buried there. The last one was: *Paul Verlaine, Poète.* On finding this, the young couple knelt for a while in silent prayer, and then Madame Ballin exclaimed: " How sad that there is no Cross on Verlaine's tomb! " The husband was of the same opinion, and related how a similar omission on Aurévilly's monument had created quite a sensation in his time. Leon Bloy had then raised such a fuss in the newspaper columns that the novelist finally got his Cross. The young wife had remained on her knees during this recital, and Ballin, discovering that she had her rosary in her hands, exclaimed with some impatience: " But Marguerite, surely you aren't going to pray your beads *now!* It is too cold here, and besides, the gates will soon be closed." Her reply was a smile, as she unfastened the Cross from her rosary.

" Is that for Verlaine? " he asked. She nodded. " But where will you put it? It will only fall off the stone." She replied simply: " I am going to fasten it to the railing." Forthwith, taking off her hat, she extracted a hairpin from her mass of dark-brown hair, drew it through the loop of the little Cross and fixed it to the railing. Verlaine now had a suitable marker, and that without speeches and newspaper polemics. It was small and plain, but Christ Crucified hung upon it. Surely the dead poet would rest quite peacefully now. Ballin could not express his feelings, and silently clasped the hand of his dear wife. How readily she had hit upon just the right thing to do! Without doubt, Verlaine's fate would have been far different had he met such a woman on his path through life.

From Milan we passed on to Bologna, the memory of whose colonnaded streets is still a delight to me. It has some very impressive churches, and of course, Raffael's awe-inspiring *St. Cecelia* in the Pinacotheca. I think the *St. Mary Magdalene* in this picture is positively unforgettable.

After resting in the hotel, we started out towards evening of the same day for Ravenna. It would have been better had we waited till the next morning, for we got no sleep after our arrival late in the night. Our small *albergho* was filled with carousers who sang and scuffled about the whole night long. I have never heard such an infernal noise in all my life. A torrent of sentimentalism seemed to have broken loose, in which all the pessimism and frustrated hope generated by centuries of faded glory, was vented in a wild orgy of Romagnese ferocity. The quondam Imperial City seemed to be in the last stages of decay, and its citizens bore their tragic fate with sullen bitterness. Nowhere have I found an atmosphere of such poignant despair as in decadent Ravenna, the scene too of Dante's exile and death. Here he lies buried, and the city seems to share his pathetic fate. It too seems to lie in exile, cut off from the merry life of the rest of the

[93]

peninsula, and even isolated from the nearby smiling Adriatic, as if it were a veritable outcast.

But artistically Ravenna is incomparably rich. Besides a number of first-class portraits to be found in the homes of many impoverished noble families of the district, it possesses several grand and well-preserved religious edifices of the Byzantine epoch which far surpass anything else in the Western world. In their noble structural lines, in the glittering mosaics with which they abound they give us a picture of the faith and religious ideals of the classic Christian age that is profoundly moving. The little mausoleum of Galla Placidia and the basilica of San Vitale affected me most of all; perhaps because they are the best preserved, and because their collective impression is more easily grasped.

Christian temples have never been given a colour ornamentation so rich and so harmonious as in the period between the fifth (or latter half of the fourth) and seventh centuries. Greco-Roman culture, suffused with the Christian spirit, had penetrated into the realm of art, and bore a fruit whose exquisite beauty and profundity of expression has been equalled only in the contemporary patristic literature. Less accurate perhaps as regards their form than their pagan prototypes, the Christian mosaics are nevertheless much superior in their warmth and power of expression, and in the amount and quality of the coloring they contain. Clearly, their creators exulted, as did the entire Christian world, in proclaiming Christ's superiority to the pagan gods; and they portrayed Him in the midst of His celestial court with a resplendent sunburst of color, a richness of symbolic design that is still the envy of the Christian artist.

But other duties were calling, and we had regretfully to leave Ravenna that same day. Florence was our objective, and our train went by way of Forli and Faenze (once the home of fine pottery or *faïence*). It was stifling hot, and our discomfort was not lessened by the innumerable dusty tunnels we passed through. Whenever we emerged from one of them I would greedily inhale the fresh mountain air. About six in the evening we reached Florence, and changed there for Fiesole, where I was expected at the Franciscan friary. At that time there was no way of getting up the steep Fiesole hill other than walking (unless one took a carriage, which we could not afford). I was so tired and the luggage so heavy that I almost despaired of making it, but at last we reached the summit and stood before the cloister-gate I knew so well. Regretfully I noticed that it no longer bore the little motto which had so deeply impressed me long ago:

> *Un anima sola!*
> *Se la perdo, che sara di me?*
> (Only one soul!
> What will become of me, if I lose it?)

I pulled the ancient bell-rope, and was heartened to hear the familiar clang again. A brother unknown to me admitted us, taking us into a new reception-hall. The Fathers were at supper, but soon two of my old friends, Fathers Norberto and Giovanni Crisostome, appeared and gave us a hearty welcome. They were rejoiced to greet their old friend

"Gianni" now as Dom Willibrordo. But by this time I was feeling really ill, and asked to be shown my room where I could lie down. Next day I was quite sick, and a doctor was summoned. He found that I was suffering from a severe stomach inflammation, and ordered me to rest and follow a strict diet. This I did, and in a few days was well enough to sing High Mass, which gave me great joy.

From that day on I went regularly with my Oblate companion into the city, and visited all my old artistic favorites again; the Giottos, Martinis, Orcagnas, Gozzolis, and many others. The Dominican cloister of San Marco in particular entranced me, as it had recently been enriched with Fra Angelico's masterpieces which used to hang in the Uffizi and in the Accademia delle Belle Arti. Without doubt, this edifying place alone is worth a visit to Italy. We viewed also, by special permission, the ancient mosaics in the Baptistery of the *Duomo,* then under process of restoration. I remember being particularly struck with the unevenness of their surface, especially where flesh was represented. The tiny bits of stone seemed to have been stuck into the mortar in quite haphazard fashion, but producd a color-effect of remarkable vividness when seen at a distance, as each one caught and reflected the light differently.

After doing a simple but very painstaking job of restoration on a newly-discovered fresco in the Franciscan refectory at Fiesole, Oblate Sarkander and I bade a fond farewell to the good friars, and set off for our goal in Monte Cassino. We passed through Rome, but could only afford to stop a few hours, as we were already overdue at St. Benedict's ancient shrine. It is located near the main line of the railway that goes from Rome to Naples, being almost exactly halfway between the two cities. You reach it after about two and a half hours' travel on a fast train, catching a brief glimpse of its imposing pile of buildings situated on the crest of an isolated mountain, a few minutes before reaching the town of Cassino which lies at its foot. This mountain rising abruptly and boldly up from the smiling plain to a height of about six-hundred metres, seems to symbolise the work begun there by the great Patriarch of the West fifteen hundred years ago. Since then it has spread to all corners of the earth, weathering the vicissitudes of time and change with an imperturbable calm, an unyielding devotion to principle that reminds us strangely of that stalwart mountain, thrusting its face into the very teeth of many tempests, and yet remaining unmoved, unchanged.

An hour's drive in a *carrozza* up the winding ascent took us to the cloister gates, and soon I was installed in the cell which was to be my home for many weeks. It was a roomy place, with a single window looking out over a magnificent panorama. Far below was the peaceful *Campagna* dotted with villages, clearly-defined farms and vineyards; while on the horizon loomed the lofty Abruzzi with their jagged peaks and dark, mysterious passes. As in Fiesole, I was here to live on an eminence high above the earth, breathing a purer air and effectually detached from the noisome distractions of the human scene.

Spiritually it was stimulating, for if the eye can range unhindered over a vast expanse of God's creation, it spurs the soul to rise above itself, to free itself from encumbrances which before had seemed inevitable. But artistically it was hardly the ideal thing, for to study nature and appreciate it, I would have been better off down on the level plain, where contrasts, perspective, dimensional details were more perceptible. The virgin forest discloses its beauty only to him who beats a path through its trackless windings, and not to the airman flying high above it. It is fascinating to watch a tiny ant exploring the mysteries of a plot of tall grass, picking its way with such steadfast courage and patience over Gargantuan obstacles which to the lordly human seem infinitesimal.

On our summit at Monte Cassino there was room for but a single path, a few metres long, where one could walk without having to climb. But this was a sheer delight, as every step revealed a charming view of mountain and smiling countryside, seen through the screen of oak trees growing along it. Among these, black mountain pigs grubbed for acorns, and sometimes a shepherd-boy would jump astride the back of one of them, at which the disgusted animal would dash away through the trees snorting fiercely. If the herd became too scattered, the lad called them with a peculiar cry, at which then they would run up to him and eat acorns from his hand quite decorously.

And the monastery! How shall I transcribe its many-sided impressions! Cool corridors offering a welcome refuge from the scorching heat outside, broad airy terraces where one could view the marvellous landscape from all angles; baroque colonnades with glistening white statues; the grand staircase leading up to the church, which was an imposing basilica decorated inside with vari-colored marbles and rococo paintings done by Fapresto. The choir was grand indeed, with its delicately-carved stalls, and the great lectern in the middle on which ponderous choir-books reposed, all of them embellished with superb miniature work. And in the dim *Toretta,* where St. Benedict once lived and prayed, we had our daily High Mass, the solemn chant seeming to bring us closer than ever to our holy Founder, its text and cadences redolent of that classic atmosphere in which he lived and breathed. And always in moments of silence, the unceasing hum of locusts, the singing of the humble *contadini* happy at their work in the gardens and vineyards on the slope below. It was refreshing too to see the merry youths from the college and seminary playing about, and to contrast them with the venerable figures of the monks in their long black cowls and hoods. And my daily intercourse with the master, Father Desiderius, his collaborator Father Adelbert Gresnigt, and with the rest of my artistic confrères remains a lively and dear memory with me now, as I look back on my sojourn at Monte Cassino.

Here I must mention one disturbing factor which has often plagued me in my work as a religious artist. People of misguided zeal sometimes are inclined to belittle the quest for *beauty* as such, thinking that, compared with *truth* and *goodness,* it is a thing of minor value — an accessory, easily dispensed with; or even something we would be much better off without from the standpoint of our eternal salvation. This is true up to a point: certainly Beauty of itself can never dispose us properly for the work of saving our souls, or even for accomplishing great and lasting worldly achievements. I myself have sometimes felt an odd fear of it, realising how fatal its charms have been for many. "And the woman saw that the tree was good to eat, and fair to the eyes, and delightful to behold: and she took of the fruit thereof, and did eat" (Gen. III, 6). Beauty severed from Truth and Goodness, her blood-sisters, becomes a seductress and a wanton. And yet, a harlot found grace with Jesus, whereas the cunning serpent, and the pharisee, were condemned. . . . God Himself is not only eternal Truth and unchanging Goodness, but He is perfect unchanging Beauty too. . . . Without Beauty, Truth and Goodness lack that transfiguration which makes them truly attractive. These three sisters must unite in affectionate embrace, if the influence of each is to have its destined effect upon the soul of man. Only then will Truth illumine him, Goodness fortify him, Beauty warm and console him, harmoniously and fruitfully.

Deep in my soul, I have always rejoiced that God has spoken in ancient times, in ways so marvellously beautiful. The prophecies of the Old Law and the parables of the New are clothed in a beauty that is unrivalled. And the Fathers of the Church, until the late Middle Ages, saw and preserved the interdependence of Truth, Goodness, Beauty. But with the Renaissance, Beauty appears unshackled from this bond, and in her new-found liberty experiences a prodigious development. But not for long, as she soon grows

[100]

pompous, self-conscious, domineering, and man tires of her. And Knowledge too, left to wander by itself, goes sadly astray. Goodness too wanes in its unnatural isolation. We of today have only to look about us and discover how little vitality she has left, how far she has drifted away from Truth and Beauty.

But now I must mention my part in the painting of the *Soccorpo* or crypt at Monte Cassino Abbey, with its tomb of St. Benedict. Shamefacedly I admit that I had but little to do in furthering that grand enterprise, which has since won the unstinted praise of experts and the admiration of many pilgrims. When I arrived on the spot, I found the greater part of the mosaics and the ceiling-work already completed. Only a few figures and one or two groups remained to be done; and for these, I made three cartoons, and two mosaic figures. One of the latter, an angel, had to be removed later as it did not harmonise with the rest. The other one, my *Father of St. Placid,* was acknowledged by Father Desiderius, some time afterward, as being one of the most meritorious bits in the entire chapel. But on the whole, I am afraid I did not come up to the expectations of my maestro. Much that I could do very well, I was not called upon to execute; and things I knew nothing about he seemed to expect me to perform. In addition, beautiful Italy had rekindled my native Dutch love of nature, and I took up sketching again. He strongly disapproved of this, holding that drawing from life, whether that of men, animals, or *flora,* dulled in the artist that perception of spiritual values emphasised in the Lenz theory of " measuring and dividing." But I kept on, trusting to my intuition and knowledge of style to avoid coming to any permanent harm.

So nearly every day I would make a sketch from life, frequently getting one of the young students of the college or seminary to act as model. These dear lads were most accommodating, often giving up an outing to sit for me. I would reward them with foreign stamps of which I had a rather extensive collection. One day they had a theatrical performance, at which several of them wore old-fashioned wigs: I did a few heads in this *coiffure,* which pleased them hugely. In this way I gradually acquired quite a fine collection of juvenile portraits, but in so doing, fell perceptibly into the manner of the old masters; which is not surprising, as every artist who sojourns in Italy for any length of time runs that risk. But it proved a blessing for my future work; and one day Father Desiderius, having carefully studied my drawings, said to me significantly: " You have served a good apprenticeship here."

As all our group of artists, including Father Desiderius himself, had never actually made mosaics before, Archabbot Krug had employed an old artisan of the neighbourhood, Oreste by name, to teach us his craft. A group of village boys also were requisitioned to help in the huge task, and early each morning they would climb up the mountain still fasting, their pockets stuffed with generous chunks of cornbread. Work started at seven o'clock, with an intermission at half-past eight during which they ate their yellow *pane* and played ball for a while in the little courtyard adjoining the *Soccorpo.* Then they worked till noon, consumed the remainder of their bread, took a short siesta, and worked again till six, when with the first clang of the great bell in the monastery tower they would be off again, chasing headlong down the mountain like a pack of greyhounds after a rabbit. At home, they found a dish of macaroni and a kind of salad made of wild herbs awaiting them for supper.

The majority of these youths were utilized only for the cruder tasks, although one or two showed ability in the most delicate phases of mosaic making. They all had nicknames: one was *Mezzafemina* or half-girl, because he always refused to play with the others and talked like a girl. Another was called Napoli, his father having come from Naples. Emmanuele, the most talented of them all, used often to work with me on the scaffolding, busying himself with the background as I did some figure or other. He was most voluble, and I soon discovered to my consternation that he was profoundly interested in murder and bloodshed. Thus, he was forever recounting some hair-raising incident he had heard of, like that in which two tax-collectors in a neighbouring town were recently murdered because they had refused, on the occasion of a great fiesta, to permit the customary fireworks since the taxes had not been paid. Another was the case of a pretty girl, " *una bella ragazza* " recently stabbed in the streets of Cassino by a jealous lover. And then, he would ask the most disconcerting questions, as for instance why it is that murderers continue to stab their victims even after they have been wounded mortally. This phenomenon he said, he had himself witnessed with his own eyes on two occasions! "These are the fellows that always go to prison," he added contemptuously. "But of course they always come out again, after ten or fifteen years; and become respectable people once more." This last was too much for me, and I queried sharply: "Surely you are not so foolish to believe that!" "But yes," he answered calmly. "It is so; they are received back into their villages and treated with the greatest respect and consideration." Perhaps Emmanuele's contempt for death was in the nature of a premonition, for three years later he was carried away by consumption.

At the entrance to the great Simplon Tunnel there is a monument commemorating those who lost their lives in the task of perforating the base of that huge mountain. There were many, too many, of them; and yet who thinks of them now that the work has been completed? A passing thought perhaps, as we glide swiftly through the dark passageway in a luxurious train. They were unfortunate indeed, but the work had to be done. If the project had ended in failure no doubt there would have been a tremendous outcry at the amount of human sacrifice entailed. So if we strive for the highest perfection in all things, perhaps our human mistakes will be forgiven us. No lives were lost in the task of decorating the *Soccorpo,* but it was a most laborious piece of work, exacting its toll of anguish, mental and physical.

Perhaps the heaviest cross was the ever-present threat of divided opinion, which was unavoidable with so many artists working, all keyed up to do their very best. That no serious split occurred is evidence that a higher Power was guiding and protecting us, and yet exacting of each the utmost of his powers. Father Desiderius too was an important factor in keeping us together. Though always an outspoken critic and a hard taskmaster, he gave us plenty of time to fulfil his demands, and never spared himself. Whenever there was an open disagreement (sometimes it seemed more like an explosion!) he was the first to make amends and effect a reconciliation. But he alone could never have brought the work to a happy conclusion had it not been for the wholehearted support of Archabbot Krug, the efficient coöperation of Father Adelbert, the patient and self-effacing toil of the lay-brothers. Thirteen long years went by before the task which the great Beuronese master had set himself, at the age of sixty-seven, was finally accomplished. That was in 1913, when with the assistance of a Papal Legate, the *Soccorpo* was solemnly consecrated. But Archabbot Krug was not there. God had called him to Himself, before being able to witness the realisation of his cherished dream.

The following year, as I was still in Monte Cassino, I was allowed to visit Rome on the occasion of the celebration in honor of Saint Gregory the Great, the great Benedictine Pope whose thirteen-hundredth anniversary was being solemnized at St. Peter's on March 12. It was a memorable occasion. Pius X celebrated a Pontifical High Mass at which the students of the International Benedictine College of Sant' Anselmo constituted the *schola* or special choir, and I was privileged to sit among them. We sang the Proper,

[105]

standing in our places on the right-hand side of the *Confessio* or Papal Altar. The Ordinary was chanted by a massed group of one thousand Roman students standing further out in the spacious transept.

In the great central nave of the basilica a crowd of over fifty thousand faithful from all parts of the Catholic world were gathered, and all awaited the solemn entry of the Holy Father with tense expectation. Suddenly we perceived a frantic waving of handkerchiefs far down near the portals, and we knew the Pope had entered. He had forbidden all cheering, which demanded some heroic restraint on the part of the volatile Italians, but they succeeded admirably well. Not a sound was heard, save a kind of rustling noise made by the restless movements of the vast throng. It was like the hum of the distant surf, of the whisper of a sudden breeze stirring in a grove of poplars.

The Holy Father came majestically toward us, carried on his *sedia gestatoria,* bestowing his blessing to right and left to acknowledge all those silent tributes of love and veneration. When he was borne past us, his paternal gaze rested upon our group of singers, and smilingly he blessed us too.

The Mass took its solemn course, the venerable Gregorian chant seeming to take on a special dignity and sonorousness for this occasion. Once the Holy Father's face was turned directly toward me, as he sang the Preface. I made a rapid sketch of his rather plain but kindly countenance. What soft, luminous eyes he had! Occasions like these make Catholics realise what a great blessing it is to have a common father, one who truly loves and watches over them, a *Pastor Vigilans.* . . .

Maurice Denis, whom I had invited from Germany to visit me in Monte Cassino if he should come to Italy, actually arrived during this year (1904). He was accompanied by his wife and three children, their nurse, and our mutual friend Sérusier. The two artists were delighted to be able to meet Father Desiderius personally, and they had many talks with him. Denis did not fail to make a sketch of our beloved *maestro,* which formed the basis of a painting he made on his return home. This work, which he entitled *Father Desiderius lecturing to Fathers Adelbert and Willibrord,* attracted quite a bit of favorable comment, and was reproduced in two different publications: the German periodical *Hochland,* and the volume *Beuroner Kunst* by Kreitmaier. In it I am represented as listening attentively, while Father Adelbert is looking to one side somewhat sceptically. When Father Desiderius was shown a photograph of it, he exclaimed: " Denis has actually made me look like a Frenchman! " Which was quite true; and demonstrates how difficult it is for an artist to free himself from the fetters of his race.

Besides Denis and Sérusier, another Paris painter whom I used to know came to see me in Monte Cassino. He was Emile Bernard, a talented artist who had early made a name for himself among the impressionists. His essay on Cézanne, with whom he had lived for some months in 1890, and his correspondence with Van Gogh, gained him some international fame as well. I had known him in Paris in 1892, and had kept up a correspondence with him ever since. But now he had abandoned the fold of the modernists, and was following the tradition of the great Spanish and Bolognese masters. Delacroix and the younger Manet were powerful influences with him, as were all the great artists of the sixteenth century. This attachment, which he got perhaps from Cézanne, together with his horror over the complete absence of fine craftsmanship among the moderns, explains his final break with them. But the result was that he was thrust from his pinnacle of fame, and was outmoded sooner than the apostles of impressionism. Posterity will no doubt decide whether he or they were travelling up a blind alley.

Bernard visited me in Monte Cassino, and later I met him in Naples, whence we made a trip to Pompeii together. Walking through the silent streets of this ancient city, whose total populace was suddenly wiped out of existence two thousand years ago, my main impression was the utter *simplicity* which characterised the lives of the people of that distant era. The houses, the streets, the artistic remains, all showed this quality. The wealthier homes showed no evidences of extreme luxury; our modern millionaires treat themselves to a much greater splendour, I am sure. Finally we sat down for a rest amid the ruins of the Temple of Jupiter, with its enchanting view of the Bay of Naples towards Sorrento. What exquisite taste, to have selected precisely this spot for the chief sanctuary of the town! On its marble steps many an ancient Roman must have sat in the warm sunshine of a winter's day, or in summer allowed his brow to be caressed by the cool sea-breeze, as meanwhile, gazing into that infinity of blue, he allowed *dolce far niente* to possess him.

Back in Monte Cassino, the terrific summer's heat began to undermine my health, and I was sent to the Abbey of Monte Vergine, which was cooler, to recuperate for a few weeks. The monks of this Abbey wear a white habit, though they are not the lineal descendants of St. William and his disciples, who founded the place in the twelfth century. This Order soon died out, but when a group of " black " Benedictines came to succeed them, the inhabitants of the district and the pilgrims who came to pray at the shrine of the Madonna there, protested vehemently, saying they did not want any " policemen "! So the monks had to don the white garb of the former religious, and have kept it ever since.

I was received with affecting kindness by the venerable Abbot and his community, and allowed to live in a special building reserved for the sick and convalescent monks, where meat, eggs and animal fats could be included in the meals, these luxuries being prohibited by the strict rule of the monastery. Here I lived in blissful seclusion for nearly five weeks, occasionally taking a solitary climb up the mountain, where a delightful breeze was always stirring. Long hours I would spend drinking in the beauties of God's creation: golden evenings with their grand and ever-changing Italian sunsets, always succeeded by nights of solemn silence, sweet and sound repose. Sometimes I would watch a show of fireworks, which on the evening of a *gran fiesta* would break out simultaneously in a dozen villages, lighting up the sky with sheaves of fire — a pretty symbol of naïve religious faith, for Love came down from heaven as Fiery Tongues, and now loving hearts sent fire up to heaven in return. . . . True, there is " the morning after," and prosaic workdays follow when feastings must be forgotten. But it nourishes the soul thus to relax at times in carefree celebration; and I at least have experienced how fertile are those idle hours spent in just studying the sky's vast expanse, or a mass of green foliage, a patch of wild flowers. Leisure that is fruitful is not idleness.

Monte Vergine still is a popular pilgrimage spot, where thousands of Italians come on the various feasts of our Lady to venerate the image, blackened with age, that for centuries has held a reputation for wonder-working. I was not fortunate enough to witness any miracles, but I am quite ready to believe they sometimes occur, as the faith and simple piety of these people is truly extraordinary. With them, the *Bambino* and His Blessed Mother are Persons whose reality and interest in human affairs is absolutely beyond all doubt. Their powerful intercession in behalf of the suffering poor takes place only when the latter manifest dispositions which to their naïve minds seem to merit it. Thus, loud weeping and lamenting, voluble praying, frantic gesticulations in the direction of the venerable statue, and even sometimes downright threatenings, are the customary attitudes visible among the crowds of pilgrims around the shrine. Touching scenes of charity are also witnessed, such as one I saw wherein a man went around giving alms to everybody, although he himself was dressed in rags.

The shrine itself is piled high with gifts of everything imaginable: articles of clothing, food, matches, workmen's tools, even knives and revolvers. One thinks of some simple peasant whose volatile feelings, outraged by real insult, urge him on to the commission of sanguinary crime. As he hesitates, the thought comes to him of the Madonna of Monte Vergine: " What would *she* say to that? " Conquered by his native regard for her, he resolves instead upon a pilgrimage to her shrine, whereon he lays at last the dread instrument of destruction.

One day, as I knelt praying in the Madonna chapel, I heard an excited commotion nearby. Turning round, I was horrified to see three women engaged in undressing a young boy of five or six. Soon he stood there just as Nature made him, whereupon the women motioned to me, saying in agitated tones: " *Si Mon,* Mr. Monk, please take these clothes and put them on the altar! " I was staggered, but complied without a word. Then the women proceeded gleefully to dress the lad in a complete new outfit; and when I asked them to explain this unusual (to say the least) form of devotion, they told me that the lad had been seriously ill, and his parents had promised the Madonna that they would give her all that he possessed, if she would cure him. This she obviously has done, so *ecco!* the vow was simply being carried out.

Of course, it was impossible to preserve even the semblance of order among these excited and simple pilgrims. Often there was a fearful crush in the little chapel, but I soon discovered it was useless to try to shepherd them. The greater the confusion, the happier they seemed to be; perhaps because it made them feel more at home, less stiff and formal. After all, they were making a call upon their Mother, not to some cranky old aunt who might be expected to greet them with a "*Please wipe your feet,*" or a "*Don't shout; my hearing is still quite good.*"

All in all, I was touched and edified by this phase of my sojourn at Monte Vergine. The faith of the pilgrims strengthened and purified my own, and I felt my soul turning towards the Celestial Light as naturally as a flower turns to the sun. And the affection of my religious brethren warmed my heart, bringing me back to the days when I had first experienced this sort of Italian *gentilezza* with the Franciscans at Fiesole.

I returned to Monte Cassino, where I remained until the following summer, when my health threatened to break down again, so I was told to return to Beuron. This I did, stopping en route in Rome, Florence, and Milan. A young man who seemed to possess great artistic gifts, Vannicola by name, had supplied me before I left with letters of introduction to two other rising young geniuses whom I wanted to visit: Giovanni Papini and Giuseppe Prezzolini. I well remember my call at the former's home in Florence, one hot July afternoon. He himself answered my knock at the door, and I saw before me a slender youth with a longish face and sharp features, which gave him more of a Mongolian than a typical Florentine appearance. He ushered me in graciously, presenting to me his friend Vaillati, with whom he had been reading Plato. I begged them to

[112]

continue and allow me to listen. This they did, Papini reading the Italian translation and Vaillati the Greek original. Whenever they came upon a particularly fine passage, Papini would cry aloud with delight. When they had finished, my host explained to me: "We meet every week to read Plato, it is an ancient Florentine tradition."

It was a still hotter afternoon when I called on Prezzolini, at his home in Milan. He impressed me as being a most captivating man, full of fun, yet extremely refined. He was very fond of the German school of romanticism, and well versed in all trends of modern thought. We corresponded for some time, and in May of the following year he came to see me in Beuron. "One must come to Germany in order to understand Catholicism," he told me then.

I kept up a correspondence with Papini also, but after a time it lapsed, as was perhaps natural, since he was still an unbeliever. But with his conversion and the publication of his famous *Life of Christ* we resumed again. This book's immediate success is perhaps due to that fact that it was written by a cultured layman, who could express the biblical facts in all their profundity with such power and clarity, such evident sincerity and conviction. I often wonder why it is that more of our modern "heathens" do not take the trouble to read the Scriptures. They would derive much satisfaction from this practice, as I once saw demonstrated in the case of a gentleman who came to visit Monte Cassino. He was a well known Roman sculptor; and when I asked him, the morning after his arrival, whether he had slept well, he told me: "I did not sleep at all. On the table beside my bed I found a book of the Gospels, and I became so interested in it that I read till very late, and afterwards couldn't get to sleep. For you see," he said (he had left the Church some years before), " we never get to see the Bible otherwise! " Perhaps his heart was touched, his soul aglow, as happened to the two disciples of the Lord, on the road to Emmaus.

Through Papini I also became acquainted with the Florentine painter Oscar Giglia. He sketched my countenance, which was very haggard at the time. It is interesting fun, this sensation of being devoured by the penetrating gaze of an artist, and watching meanwhile the changing expressions on his face, now cloudy and puzzled, now lit up with pleasure and satisfaction as he pinions your veritable self upon his canvas.

CHAPTER SIX

IN VIENNA

I ARRIVED in Beuron on August 1, 1905, during the noonday recreation of the brethren. They gave me a cordial welcome, and invited me to join them in picking currants, a task that was just then engaging their attention. I complied, and thus began again that monastic routine I had learned to love so well, wherein humble service and self-sacrificing fraternal charity are ideals so thoroughly practised. The delightful coolness of the climate soon revived my lagging strength, and after a month or so Archabbot Placid requested me and another monk to go to Vienna, to investigate the advisability of exhibiting some of our art there. The so-called " Secessionists " under the leadership of the poet-philosopher Richard Kralik had invited Father Desiderius to join in an exhibition of religious art they were planning. At first our people were loth to consent, because of the ultra-modern ideals of the group; but when the invitation was repeated and several of our community were in favor of accepting, it was decided that a study of the situation *sur place* was warranted.

So we set out on our diplomatic mission, and duly arrived in the ancient capital, now more interesting than ever, since the addition of modern suburbs which harmonised so well with the *Altstadt*. Modern progress had not yet spoiled the dreamy *Ring* with its series of imposing palaces, parks, rollicking cafés; no raucous motor-horns, no acrid smell of petrol, no mad speed-demons on hand to disillusion the seeker for historic atmosphere. The hoary old Cathedral of St. Stephen was still the nerve-center of the city, and from it narrow picturesque streets radiated out to join the broad *Ring* and its colourful flow of life. Even if one boarded a tram and rode out to the old suburbs of Doebling, Heiligenstadt, Grinzing, or Sievering, there was always that same atmosphere of haunting beauty so peculiar to old Vienna. How much more interesting it was (thought I) to see the numerous hansom cabs and carriages about, than to behold a monotonous stream of taxis and limousines gliding correctly and swiftly down the street. What a joy it was to watch a pair of spirited horses dashing along, with a smart coachman expertly checking them! It harmonised so well with the animated tone of Viennese life — life on a background of life. The Royal Guard still held its smart drills inside the courtyard of the *Burg*, and crowds would congregate to watch the " Changing of the Guard " ceremony. The beloved Emperor still governed his people from within those portals, holding them united by the power of his intelligent sympathy rather than by force. Lueger, probably the most distinguished Austrian of his day, still was mayor of the city, an office to which he had been elected by a vast majority in 1897.

Our business with the " Secession " group was soon finished. Its directors were most accommodating in every way, and when we learned that the Munich *Society for Christian*

IN VIENNA

Art had agreed to send an exhibit, our last objection vanished and we accepted. Our plan was to have a monumental representation of the Sacrament of Baptism, as a setting for the samples of Beuronese art we were to bring. This was to be painted by the artists of the " Secession " group, in seven subjects: *The Blessed Trinity* (in whose Name Baptism is given), *Original Sin* (Eve and the Immaculate Virgin), *The Passage through the Red Sea, The Slaughter of the Innocents* (Baptism of Blood), *The Repentant Thief* (Baptism of Desire), and *The Baptism of the Ethiopian*. But as none of the artists felt willing to undertake the second subject (*Original Sin*) I was commissioned to do it; and so after completing all our arrangements I set out with my companion for Beuron again, to begin work.

After making a sketch of my projected picture, I began drawing the cartoon. Keenly feeling the lack of female models, I nevertheless did the best I could with the help of pictures and plaster-casts, and at last had what I wanted. Meanwhile, my companion had gathered together, packed, and shipped all that we needed for the exhibition, and off we went again for Vienna. This was early in October, and as the show was scheduled to open on the thirtieth, there was no time to lose. I had first to trace my large cartoon on the surface reserved for it in the Exhibition Hall, and then paint the actual picture on the spot. The other six artists, Andri, Lenz, Mueller, Jettmar, Engelhart, and Koenig (all Secessionists, of course) had already started working on their portions of the plan; and so day after day we painted

[117]

together in merry unity. Now and then I could hear a word or two spoken that would hardly grace a drawing-room, but this only showed that the gentleman in question was hard at work. Or sometimes there would be comical horseplay, as when Lenz pretended he was Engelhart's long-lost friend, begging to be reinstated into his good graces. But Engelhart rebuffed him with such droll severity that we were in fits of laughter. Whenever the telephone would ring, there was a rush to answer it, to see whose " girl " was calling now: if the caller turned out to be really a female friend of one of the artists, she was given a thorough teasing. If the fun grew too boisterous, Andri who was the president of the committee, would call out entreatingly, " Brothers, we must work! " and he was generally faithfully obeyed. Plecnik, the architect and real instigator of the exhibition, often called to watch our progress, and on these occasions he would run ferret-like from one painting to another, his face a picture of delight or woe according as he approved or disliked what we were doing.

The principle of the " Secession " in regard to art exhibitions was that the arrangement of the objects was as important as the paintings themselves. A minimum collection well arranged, they held, was more effective than a great number and variety of pictures all contending for space. This of course limited the representative possibilities of our exhibition, but I was overjoyed to see Maurice Denis and Gauguin, old friends of mine, represented by samples of their work. The former had sent three paintings, one of which, his *Notre Dame de l'Ecole,* now reposes in the National Gallery at Brussels; while the *Dream of St. Joseph* which Gauguin contributed has since been acquired by the new Bavarian State Gallery in Munich.

When the exposition opened it met with immediate and great success. Andri and Engelhart were much perturbed however, as the numbers coming were not great enough to insure payment of our overhead, and there was scarcely any criticism. But all went off smoothly, and though the " Secession " was left with a deficit in its treasury, enough paintings were sold later on to reimburse them most munificently. And I, after my return to Beuron, was rewarded too when one day during recreation, Archabbot Placid read out the following telegram: *" Picture sold. One thousand crowns. Andri."* My *Eve with Mary Immaculate* had also found a lover. It now hangs over the inner portal of the Wittgenstein Palace in Vienna, where (as the caretaker has since told me) many people are charmed with what they claim to be a mysterious unearthly beauty emanating from it, transporting them to a higher world.

Chapter Seven

IN THE HOMELAND

My parents had never been quite resigned to my "desertion" of the family hearth, although they never admitted it to me. Here for instance is a typical letter from my mother: "Tonight I am all alone, your father is out to a meeting, and of course none of the eight children are with me any more. They have their own homes now. A few moments ago I cried a little . . . for I am really quite alone . . . Yet I have every reason to be happy, which I try to be. . . . And my boy, you know I am always with you in spirit, in my thoughts. . . ."

My Archabbot however was averse to my going home for a visit, unless for some serious reason. But when my brothers wrote that they were having a grand reunion to honor my father on his seventieth birthday and were anxious to have me come, this was deemed a sufficient reason and I was told to go. But I hated the thought of having to put off my monastic garb even for a short time. Surely I thought, my people would not let me in the house, dressed in such a fashion. However, I put out a diplomatic feeler in one of my letters, and being told that there would be no objections on that score, set out at once. It was an early morning in November (1905), and I recall as if it were yesterday the thrill of joy that filled my heart as I boarded the train at the Beuron station, to go back to my dear home and parents after an absence of nine years.

I went to Hilversum, a small town between Amsterdam and Utrecht, where my parents were living since their removal from Haarlem. It was a place where many business and professional men of the capital had their country homes. My little mother met me at the station at about ten that night, welcomed me profusely, and in the carriage as we rode to Villa Tromp, the new family residence, gave me all the news of her small world. My widowed step-sister with her three children lived across the street; the hack-driver, right next door: I was to take a carriage whenever I wanted to, and it would go on the family bill; father had reserved two rooms for me in the hotel nearby, so that I could be comfortable and at the same time independent, able to receive whomsoever I wished. We had a fine big dog, who went with father on his daily walks. I must be dreadfully hungry and tired after such a long journey. How was my health? Wait till we get inside where the light is good, and mother can inspect me thoroughly from head to foot! The carriage stopped; we had arrived. " Have you got all your belongings? What! No umbrella, and only that small bag? But I suppose it is convenient, after all, to have such small wants."

Father was standing in the living room, waiting. He was no longer the robust, keen man of yore; the years had taken their toll. In his eyes there dwelt a kind of fear, a wavering look that came from the paralytic stroke he had suffered five years back, as though he had seen death, and quailed before

it. He took me in from top to toe — *his* son, black Benedictine monk — we clasped hands firmly. True, he had seen
me in my habit before: once in Carlsbad whither he had
gone to take the waters, when I had come up to see him
from nearby Prague (1896); and another time when he had
come down to Prague himself, before returning to Holland,
to see our paintings in St. Gabriel's. But it was different
now, this meeting in the family home. Somehow as he
looked at me, I could not help thinking of Ballin's remark
on first seeing me in the habit: " You never in your life
looked so decent as you do now." We sat down. Soon the
maid served supper, during which we talked quite uncon-
strainedly. All had gone off smoothly indeed.

Four of my brothers, and two sisters (the third was unable to come) arrived at Villa Tromp for my father's
seventieth birthday anniversary. All brought their children,
so that my father was soon surrounded by a veritable flock
of grandchildren. He looked like a classic patriarch in their
midst, with his tall spare figure, his dignified bearing, his
finely-shaped head with its crown of snow-white hair. His
firm mouth, so expressive of a strong will, was yet the evidence of his sensitive nature; his lips would tremble, and
tears gather in his eyes, whenever a grandchild approached
to wish him good-luck. Happy to overflowing he unde-
niably was, doubtless because he had the instincts of a true
father, who sees himself extended, as it were, and living on
in the members of his progeny. Proudly he looks upon them,
seeing in them himself and his own ancestors surviving,
continuing into the distant future. Perhaps he has been dis-

appointed with some of his own sons and daughters, but no matter: these grandchildren, now, give him renewed hope of the fulfilment of his most cherished expectations.

After my father's retirement from business, my twin brother and two of the younger ones had kept his two oil-refineries going. "The boys are doing well in Zaandam," he told me, "but I am not completely satisfied; they are wearing too many borrowed plumes." By this he meant the loans they had succeeded in floating for the extension of the business, which went against his principles. He admired the enterprise and daring of great captains of industry; but for himself preferred to keep within more restricted limits. I am more like him in that respect, feeling more at home in an unpretentious dwelling, where everything is spick and span, than in a vast palace where neglected rooms adjoin luxurious stately chambers.

During my stay at home, I had the joy of singing High Mass over in Zaandam, the town where I was born. It was celebrated in the large new parish church, and my three brothers attended. I was sorry that the old church had been torn down, for it had been next door to my father's first oil-refinery. As a lad I used often to peer into the windows curiously, sometimes shouting in derision, "*Pater noster, Pater noster.*" And now, I was a *Pater* myself.

When I came out to start the Mass, some of the congregation could not keep from smiling, so exact was my resemblance to my twin brother. It was as if "Director Verkade" had suddenly taken his stand at the altar. But no, there he was sitting in the front pew. Yet it was clearly

[123]

a member of the family, which gave great satisfaction to the local Catholics. Old Freerik, a former employee of my father's, whom we twins used to adore because he always made such fine arrows for us to play with, came afterwards to the sacristy to receive my blessing. He was a Catholic, and there were tears of joy in his eyes as he knelt humbly at my feet. I made the sign of the cross over his bowed and grizzled head, showering upon him, together with God's blessing, all the warmth of the love I felt for this kind friend of my childhood days.

After visiting some days with my brothers in Zaandam I went to my married sister's in Hattem, stopping on the way at the home of my youngest brother in Amsterdam. All the while I felt under a peculiar sort of constraint, as I still was wearing my habit; and Hattem especially had been the scene of two critical years of my life. The little town had not changed much; its old Romanesque tower still chimed out the hours with the same old song, if somewhat more hesitantly than before. The same trim houses poked their varicoloured gables toward the sky, the same narrow streets were still kept spotlessly clean. But beyond the old moat a hideous modern schoolhouse had arisen, while skirting the forest there was a row of pert little bungalows.

Thus it is generally with picturesque country towns: the artists first discover it, exploit its beauties and make it famous. Then come the tourists, who are succeeded by the more persevering summer-resorters. A few of these are induced to settle down permanently, imagining their dream of:

IN THE HOMELAND

" A lonely cottage on a heath,
Far from the madding crowd,"

to have come true. Some want to improve the soil, or to raise chickens, an orchard; while others only desire to enjoy the salubrious air and quiet. But they are doomed to disappointment, all of them. The soil is stubborn and refuses to be " reformed," the chickens die of some plague, the trees simply will not bear. The atmosphere remains as healthy as ever, but somehow the quiet solitude becomes irksome. Then, it is discovered that living is expensive instead of cheap, as everything has to be brought from a distance. And so the noble experiment ends in discouragement and failure; unless (as happens more frequently nowadays) it is carried out by an organized group, whose members plan everything thoroughly and agree to share both profit and loss with one another.

Near Hattem is the town of Zwolle, the burial place of Thomas à Kempis. I went there to pay my respects to the remains of this holy spiritual guide, and called also at the residence of the Dominican Fathers, famed for their particularly fine rendition of the Gregorian chant. I was received with such extraordinary warmth by the guest-master and several of the other Fathers that instead of staying but a few hours I remained three days. The interchange of thought between us was most refreshing to me. I have rarely found religious so full of vitality as these Dominicans of Zwolle: they were *robust* men! This peculiarity would have disconcerted me, had it not been so crystal-clear that their

[125]

minds were directed wholly God-wards, their hearts filled with a devotion, sincere and touching toward our Blessed Lady. Perhaps no other order in the Church has emphasised *personality* so thoroughly, which is probably why it has produced so many men of distinction in the realms of mystical and speculative theology.

But in spite of many pleasant visits like these among my old haunts, the most precious hours of all were spent with my dear parents. Usually these were in the evenings, when all was quiet and there was no one about but our three selves. It was then that my childhood days seemed to live again. The same curtains as of yore hung on the windows, the same familiar table and chairs decorated the living room; even the gas-lamp seemed to hum softly its old familiar air. A cab rolled by: *that* sound I knew too from long ago. We would have tea; then mother would write a letter to one or other of her absent children, and father would read his paper, I a book. But the silences did not seem to last long. We were content, we three, just to be together for a while. Soon it would not be possible any more, this loving communion of our hearts, in the warm cosiness, the *sacredness* of our family home.

My parents were extraordinary, I think, for two things: their love of domestic life, and their loyalty to their children. These may be characteristic parental virtues, but they possessed them in a degree that I have never seen excelled. And for that, my gratitude to God and to them has been unceasing. What blessings this devotion has brought to us their children! The eight of us have all, so far at least, made our way successfully in life, and yet we were not brought up according to fixed rules or complicated pedagogical standards. My father, when I had thanked him on his birthday for all the wisdom he had taught me, said that I was exaggerating matters: he was no pedagogue, he said, but had only followed the promptings of the moment. And indeed, both father and mother had little time to give to each one of the eight individuals demanding their attention. It is better this way, I think, than trying to impregnate fewer children with a much greater number of principles. A few general ones, consistently and clearly instilled, sufficed amply for us. We knew right from wrong, and my parents took pains not to allow us to expect praise or rewards when we acted rightly, but made us view it as a matter of course. Vulgarity and meanness were treated with ridicule rather than with severity. Their chief aim was, I think, to make us all good members of society, worthy occupants of the position in life to which we were born. Yet if they nourished ambition in us, they were always careful to see that we kept it within the bounds of reason, and of justice.

Thus if our up-bringing cannot be said to have been Christian in that it failed to hold up God and His rewards as the highest of all goods, it was still animated by a truly Christian spirit. In my case at least, it has proved to be the basis for a true religious ideal as opposed to the purely secular — an exception, perhaps to the rule; just as is the case with those unfortunates who, having had all the benefits of a religious education, turn in the end to unbelief.

IN QUEST OF BEAUTY

And yet, in spite of all my dear parents could do for me, in spite of the charms my native land, so cozy and comfortable, woven about my heart, I grew uneasy. A barrier had somehow grown up around me, keeping all that I had once loved at an appreciable distance. I was definitely no longer at home with my parents nor in my quaint Holland; and my habit reminded me that I had duties that could not be shirked for long. So I made up my mind to go.

But before I went, my friends insisted on holding an exhibition of my paintings. I had brought along the charcoal portraits made in Monte Cassino, and a few sketches, to show my parents; and when the Dutch artist Jan Toorop saw them one day at our home, he immediately demanded that they be publicly shown. He took me to an art-dealer in Amsterdam, Van Gogh (a relative of the famous painter), who agreed with the suggestion and offered the use of his rooms for the purpose. So I was given the satisfaction of seeing my works, well-framed and hung, on public exhibition. My satisfaction was not, I hope, due to vanity, but rather to seeing all my paintings together side by side. Only in this way can the artist's personality and ideals be correctly seen and valued, as a complete whole. An unexpected number of people came to view the exhibition, and it had to be kept open a fortnight longer than we had planned. So I felt some reward for what I had done in quest of my ideal, especially when the leading local newspaper gave this verdict: "Although it was somewhat academic, and obviously under the influence of Italian art, the exhibit had an undeniable air of purity and refinement about it. There was something typically *Catholic* about the faces and the expression of the eyes, which bespoke a deep piety and a sincere faith: qualities which are found only when the artist himself is an ardent believer."

I realised however that my drawings lacked the robust synthetic character that had stamped my works in the Parisian period, and that I had therefore perhaps deteriorated from a purely artistic point of view. But what I had succeeded in portraying was something that had been born within me since that time: a dim vision of Unseen Beauty, a love for an Ideal that far transcended all things earthly, so that my creative strivings could no longer be satisfied with merely individualistic expression or mere sensual beauty.

Another episode that took place before my departure I must also recount. One day, in the little hotel where I put up in Zaandam, a Chinese woman passed me on the stairs. She was dressed in her native costume; and noticing my look of some amazement she stopped and said: "I too am a Catholic, and so glad to meet a priest." She spoke in English, evidently unable to talk Dutch. So I replied, in the same tongue: "Where do you come from?" "Shanghai", she answered. "I am with the Dutch Consul's family, as nurse for their little child. But I am so homesick!" And then, looking furtively about, she exclaimed piteously: "Father, if only I could get to church oftener, and go to Confession and Holy Communion, I would be happy. But it is so difficult to get away, and when I do go the people stare so at me and I can find no confessor who understands

English." I promised at once to help her and soon located a priest in the neighbouring church who could hear confessions in English. I then got two girls to accompany her, and when I next saw her some days later, she was radiantly happy. " I have been to the Sacraments," she explained simply. Before my departure I gave her a bronze St. Benedict's medal as a farewell token. At first she took it for a piece of money, and flatly refused to accept it. When I explained what it was she thanked me with profuse apologies; and then, to my consternation, threw herself down before me Chinese fashion, touching the floor with her forehead. I gave her my blessing, and retreated in confusion.

On the day of my departure, my father was unwell. I went into his bedroom to say goodbye. Anxious to avoid any effusions of sentimentality, he bethought himself of the various presents he knew I was taking along with me, for my brethren in Beuron. " Beware of *pickpockets*," he warned me (using the English expression). " I dreamt of them last night; and you know, I myself was their victim once." I promised to be careful; and then he said spiritedly: " Well, Jan, goodbye! Or rather, I'll just say *au revoir!* " These were the last words I ever heard him utter. And my mother? But I was destined to see her again, so let me draw the veil of silence over our affecting farewell.

On the homeward journey I stopped at two Abbeys of the Beuron Congregation: St. Joseph's at Coesfeld in Westphalia, and Maria Laach near Bonn. These two houses greatly interested me because they had been founded during the incumbency of Archabbot Placid Wolter (1890–

1908); and in addition, I was curious to see how their observance compared with ours. Though of a different stamp
and character, they both edified me extremely: for, while
remaining true to the basic traditions they had brought from
the Mother Abbey, they yet had developed a distinctive
ethos of their own, which, of course, is the natural thing
with all Benedictine communities. Both of them were still
in their formative period, which gave them a somewhat
different cast from a monastic family that has overcome its
initial difficulties and has a more settled tradition. Also
each had its own special work, demanded by local conditions; and this likewise influenced the character of each. I
met many old friends here, brethren who had been with me
in Beuron. They were all fired with a youthful enthusiasm
which promised great things for the community, accepting
their many deprivations with heroic patience and even joy.
I spent Christmas at St. Joseph's, and the feast of St. John
the Evangelist (my former patron-saint) at Laach. On New
Year's Eve I was back in Beuron.

CHAPTER EIGHT

AICHHALDEN

THIS year (1906), which I had commenced so well by arriving in my monastic home on the eve of its birthday, brought with it another welcome assignment: the decoration of the parish church at Aichhalden, in the Black Forest. This little town, nestling in a valley high up in the famous woodland region, was the centre of life for quite a sizable group of Catholic peasant families, despite the fact that its only link with the outside world was a rickety mail-coach that came up from Rottweil-on-the-Neckar once a day. Its church had been built in 1832, during a " utility craze " in Wuertemberg which produced so many of those barn-like religious edifices still to be seen in the province. All seem to have been fashioned upon a single prosaic pattern: plain rectangular structures, with high Romanesque windows and a flat ceiling; an uninspiring hexagonal choir with the high altar in the middle, two side altars to right and left of this, and an elevated arch connecting apse with nave. But strangely enough, this type of structure had its merits: the whole congregation got an unobstructed view of the high altar, and preaching was made easy as there was but little echo; while the vast reaches of unadorned space facilitated immeasurably the artist's task. By dividing up the surface harmoniously, and by judiciously choosing his colours, he was able to produce rhythm and life as if by magic.

Father Herman Buehler (1873–1920) was the beloved *Pfarrer* (pastor) of Aichhalden at the time, and true shepherd of his flock he was. The program he had set before himself on taking up his duties was characteristic of his unique personality. It had three points only: to acquire more bells, to decorate the church, and to have a mission for the people. He accomplished all three objectives, and when after eight years he was promoted, his successor found a thriving parish awaiting him in Aichhalden.

One of the best means of rejuvenating a parish is to decorate its church (a work to which rich and poor alike contribute), especially if the house of God has become shoddy and neglected. The people of Aichhalden had always been generous in giving toward their church, as was shown by the various interior furnishings. The three altars, the statues, the sacred vestments and other equipment were of the finest; but the walls were sad to behold. Dreary and sodden, like the sky on a rainy day. Distemper must be renewed frequently, especially in an unheated church, where during the winter the north wall is coated with ice for weeks on end. After ten years or so the lime will have disintegrated, leaving only coloured dust.

When I saw the nature of the task before me, I knew it was hopeless to attempt single-handed. All my artistic confrères in Beuron happened to be otherwise engaged; so I asked the painter Karl Mayer, of Neunhausen, to assist me. He accepted the invitation and arrived in Aichhalden about the middle of May, bringing two assistants and his son Karl junior, aged fifteen. As soon as the scaffolding had been put up we began to work, I at the figures and the others at the background. We were guided by a small water-colour sketch which Father Paul Krebs had made, he having been designated originally to do the work. This helped us considerably; but there were many hard nuts to crack nevertheless. Everything had to be experimented with first, such as the exact division of the surface, the size of the ornaments, the intensity of the colours. As I was the director, there was continually this question to be answered: " Well now, Father, what next? " For once the details of the work assigned to each section had been decided on, execution went on rapidly.

But still I found enough time to work upon my figures. To start with, I did two angels, more than life-size: St. Michael, patron of the church, and St. Raphael. Standing on clouds, they filled the space above the side altars to right and left of the choir-arch, symbolising their guardianship of the sanctuary. Next I painted a large half-length Christ, in an oval on the choir-ceiling, and then a six-winged angel in the space on either side. Finally between the windows of the choir I placed eight smaller angels, using for these, sketches I had made of some children of the village.

The latter effort turned out so well that I formed the idea of using more of the young people of the parish as models for further figures. Father Paul's plan called for dividing up the wall-space in the nave into six large sections which were to contain texts from Scripture; but my idea was to make this into twenty-two panels, each containing the figure of a saint garbed in white, on a dark background. The pastor consented to the change, as did my Abbot; so as soon as we had finished the choir early in August, I set to work with great enthusiasm. Mayer and his assistants had already left, their task of putting on the colour background having been completed. The church was radiant in its bright new garment, like a bride on her wedding day. The glistening ceiling, the front wall of the choir with its imposing angels on a background of dark blue and a cluster of golden stars overhead, made a profound impression. "Now we see how dirty and dismal our church was before," the villagers said.

I can imagine nothing more calculated to delight the true artist's heart than painting figures in a church where the whole setting and background have been completed. It is like putting precious jewels into their delicate band of gold, or gorgeous exotic flowers into a fragile bowl of crystal. And what bliss, to paint all day in the sacred atmosphere of God's house! Even the lordly sun seems interested, peeping in through the choir-windows just as the morning's work begins, and again towards nightfall, he sends his last rays through the rose-window in the western wall, making the colours glow and live. Outside, it is burning hot, but here, so cool and restful. The clock in the church-tower strikes the hours with an amazing swiftness, for time flies quickly by, when work is pleasure. At eleven, a schoolboy rings for prayers, as the morning's classes end. The ringing stops, but the mischievous lad must be hanging onto the rope, as I hear his feet striking on the floor of the sacristy several times. Now a farm-wagon rattles by, as I can tell by its heavy rumble, and the resounding crack of the driver's whip. He swings it gleefully, for the harvest has been good this year. . . . Children are playing by the church-door; now suddenly they enter. There is a sound of bare feet on the stone pavement, a murmur at the holy-water font, a rustling in the benches, then silence: they are praying. The smallest one is bored: he soon sets up a howl. Suddenly they all rise and dash out, banging the door. . . . Quiet reigns. . . . It is sweet thus to be alone with God, working in silence, for Him. . . .

In the afternoon, other visitors come. Sometimes it is a healthy-looking mother with her baby, both serenely happy. If the day is particularly fine, an aged couple hobble in, to sit for an hour or so in one of the pews, the picture of patient resignation. It is hard to be unable to do any work, and thus to be a burden for others. Poor old souls, they long for death, and yet they are afraid.

But I could not allow myself to give way to my poetic moods, great as the temptation was. Creative work is impossible unless one fully concentrates on the plan in mind; and yet, sometimes the best results come about as if by chance. A sudden light flashes through the soul, a new road opens up as of itself, leading easily and directly to one's goal. But such heaven-sent aids are usually given, in my experience at least, as reward for superhuman effort, which bars all sense of repose, just as swift journeying permits us no feelings of tranquil enjoyment, however fair the landscape may be.

I completed three figures almost every week. Each panel

was 43 inches high and 27 broad, which left room only for the upper half of the saint's body. But this made a fine effect, high up on the wall. On Sunday, the people coming to church would always inspect the work, being pleased to note the progress made since their last visit. They would try to guess whom I had used as model for this or that figure; and enthusiasm reached a high point (especially among the children) when Father Buehler was recognised as St. Thomas Aquinas and myself as St. Bernard of Clairvaux.

One day I was pleasantly surprised with the following telegram: "Arriving today. Toroop." The famous Dutch painter arrived in the early afternoon, in the midst of a fierce thunderstorm. In spite of his noticeable limp, he insisted on climbing up a high ladder to get a close view of my work. We remained on the scaffolding a long time, during which he gave his comments in a most cordial and kindly manner. He approved most thoroughly of the division of space and the harmony of the colors, criticising only a few minor mistakes in detail which could easily be corrected. This visit was a godsend to me, as it gave me confidence in what I was attempting and saved me what might have proved to be costly blunders; I deeply regretted that it had to be so short. The painter could only stay a few hours, leaving by carriage late that evening. Needless to say, he took with him my affectionate gratitude.

The end of August brought me another distinguished visitor, in the person of my old friend Johannes Jorgensen. We had not been together since 1894, an interval during which, as the poet wittily says in one of his books, we had

[137]

been "playing hide and seek with each other all over Europe." When he was able to visit Germany I happened to be in Prague or Italy, and when he tried to see me once in Italy I had just left for Vienna. But now we had arranged for a good long visit. Father Buehler had been kind enough to offer him a room in the parish house, and one fine day he arrived, in the best of spirits and full of great plans. His leisure time was to be spent, he said, in writing a brief history of Danish literature, which the firm of Koesel and Co. in Kempten was already arranging to publish. I had gone to meet him at the nearest railway station, driving the carriage myself. As the horse turned out to be a skittish young colt which shied under the slightest provocation, our homeward trip was quite exciting: an incident which Joergensen did not fail to describe most amusingly in his essay *Von Vesuv nach Skagen* (*From Vesuvius to Skagway*).

My friend's arrival produced no great change in my routine at Aichhalden. We both had our work to do, and were in such perfect *rapport* with each other from previous intercourse that there was nothing pressing to discuss. Our tasks took all our energy, and we found nothing strange at all in our having so little to say to each other. For diligence makes one silent, and true friends find solace in a kindred task more than in loquacity. Joergensen has a charming passage describing this phase of our visit, which I here transscribe:

"The days passed swiftly by in sunshine and in work. Each noon the *Post-auto* brought us letters, the *Deutsche Volksblatt* from Stuttgart, and a local paper from neigh-

[138]

bouring Rottweil. After dinner we three would remain sitting at table in contented ease, each one absorbed in his own bit of printed matter. No one would speak, and the only sound would be the rustling of turned pages, or an idle flicking of someone's hand at busy flies settled on the remains of our meal. Coffee was served, which roused us from our reveries somewhat; but immediately Verkade would jump up, don his artist's smock and go out into the church, crawling carefully up the long ladder onto his scaffolding under the ceiling. I went to my room, and was soon buried in my notes on Danish literary history. Thus the day went, until we met again at the supper-table, under whose hanging oil-lamp three faces beamed with the satisfaction of work well done, and with the pleasurable anticipation of good food followed by a well-earned repose."

And those precious daily letters! What comfort, what inspiration they would bring! I quote for instance, from one of Prezzolini's: "Your visit to me was like that of a strange meteor falling from the skies, leaving behind it a bright trail of light, and phosphorescent odors that made one giddy. This is the only way I can describe how your rare combination of worldly asceticism and abstemious hedonism has affected me. I cannot but believe that your cloister-walks are simply a spacious promenade whither you have escorted your fair Lady Imagination, to revel in what dreams of the world and life your mystic surroundings can call up. And your life of mortification and penances, isn't it simply to provide more *salt and pepper* for those cloying dreams? And your Rule, your Abbot, do they not provide a convenient, if restricted background upon which to display your new-found wisdom? "

These were extraordinary notions, but they often contained a grain of truth. The expression " abstemious hedonism " fitted well my natural inclinations, which have always been in the direction of life's joys, even now that I am a monk; and it is only my native love of moderation and frugality that keeps them in check. Early in my life I must have realised that genuine happiness demands surrender to, assimilation with a *bonum,* a true good, which in its turn exalts and transforms our limited selves. But of course, such happiness is not possible without renunciation.

During our visit in Milan, Prezzolini and I had discussed St. Augustine, and painting. But during our subsequent correspondence we abandoned pompous theorizing, pouring out our inmost thoughts in a curious mixture of gaiety and seriousness that was most diverting. My friend, too, had since come to know what love is, which mellowed and softened his talented nature. His wife had taught him how (as he put it) " to treat simple people with benevolence "; a precious lesson which I too have learned, I believe, *ex ore infantium:* from little children. And thus, as in some pleasant game, we two friends exchanged with each other the latest pretty fruits we culled from the garden of love and beauty all about us.

Besides my painting, I also performed my first priestly labours in Aichhalden. For the first time I entered the confessional-box to hear those tales of guilt and penitence, and in Christ's sweet name, to absolve and comfort harassed souls. I administered Baptism for the first time and preached my first sermon in that humble house of God whose walls I was being privileged to beautify. Incidentally I made my first oratorical *faux pas,* during a funeral sermon in which I called the deceased a *poor* woman, only to be informed afterwards, by a somewhat disgusted parishioner who came to the sacristy to tell me about it, that the lady in question had left an estate of considerable value. My first penitent happened to be a schoolboy whom I had often sketched and I am still in doubt as to which of us was the more embarrassed. Certainly we were both glad when the ordeal was over, and another penitent had entered. What a joy came to me when first I baptised a little child! But shame too, as I read those moving promises of fidelity to God, which I had kept so imperfectly. It is indeed a grand privilege, thus to be the instrument of life, unending life, and splendid divine grace to a human soul.

When October was ushered in, the church in Aichhalden was almost complete in its new garb; and none too soon, for the solemn dedication was scheduled for the fourteenth of that month. On the fifth I started on the last two figures; but there were still many finishing touches required throughout the whole. Delicate work, too, because any attempt to change a figure usually spoils it. It is better for the artist to execute at once, with as little intermission as possible, what he has in mind for the individual components of his plan. Delacroix well says: *Finir une chose lorsqu'on tient, la seule manière de faire beaucoup.* Experience of many years has taught me that the painter must finish his work with dispatch, or if this is impossible, he must approach its termination with the greatest caution, even though he has visualised the end-in-view from the start. In this latter way, the only way to handle monumental projects, the work reaches maturity slowly, gradually; so that undue haste in its final stages invariably does harm. Restraint is difficult, of course, as one views the proximity of his goal; but it is indispensable. I tried to visualise the final effect of my entire work as if it were a star approaching from the far-off heavens, increasing in vividness and brilliance of colour with each passing day; or as a massive, shapeless form emerging from thick fog, unrecognisable until the very moment it is before you. Finally came the day when only a few contours here and there, or an accentuation of colour, remained to be done. It was the day on which everything depended, but it brought success, complete satisfaction. I saw absolutely nothing that remained undone to mar my plan. " *Deo Gratias, it is finished!* " I cried out at last, and the workmen came to remove the scaffolding.

Various people came at once to view the church, among them Herr Mayer, and Father Melchior, the aged Subprior in Beuron. He preached a congratulatory sermon the following Sunday; and in the afternoon there was a farewell party, in my honor, at the village inn. When I drove off next day, many of the villagers came to their doors to wish their artist *Herr Pater* a fervent Godspeed. Some time later, Father Buehler wrote in his parish chronicle, that the renovation of the church had acted like a mission upon his community.

Chapter Nine

MUNICH

On our way back to Beuron from Aichhalden, Father Melchior disclosed the " happy secret " which the Arch-abbot had hinted about in a recent letter to me. I was to go at once to Munich and continue my art studies! This pleas-urable prospect at first filled me with happiness, but sud-denly when I realised that it would mean leaving my dear Beuron again, and that after my latest absence of five whole months, my joy was mixed with sorrow. However in the end, faith triumphed over feeling. " My superiors wish it, so I must take my medicine and make the best of it," thought I. On October 29, scarcely a fortnight after my arrival, I left my monastic home again, this time for Bavaria's pleas-ant capital. I took up residence in a college belonging to the Benedictines of Scheyern Abbey, in the Veterinaerstrasse. Nearby was the studio of the artist Karl Hornung, where I was to be afforded facilities for drawing from life.

Every one of us, on looking back over his or her career, discovers periods wherein we have made distinct and rapid progress towards the success we aimed at. Yet rarely are these periods unaccompanied by their more negative phases of mistakes made, sufferings undergone, or even of serious lapses committed. It has not all been one triumphal prog-ress; no, not even those " dear old days " of our youth when so much was learned, so many new things tried and accomplished: its turbulent storms and fierce battles, the continual ferment in the depths of our souls we now would fain forget, were factors too in our fashioning.

Now, my stay in Munich was, alas! not among the most progressive periods in my life. Though I profited much, I also suffered sharp and serious losses which it took me years to counteract. The heat of summer, invading a well-stocked wine cellar, causes the wine to ferment anew, especially if it is young wine. And this of course is harmful. So also it is with the soul of him who is forced to fight and conquer for the second time those attractions of worldly life and pleasure he had mastered once (or so he thought) for good and all. I was still extraordinarily young and alive, despite my thirty-eight years, perhaps because I had been spared the anxieties of having to earn my daily bread, and had always been associated with younger men since my rather late start in religious life. Then too, the monk is always in one sense a child, as he must ever look to his Father Abbot with filial love and reverence.

But now I was to enter again upon a period of conflict in the turbulent, pleasure-loving world, a world which was now more bewildering than ever to me, due to my new habits. To step out from the cool peaceful seclusion of the cloister into the heated arena of secular art and life was madness itself, for me at least. My every aspiration was tending, earnestly and happily, towards a far higher Good than I could find in Munich's tinselled ateliers. In Aichhalden, it had been different; artist-monk-priest in perfect harmony forming a single unit of action. Each successive picture that I painted there set off the other, to form a complete totality. But now in Munich, all this was changed; and when I left after painting for nearly a year and a half, my studio blazed with pictures (mostly still-lives) as varied in subject as were the rich colours they contained. And not one of them portrayed what was going on in my soul (mostly nostalgia and bitter heartaches, as God knows!), in spite of the undoubted vigour and artistic finesse they displayed. A few, indeed, now grace the parlour of a certain parish-house in Württemberg; but I fear, with scant hopes of staying there long. And small wonder, for they were done in six to eight hours, like most of my works of that period. One or two I think took me from two to three days to finish. The artist would have to be a genius indeed to create the small cosmos every non-serial picture should be, in so short a time.

At the *Scheyern Kolleg* our hours of prayer (all the students were monks attending courses at the University) were so arranged as to leave most of the day free for study. We said the Divine Office daily in common, and attended Conventual Mass together, but all morning from seven o'clock and in the afternoons, we were left completely free. And so it happened that the priest-monk gradually gave place to the artist in me, for art if not kept strictly within bounds, tends to absorb, possess. . . . There was of course no serious open rupture between my two selves, but only constant friction. My Benedictine motto of *Ora et labora* (Pray and work) was not so nicely balanced as in Aichhalden. Prayer became, I fear, a minor thing, an accessory to a feverish labor that

[145]

threatened to consume, destroy. This is the harm, the sad and serious harm, that as I have said came to me in Munich. Luckily, it was not irreparable; but it was only through God's grace, and a heroic effort of my will, that later I could finally re-unite again the artist and the monk in me, and bring from that union a mature product which displayed, in proper harmony and proportion, all the elements from which it had been fused.

My first months in Munich were like a nightmare. When in the *Kolleg* I felt stifled and pent-up, as in a prison. Its confined space and narrow cells made me homesick for my " Mother Beuron," whose long corridors, vast refectory and spacious garden were so like a paradise on earth. Now plain unadorned walls confronted me, instead of the tastefully decorated, cheerful appointments in my home. And then, instead of painting the heads of saints in some lofty church, I now worked daily with two other artists in a small studio utterly devoid of anything that could uplift my soul. Certainly the professional models whom we paid to sit for us were anything but inspiring! And thus I became soon dissatisfied, impatient; our work was hardly more than photographic copying, while wild impossible desires and plans that I had thought long since dead began to torment my soul. With such explosive ingredients seething within me, it was no wonder that sometimes I boiled over completely, and much that I had gained was lost forever. No longer could I control my feelings, no longer could I create peacefully and naturally; but instead, began to force myself with a kind of wild and violent fury. It showed that I no longer had riches within me to dispose of, but had become poor, impotent. And of course, with but one result: paltry success, which only increased my bitterness and feelings of inadequacy. Much modern art I think betrays this same trait of incompleteness, artificiality, violent forcing, as though providing us with a sumptuous banquet on borrowed money.

Whenever I would visit the *Neue Pinakothek* (New Art Gallery), the sight of the paintings there only plunged me into deeper gloom. Whether I liked them or not, it was always the same story: each one had been created at the price of an anguish similar to mine. Each one was a world of suffering and sacrifice; I could hear all the complaints, criticisms, curses uttered by their creators in their uncontrolled rage, all the sobs and tears of dear ones neglected because art counted more than they. What a prodigious, costly expenditure of human energy! The true value of it all must perhaps be measured by God's eternal standards, as Baudelaire intimates in his well known lines:

Car c'est vraiment, Seigneur, le meilleur témoinage
Que nous puissions donner de notre dignité
Que cet ardent sanglot qui roule d'âge en âge
Et vient mourir au bord de votre éternité.

For it is true, O Lord, the proof sublime
That we can give Thee of our dignity:
The scalding tears that flow through endless time
To reach the shore of Thy Eternity.

(from " *Les Fleurs du Mal* ")

[147]

Even the *Alte Pinakothek* (Old Art Gallery) failed to satisfy me with its maturer paintings, its creations from a happier and more leisurely age. A bad sign indeed! Even the old German crumble-fold painters seemed to me too stiff and dry. Durer's *Apostles* and Gruenewald's *Erasmus and Mauritius* found some favour in my eyes, but the works of Dutch masters such as Tenniers and Brouwer struck me as being insufferably vulgar and commonplace. " How dreary it all is! " I said to myself. "This museum is just like a cemetery." And most of the time I found it more interesting to watch the visitors than the paintings. Only one master, Rubens, succeeded in inspiring me as of yore; but he is of course the best represented artist at the *Alte Pinakothek*.

Why is it that we are attracted most by objects wholly unlike ourselves? The law of compensation, or of equilibrium, perhaps explains it. At any rate, Rubens was my first love, and I still remain faithful to him, in spite of our divergent artistic conceptions. Perhaps it is because his innermost, most sacred sentiments entered into everything he created. But all that he was, all that he suffered, held me strangely fascinated. All my ideals as a religious artist I saw realized in him, if on a far different background than my own. For he had known how in youth to wait and be submissive, until at long last his genius burst forth in all its shining glory, like lightning from a storm-cloud. He had known how to draw his inspirations from the immediate surroundings of his home: his wife, his children, his servants, and even his domestic animals were the means he

[148]

chose to vocalise his talents; and thus he had remained natural, true, sincere. Though wealth and ease had come to
him, he had not been spoiled. Fully conversant with all
the trends of his time, he had yet not been led astray. The
very embodiment of healthy vigorous life, he spread this
quality over everything he did, giving with a joyous aban-
don of the rich abundance within his soul. His fiery temperament was always kept firmly in hand, like a mettle-
some horse ridden easily and securely; and yet this
restraint never caused the vivacity of his work to diminish.
In fine, there seemed no limit to his vast powers; and I
still regard him as the most remarkable genius of his age,
whose influence remained for a century at least, dominant
and fertile in the world of art.

All great artists have known the thrill of ecstasy. Moments come in their lives when they are literally beside
themselves with some vision of great beauty, and are conscious only of a higher world, more sublime and real than
that in which they live. A strange mystic power seems to
have transformed their senses, so that these can now per-
ceive heights and depths unknown before. Qualities like
strength, beauty, greatness are intensified and exalted far
above their ordinary state, appearing as realities shorn of
all human dross, in all their pristine splendour. Moments
like these explain the *fertility* of all great masters such as
Rubens. For during them there was transformed and en-
nobled all that the artist had seen or felt or heard in that
ordinary existence he as mortal man was forced to live.
The seed had fallen on good soil and, thanks to that pa-

tient waiting for a proper harvest-time, had borne good fruit in season.

Rubens had a profound admiration for the classic period, surpassing most of his contemporaries in a knowledge of its history and literature. The true artist in him perceived the beauty and grandeur of the ancient creations; and this combined intellectual and psychological background enabled him to represent the spirit of the Greeks and Romans with lively accuracy. Like Shakespeare, he seemed to live in that ancient atmosphere, crossing with an easy bound the bridge of time to express in moving accents thoughts and ideas his own world had long since forgotten.

Yet Rubens was " Greek of the Greeks " in his own peculiar way. Much of his treatment of mythological subjects was in glaring contradiction to ancient conceptions; and yet he was faithful to antiquity by consistently making the *idea* and not the *event* dominate his pictures. This is true even of his representations of unfettered human passion. In his *Slaying of the Amazons* for example he has not allowed the impression of bloodshed and rapine to stand out, but rather the concept of battle, or struggle between life and death. Bloodshed there must be, but its horror is subdued, made subservient to a higher idea. And yet the picture is thrillingly beautiful, like a destructive conflagration. It is the same with his masterly *Last Judgment,* and his *Slaughter of the Innocents.* But this is certain: not everyone who views Rubens' paintings will grasp this *idea.* Especially nowadays when people's minds have been spoiled with so much folly masquerading in the rôle of art. The " man in the street " will hardly grasp it; but of course, Rubens was painting for a different public, and in a far different age.

Among my artist friends during this period were the talented young painter Hugo Troendle, whose ideas intensified my interest in drawing from living models; and the Russian neo-impressionist Alexei Jawlensky, to whose influence I owe the few really good things I was able to accomplish in Munich. I had been invited one day in February (1907) to the home of Dr. Schwarz, editor of the art journal *Kunst fuer Alle*, and met there Kurt Hermann, the Berlin neo-impressionist. He knew many of my Paris friends, among them Bonnard, who had painted a portrait of his wife. During the afternoon, we visited his private exhibition at the *Kunstverein* (Art Association); where we were joined by Jawlensky. A stout jovial man of about forty, he literally bubbled with enthusiasm for the exhibit. He was of similar bent himself, he said; and begged us both to call on him the following Sunday and see for ourselves.

I duly turned up, and received a most agreeable surprise on entering his studio. One whole wall was literally covered with richly-coloured landscapes and still-lifes, conclusive proof that he was no long-haired crank, but an artist of wide-ranging talents and human sympathies. We soon became fast friends; and from that day on, I worked often in his *atelier*. Never have I met an artist of such unerring judgment as Jawlensky: he was infallible in picking out the wheat from the chaff, and could always tell exactly what was coming next in the development of painting. Yet he was no pedant, but a modest, lovable man, whose great tact was equalled only by his charming Russian *naïveté*. His zest for life was boundless, but art always kept its hold over him. Thus his spirit remained wholesome and sane; for art, if exercised in accord with reason, is a strong protection, and makes one truly wise.

On another Sunday at Jawlensky's I met a distinguished looking, bewhiskered gentleman who appeared to be a diplomat, and his wife. It was true: he was none other than Goeremykin, former Prime Minister to the Czar of Russia. He was visiting his niece, the Duchess Werefkin, who was herself a gifted artist and close friend of Jawlensky's. As I looked at him, I felt awed with the power over life and death he must have wielded once. What blessings and what woe it had been his to cause! A single stroke of his pen, and many a poor exile would have been liberated; but a final " No! " from his lips, and black despair in the hearts of thousands. Yet he was obviously a most kindly man, looking as though he might be a prosperous banker, or professor in some university. Some time later I recognised him in a newspaper photograph of the Czar's entourage; he had been recalled to his ministerial functions. But during the Revolution both he and his wife were slaughtered, along with the Russian royal family.

The new ruling class in Russia is no less despotic than the old. It may have lessened some material misery, but there are other and deeper distresses afflicting society. It really looks as though spiritual suffering has increased in proportion to the much-heralded alleviation of social suffering. Today in Russia there are probably more prayers being addressed to God than ever before in her history for in the fierce tempest the mariner learns to pray. If Communism means social solidarity, why can it not see that no such solidarity is possible without a foundation of love? Perhaps, because it has rejected God, for without Him there can be no love that will endure.

During this month (February) I also received sad news. My father died on the night of the seventh, resigned and peaceful. He had been conscious to the last, and quite cheerful. He spoke often of religious matters, and of his hopes regarding the life to come. His last words were these: *Sister, now suddenly I can see the sun!* " I was unable to come for the funeral, but a month later visited my mother for a few days. While in Holland, I received a letter from Beuron granting me permission to return to Munich *via* Paris, where I wanted to study some recent developments in modern art. I wrote to Maurice Denis asking if I could stay with him, and received his reply: " *Quelle joie, quelle joie!* " (What joy, what joy!).

I arrived in Paris on Monday of Passion Week, March 18, 1907. Sérusier met me at the Gare du Nord, and took me over to the Gare St. Lazare where Denis joined us, whence we took a train for the latter's home in St. Germain-en-Laye. The following days were full of activity: a trip to Le Vesinet, where Denis had decorated two chapels in the parish church; a visit to the Salon des Independants, where the grotesque creations of Matisse's group (known among artists as *Les Fauves,* or " The Wild Beasts ") were attracting curious crowds; calling on numerous art-dealers

and collectors; a dinner in the home of Denys Cochin, a
Deputy and leader of the Catholic party; another with
Mithouard, editor of *L'Occident;* a concert directed by Vin-
cent D'Indy in the *Schola Cantorum.* And needless to say,
I was often to be found browsing about the Louvre; nor did
I fail to get in touch with all the *Nabis* again. Success and
fame had come to each of them, with the exception of poor
old Ranson. When Vuillard and I called to see him in his
studio, he greeted us with a wry face, and said mournfully:
"*Je suis foutu, je suis fini* (I am ruined, I am done for).
Yet I feel sure that my great efforts will be good for something or other, some day." And he was right; recognition
came to him finally, and before he died in the spring of
1909 at the age of forty-seven, he founded the still famous
Académie Ranson.

But my Paris sojourn would not have been the success it
was, had I not stayed at Denis' charming home. An atmosphere of peace and contentment dwelt there, charged with
those genial qualities which had made its master not only
eminent artist, but likewise incomparable husband, father,
friend. And in all its rooms, there breathed the presence of
his lovely wife, of whom marriage and children had not
made an anxious careworn " Martha." Devoted to her children, she yet remained the radiant bride of their honeymoon. Her girlish countenance smiled down from numerous paintings throughout the house, now in the guise of a
Madonna or some saint, now as some fairy-sprite, or young
maiden, or proud mother with her offspring. Only one lack
so far marred their happiness: an heir to the name. Four

girls had come to them after their first child, a boy, had died in infancy.

Wednesday was my friend's *jour,* or " at-home " day. The visitors first went out into his garden-studio to examine the master's latest creations, and then assembled in the drawing room for tea and conversation. There were great comings and goings, and once more I experienced the joys of social intercourse which is both highly intelligent and refined. What an art the mere exchange of thought can blossom into! But only when he who is speaking knows that no cutting remark nor trivial joke will interrupt him, but only an occasional " Very interesting " to spur him on in the elaboration of his ideas. Such an exchange is like a game of ball, wherein one player throws the ball into the hands of his fellow, and *not* into his face. It calls for culture, education, respect for human personality, as well as a certain suavity of manner, the graceful art of dissembling which makes possible the expression of strong emotion without loss of poise.

As recently as the year 1924, Denis' paintings were exhibited at the Louvre, in the *Pavillon de Marsan.* It was springtime, and all who were fortunate enough to view the pictures experienced a true thrill of spring. For few painters have been able to combine in such exquisite fashion, the two contrasting qualities which constitute nature's strongest enticements; a forbidding *noli-me-tangere* attitude, and that of compliant full surrender. He had a decided preference for young life, and with his masterful style, always seemed to capture its air of budding promise. Radiant

[155]

mothers lost in bliss carrying their first-born child through flowery gardens, dainty maidens and little children dancing on a background of glowing landscape or playing on the strand of some foaming sea. Royal Nausikaa exuberant with life, seated on her rocky throne, converses with the exiled Ulysses. An Arcadian atmosphere surrounds her: two of her companions are feeding some gentle goats, while others are bathing in the cool waves. And such an air of delicate chastity over all, that I can think of but one word that aptly characterises Denis' work: the word *adorable*. It is unfortunately a hackneyed term, but it certainly was passed from lip to lip among the spectators on the very inaugural day of the exhibition and understandingly so, for they were thrilled, captivated completely, with that sensation of chaste joy coming from all they saw.

This description of Denis' work should not lead the reader to set him down as a mere poetic dreamer. For he was quite the opposite: he was extremely well-balanced, and even as a young man always knew exactly what he was after, and how to express this in few but pregnant words. His numerous and varied paintings show his extraordinary fecundity; whereas the dreamer is limited and barren, barely able to rouse himself long enough to write a few verses for some autograph album. To achieve the heights Denis has, an artist must be endowed with real virility of temperament combined with an imagination both fertile and lively; and in addition that peculiar *sense for order* which always distinguishes the genius from the hack.

One afternoon I went with Denis to inspect Delacroix'

chapel at St. Sulpice; and after consuming this tasty mor-
sel unhurriedly, we moved over to the Pantheon to see the
frescoes Puvis de Chavannes had done depicting the various
branches of science. Unfortunately it was closed, on account of the death of Berthelot the chemist. Denis consoled
me by saying we could see other frescoes by Puvis in the
Sorbonne, and we repaired thither. On entering the *Aula*
of the famous university, one faces a semi-circular wall on
which the artist has painted separate frescoes for each
science.

Gazing upon the whole, one is transported into a sublime
world where all is *in harmony:* youth respectful and docile,
man strong and noble, woman chaste and fecund, old age
wise and mellow — a world in which beauty holds sway
without leading to perdition. There in the home of the
Muses, where all is serenely quiet save for the strains of
heavenly music, and wisdom is taught, not in the confine-
ment of a dusty classroom, but under the free skies, close to
invigorating nature. Learning appears as some pleasing pastime, in which the sense of struggle and constraint is con-
spicuously absent; while the silence of the listeners resembles
that of those who are absorbing delicious wholesome nourishment.

The reflective artist always admires in this work a sort
of polished skill which has avoided all that is stereotyped,
all suggestion of ponderous pedagogy, in spite of the obvious difficulties presented by the subject. This effect is
given by the classically beautiful movements of the supple
bodies, the simple forms and precise contours, the subdued

[157]

harmonious colours, the happy distribution of light and shade. Remarkable too is the integration of figure with landscape, whereby they seem to melt into each other and yet preserve in clear relief their mutual forms and colours. I was fascinated to note the various influences involved: Ancient Greece, Giotto, Pier della Francesca, Luini, Poussin, Ingres, Chasseriau — all were recognizable in some way. But in the end, I had to solve an enigma: how was it possible to create such a transcendent world, and still be so true to nature? Whence this loftiness of concept, this almost religious sanctity of expression, this beauty touched with the very breath of eternity? Undoubtedly, Puvis de Chavannes must have once been granted a vision of celestial beauty, in the depths of his soul; nourished by some inner flame, he too had quested for a perfect ideal, and found it — but not on this poor earth.

Directly under the long frieze in the *Aula* is the instructor's desk. What an exquisite preparation, thought I, for the words of him who has something valuable to say! And if he has not, but bestows stones instead of bread, then there is consolation in gazing at that marvellous frieze. At best, mere words soon lose their impression on the soul, but a fine picture continues to attract and captivate, never losing its power — just as a man's good example moves us more powerfully and lastingly than do fine theories.

On the last day of my stay in Paris, Denis insisted on painting my portrait. It was Palm Sunday; and I let him have his wish that afternoon. It took him but two or three hours, after which I packed and was off on the night train

[158]

for Holland. A brief farewell visit with my family, and I set off again for Beuron, where I arrived on the following Wednesday. Soon after Easter I was told to go to Aachen, and arrange an exhibit of our art in connection with a large exposition soon to be opened there.

The experience I had gained at the Secessionist Exhibition stood me in good stead with this latest assignment, and I found it pleasant indeed. The day (and night) previous to our opening I shall never forget. Feverish excitement and working at tense speed, yet with everyone in good humour and mutually helpful. Perfect teamwork, and yet no one slighting his own individual task; as for instance when a ladder was finally captured by a workman, he always saw that its absence discommoded nobody, and that it was duly returned. All of us really accomplished miracles, and yet good Brother X. (carpenter at Maria Laach Abbey who had been loaned to me) said that he had never made such a muddle of things in all his life. A thousand things requiring the attention of two men, and yet we dared leave nothing unfinished for the opening of our Beuron Room on the morrow. We both were tired to death, and only an occasional glass of beer and a sandwich kept us going. At last, a scant hour before the opening, the miracle took place.

In the twinkling of an eye, everything was ready. All had been attended to down to the very last detail (save for carrying away the rubbish, which had to be hastily swept behind benches for lack of time), and when our two powerful arc-lamps were turned on illuminating the whole exhibit, it looked like fairyland indeed. The dominating effect of

gold and white was truly dazzling, and many were the
" Oh's " and " Ah's " we heard from the onlookers, who
saw it for the first time on coming in out of the prosaic
world. I had done a border-frieze around the walls of the
room, high up; and below this we placed some of Father
Desiderius' best sketches on a background of white flowers;
while in the central space of the room we had glass cases
containing our samples of vestments and sacred utensils.
In a niche opposite the entrance was a magnificent carved
and gilt altarpiece, which now adorns the St. Boniface
altar in Maria Laach Abbey-church. All in all, it was a
fine and very successful exhibition, thanks to God's kind
Providence.

And now, if I trespass by indulging in some further re-
flections on my sojourn in Munich, I beg pardon of my
readers. It is difficult to keep an old man's vanishing memories within an orderly sequence, and, after all, my story
is (I like to think) more of a commentary than it is a
narrative. In Munich, when I had been scarcely two months
there, I made some interesting discoveries. Hans von Marées'
(1837–1887) at the *Watering-trough,* which I had scarcely
noticed in former years, now astonished me with its colour-
ing, so rich and yet so ethereal, and with its consummate
deftness of pictorial effect. Here was one of those very
German masters I had affected to despise; and yet, not a
suggestion of clumsiness about him. " He must have been
truly a fine man," I thought. But I was to get better acquainted with him.

One day Troendle took me out to Schleissheim, where

the best Marées' paintings are kept in a collection; and here for the first time I was wholly captivated by a master of the German school. Not only did I witness an ideal world ravishingly disclosed, but I was made to live through poignant tragedy, the tragedy of an artist who achieved an early greatness, but who thrust it aside, using it only as a stepping stone to the higher, more universal end he saw but dimly. Ever advancing, despite the ever-increasing burden of his pain, until he at long last reached the summit of his powers, and his last works touch the sublimest heights of artistic genius. The long and toilsome road he travelled can be seen by comparing his *Diana in the Forest* and earlier work with his last painting *The Rape of Ganymede;* and by studying two of his self-portraits, made at different periods of his life — pictures that reveal a truly terrible suffering. In the portrait of himself and Lenbach, painted when he was about twenty-five, Marées looks considerably the younger of the two. We see a happy carefree youth, with an almost girlish face framed in long silky hair. His eye (the picture shows but one), so affectionate and tender, discloses a soul deeply touched with beauty, enraptured with it, so that its owner sees all things transfigured. Even his sensitive mouth seems to inhale some beauteous perfume as, half-opened, it tastes the sweet morning air. So it was that the young Marées, in painting pictures of such vast limpid beauty, was but giving of himself, and of all that his soul saw.

But his self-portrait painted some twenty years later is a shocking contrast. We can scarcely recognise that it is the same person, or that the same hand painted it, so filled with anguish are the stern, tormented features. The noble head, sitting squarely upon the somewhat bent shoulders, reminds us of some storm-bound rock thrusting its face grimly through the seething tempest. Itself unmoved, unshaken, it knows naught of clemency for others. Clearly this man gazes unseeingly on nature's beauties, his eyes searching steadfastly for a still grander vision far beyond. His vaunted powers of sense are useless now, only mind and will can count, in that relentless questing of a higher world. Those flowing locks too are gone; and a small black skull cap crowns his head, setting in sharp relief his broad, striking brow. The mouth now obscures itself below a bushy moustache, the lower lip seems trembling with suppressed emotion. The right hand grips a long paint brush, poised expectantly. Truly, the picture of a man abandoned in his loneliness, forgotten by a world he in his turn also had forgotten, caring only for that vision of *the perfect* in art to which he was a willing holocaust.

After that memorable day at the Schleissheim gallery, I went many times again, once in company with Sérusier, who, however, got an impression quite the opposite to mine. The *Nabi* was much disappointed, saying that only the earlier paintings pleased him. "The later ones convey hardly anything to me," he said. "Marées had some good theories, but spoilt everything by his colours. And his whole effect is so hopelessly *sad*." Another time I went with Meier-Graefe, the well-known author, who was at the time engaged in writing a book on Marées' career. He was wholly on my side, probably because of the deep study he had made of the master's life and character. He had travelled far and wide collecting material for this and other artistic essays he wrote; and gave me many interesting side-lights on Marées and on some of his contemporaries. For instance, he told me of having interviewed Dr. Gachet, the physician who attended Van Gogh (1853–1898) at his death, which occurred in an insane asylum, whither he had gone after a nervous breakdown. But his written account of the artist's tragic end needs some correction. True, Van Gogh was a suicide; but it is *not* true to say that " he had to go suddenly in all his beauty, to avoid the fate of decadence, gradually sinking into the inane slough of ugliness." This fate *should* be avoided, but not by committing suicide.

Nor did Van Gogh die in the Socratic fashion Meier avers, on the testimony of Dr. Gachet. I happen to know the facts in the case, which were given me by a young Dutch disciple of the great painter, whom I had known in Paris in 1892. He had been present at the latter's end, and in fact had been often with him during the days of terrific pain that had led up to it. Once during a particularly severe spasm Van Gogh had cried piteously: " Is there no one who will open my body for me? " And then one day, seemingly much better, he had been allowed to go for a walk, alone — and in a clump of trees, fired a revolver into his abdomen. Mortally wounded, he managed to drag himself to his home, where his landlord found him bathed in blood, lying on his bed. " I tried to kill myself," he had told him; " but it was no use. Now I'll have to do it all over again." But he

[163]

died the following day. Great throngs attended his funeral, among them Emile Bernard who told me how deeply moved all were. " For he was so universally loved," my friend had said.

There are thousands of studios in Munich. There are streets where there is one in the attic of every house. In these the painters live. There they work and sleep, make merry, are filled with hope or plunged in despair. Since the inflation their number may have decreased, but it must still be very considerable. The reason for the great number today is to be found in the schools, where the drawing instruction is such that the least talent is awakened, discovered and encouraged. If a boy draws better than his companions, these admire and try to copy him, and he begins to feel that he is an outstanding personality. The time comes when his friends begin to say that he should be a painter and he believes them. From the day school he passes to the art school, or even to the Academy of Fine Arts, often at great financial strain to his family, and there he acquires a certain manual dexterity and becomes a purely academic painter.

Others who have not distinguished themselves in drawing at school, but are, nevertheless, intelligent, feel themselves drawn to a painter's career by their love of art. By hard work such as these may really accomplish something and go much further than those who start with a mere talent for drawing. Others, again, revolutionaries, peasants and libertines, for example, become painters as a means of escape from their surroundings or from the ordinary conventions of society. Finally, there is the considerable number of the *dilettanti* who choose art because they have a feeling for it and who then drift along without any sense of the responsibilities of their vocation.

The recent abstractionist tendencies in art have increased the number of painters enormously. As art has turned away from the representation of tangible things towards an abstraction hard to understand and harder to evaluate because unrelated to any definite canon, it has become possible for charlatans with a minimum of artistic power to pose as artists of merit. Adverse criticism of the work of such painters has been silenced to a considerable degree because in the last decade, works of which the general public could make nothing, or at which they could only laugh, have been bought for large sums. In work of this type suggestion takes the place of representation and into it all manner of things are dreamed by the credulous observer. To many who have worked hard to learn the mysteries of their art, there is something sordid about such methods of work as these.

It is bad both for art and for the artist that there are so many painters today, and I would advise parents to encourage their children to do woodwork and the like rather than to draw. Often I find it difficult to know what to say when a boy's drawings are brought to me for my opinion as to whether or not he has the talent to become a painter. Sometimes the boy himself is brought. Some of the boys are very confident and others watch me shyly while I examine their work. Almost always I can say there is talent there, but I always add that talent in itself, is not enough. Besides talent, in all professions calling for natural ability, but above all in painting, it is necessary to have opportunity for intensive study, isolation to permit of this, and commissions on which to work. In face of all difficulties, truly, the greatest have succeeded, but only at enormous cost. I can never believe, as we so often read, that the misfortunes of these great ones brought them to the heights.

Even when material circumstances are relatively favourable, talent is still not enough. Imagination must direct, encourage and stimulate the other faculties of the soul, and the creative impulse must be nourished by the experiences of the senses. Every such impulse strives to give itself expression, but of itself it has no permanence. The artist must therefore have endurance, patience and perseverance to reinforce his creative impulse, and he must develop his judgment and artistic conscience to guide it. Without the moral force of the will to refine and spiritualise the creative impulse it may easily become perverse, imprudent or superficial.

The most talented beginner still needs to exercise perseverance in the highest degree. Before he can paint successfully the simplest picture, the necessary knowledge of form must be acquired by strenuous effort. Then, when at last he has gained this knowledge he makes the troubling discovery that he has lost vision which he possessed as a boy. He cannot go back to childhood. Growth must always be onward. There is only one thing he can do; to create a new thing in which the old is embodied in a maturer form, although the warmth and vivacity of the earlier manner

[166]

cannot be recaptured at once. Fruit can never be the same as blossom, but even when ripe it has its own beauty of colour and scent. In ripening it has become palatable and nourishing, and in it is the seed of life, even although the alluring delicacy of the bloom has gone. Some fortunate natures find themselves again comparatively quickly after a period of such mental disturbance in their student days, and these, without great crises of change produce works, often of importance, in an unbroken chain of development.

It is seldom, however, that the aims and manner of the painter escape changes. These we see in the works of almost all the old masters. These changes are always accompanied by sacrifices, sufferings, and dangers. This is specially true of the modern painter, who inevitably lacks the support of a strong tradition. When a business man turns over his business to his children and starts a new one it is no easy matter for him. But, at least, he does not need to change his business methods. The changing artist, on the other hand, stands with a new, uncharted world before him. As with the business man, making a new start, industry and patience are necessary here too, and in even greater measure. This is particularly the case because good intentions count for so little in art. The artist must first know what he wants to do. Until the concept of what is to be made is formed in the imagination, the will cannot act. It is not necessary that this concept be complete; and it is probably better that it should not be. The concept should grow with the work, thus preserving spontaneity, and allowing the whole to develop organically so as almost

[167]

to appear to live. Always first there must be the idea in the artist's mind.

Even for the artist working from nature this holds good. One must never copy nature but present a concept of it. Such a concept will never come suddenly in its complete form and so it was Cézanne said: "*Cultiver sa petite sensation.*"

Many painters, while waiting for their concepts to assume intelligible form, go for a walk or otherwise amuse themselves. This has its good points but I hold it is better to sit, brush or charcoal in hand, before the canvas, like a cat at a mouse-hole. For just as the cat must seize the mouse at the precise moment it emerges from the hole, so must the painter grasp his concept the moment it presents itself. He makes a preliminary sketch, but has still a long road to travel before the work is complete: and it is a road on which many an artist has lost his way. The original concept is easily lost sight of, and then the artist flounders about trying to patch it up again with details from nature which do not match. Perfection is accomplished only when the exterior concretion fully represents the interior concept.

My sojourn in Munich consisted to a large extent in trying to regain what I had lost since my association with Gauguin and Sérusier in Paris sixteen years before. But I had only meager success in this, and had to admit, on comparing my best Munich efforts with those of my Paris days: "You can no longer equal that! Your horizon has indeed been extended, but at the cost of pure artistic quality." That was a shaming confession! And yet, I hated to give in, even though I knew (as I have so often written and said) that we have to pay for every gain by some loss, especially those of us whose talents are limited. I told myself: "You are only exhausted, drained completely out because you have kept away from nature too long. And you have become immoderately cautious and timid." Thus I blamed first my surroundings and then myself, and even my companions, whom I accused of pettiness, narrow-mindedness, mediocrity. I blamed the times, and the worldliness in "voluptuous Munich."

The sharply critical attitude always denotes an exaggerated and unhealthy self-consciousness, which is fatal in the artist as it cramps his whole style. It is the bitter fruit of failure, an attempt to compensate for a fault which was our own. Either we did not know what we were aiming at, or we aimed at something beyond the reach of our abilities, or we were too slack and lazy to do what we were able to. But I fortunately did not have total failure to record, for my perception of form had definitely improved, my taste become more refined, my dexterity in drawing and painting increased; and here and there I had produced something original which could be traced to very strong impressions received from nature.

My occasional visits to Beuron during my Munich stay also did much to keep me spiritually refreshed. As soon as I was back I felt sustained and soothed by my contact with the community, and by their zealous pursuit of purely supernatural ends, in the quiet of rural surroundings and enclosed within high walls from the world outside. The religious inspiration of the great feast-days I came home to celebrate (Christmas and Easter) especially revived my drooping soul; and if any of my readers happen to have spent a Holy Week at Beuron they will know what I mean. Thus the monk in me was reinstated in his proper rights, giving himself unreservedly to the liturgical functions, and singing the grand Gregorian to his heart's content. And as a priest, I had the consolation of hearing Confessions again, consoling in my turn many souls plunged too in deep affliction — erring souls, often, whom the soft clear light of Bethlehem's star had led back to the Saviour.

Shortly before Easter 1908 my Munich sojourn reached its end; and none too soon, for I was at the end of my endurance. I had made no progress at all during the final few months. In December Sérusier had come for three months, having taken a studio. He worked hard, and three young painters who had placed themselves under his supervision, Freitag, Schulte, and Hartmann, had progressed well. But I could not adapt myself to his new method of cold and warm tints, so we remained apart. This led to a certain estrangement between us which has never wholly subsided. Towards the end of my stay I came across the painter Slevinsky, a disciple of Gauguin, whom I used to meet regularly at Mme. Charlotte's *Crémerie* during the good old Paris days. With Jawlensky I paid him a visit on the eve of my departure, and we had an interesting talk about Gauguin, two of whose pictures, a self-portrait and a Tahiti landscape, the artist had in his studio. " Gauguin was highly intelligent," he remarked to us, " and endowed with great self-confidence, which made him succeed in everything. But he was also extremely vain. He would lend hundreds to the first comer, just to display his generosity. It was a mistake for him to return to Tahiti, but two years among the Maoris made him unable to be at home in Europe."

Willing friends helped me with my packing — and there was much to do. I had accumulated such a lot of rubbish during that year and a half! Now it is all scattered to the four winds, and the last resting-place of most of it will probably be some ash-heap, after a more or less prolonged sojourn in some hospitable attic. So be it!

Chapter Ten

IN THE HOME CLOISTER

In the country you often notice buzzards wheeling idly through the air, their wings motionless save for an occasional flapping which enables them to maintain their altitude. The wind does the rest. It is doubtless an amusing pastime for them, but it cannot last forever; they must eventually come down to earth for food and rest. Something similar happens often in the life of a monk. Long intervals of enraptured soaring between heaven and earth are given him, during which he can adjust the natural to the supernatural in most ideal fashion. But then ensue periods of battle wherein nature strives with the supernatural for supremacy, or, at least, tries to find perfection and completion within the limits of itself. At such times the monk finds himself drawn to follow so-called "common sense" in preference to mystical principles, and tends to place a greater reliance upon his own character, abilities, and learning, in living his life, than he does upon the practice of loving God purely and simply. Thus has his centre of gravitation become shifted from God to self; though not necessarily without some relation to God. There is no severing of connection with the supernatural, only nature has, for the time being at least, gained the predominence.

This phenomenon occurs so often, as I have observed,

with men in their middle thirties, that I regard it as an almost normal phase before the attainment of full maturity. Perhaps it is because nature herself, when given her due, can help wonderfully in strengthening and deepening one's spiritual life. But of course there are exceptions to this rule: great saints whose entire life seems to have been spent in soaring at dizzy heights, and on the other hand, religious persons who descended to earth and remained there ever afterwards, seeming to have lost, like the chickens, their ability to fly.

I went through this phase after my stay in Monte Cassino. I began to feel more and more an aversion for the religious ecstatics, and for those mystical writers I once used to delight in. Joergensen noticed this in me at Aichhalden, and mentioned it in a letter to our mutual friend Mogens Ballin. The latter was at the time himself undergoing severe temptations in regard to faith, and as he lacked the advantages I enjoyed of daily intercourse with the liturgy and the divine office, he sent me a letter of gentle reproof.

Whether or not " living with the Church " in her liturgy supplies the soul with all the spiritual nourishment it may require, can hardly be discussed here. I only wish to remark that I have been ofttimes amazed at the varied means by which spiritual awakening has been evoked, spiritual progress stimulated. Circumstances of time and place, as well as the condition of the " stomach " must be considered. Thus, at the period I am speaking of, I found the greatest profit in reading purely ethical literature, such as Carlyle, Ruskin, and Foerster; and for the first time became deeply

interested in the great moral dramas of Æschylus, Shakespeare, and Schiller. The *Feigenblaetter* of Bogumil Goltz
also captured my attention. It is almost forgotten now, but
its peripatetic philosophy so exactly mirrored my own state
of mind that I was fascinated by it.

But this is certain: whenever I returned to Beuron after
a protracted absence, I always felt keenly the need of
following out the monastic routine in its smallest details,
even though I would be exempt from attendance at the
daily High Mass because of my artistic duties. I felt the
need of something solid and regular to bolster up my soul,
and would even sometimes lay aside my brush for weeks at
a time in order to read and meditate. Besides, I was always
conscious that I might be called away again at any moment
on some new assignment. At any rate, I never became alien-
ated from my monastery and the life there; and after being
away for long periods could always come back and feel at
home immediately, like a soldier returning from his leave.
It had been different in the beginning, of course; but now
the life was *my life,* and whenever I came in contact with it,
I was in my natural sphere and simply let it take me in tow.

Our annual retreats or days of special concentration upon
the spiritual progress made during the past year, were also
a great help to me. They were held during the Octave of
Epiphany each year, and lasted for seven full days, during
which we observed complete silence, and attended special
conferences given by the retreat master, in addition to our
regular offices in choir. I found them burdensome however
if I happened to be engaged in any particularly stimulating

[174]

artistic work at the time. This work would give me so much spiritual food that anything additional seemed superfluous; and after the retreat was over it usually took me a fortnight or so to recover from such gorging. But generally the spiritual exaltation produced through the retreat acted like a tonic to my soul. The silence was so edifyingly kept, and the fervour manifesting itself during the psalms and chants in choir was so intensified that I felt truly uplifted.

But the monk sometimes stands in need of more than mere strengthening and refreshment for his soul. For those dark hours can come to him too, when he leans over dangerous precipices to pluck some pretty flower — or descends from the high plane of his spiritual calling into the world's arena, there to satisfy some personal ambition. Sometimes he forgets how precious those possessions are that he has won, falling asleep, as it were, and leaving his door ajar, toying with thoughts and ambitions that should be sharply rebuffed. Thus deteriorating, thus losing his true balance and perception of what he is and is responsible for, he needs to be awakened, renewed, regenerated. Like a wayward child who foolishly jabs a stick into a wasps' nest just to see what will happen, or torments a sleeping dog until the animal rouses and nearly bites him, such a religious chooses the most painful manner of learning. The eyes of a most loving Father are upon him all the time, who grants His child freedom hoping he will learn from sad experience, at least; and intervenes only when absolutely necessary.

IN QUEST OF BEAUTY

Of course our retreats differed greatly as to their subject matter and the methods used in giving them. But their effect on me was always substantially the same: a joyous exultation over God's magnificent bounty, an ever-new amazement at the sublimity of our calling through Christ. And yet at the same time an *obligato* of horror and disgust at the ingratitude and incomprehensible flippancy with which we miserable mortals dare to cross God's evident designs. While He was aiming only to bring us into closer, more sublime union with Him, we, through our sins and negligences, have made such wondrous intimacy impossible, thus truly cheating Him from carrying out His all-loving intentions.

During the retreat, the ugly nature of sin was always most apparent to us. Even the smallest imperfections, the negligences or faults that were only partially voluntary, were brought to view. All the good intentions that we had never carried out, all the abilities in us that our sluggishness had frustrated: what heinous omissions, what a mountainous accumulation of infidelities! And our pettiness, coldness, brusqueness with our brethren, our meanness and selfishness in a thousand little ways, all passed in sad procession before our mind's eye. Then the soul became sorrowful and contrite, and with tears of remorse carried the heavy burden of its sins to God. Christ through His priest then spoke the words of full forgiveness, *Absolvo te,* and guilt was no more. Tears of sorrow gave place to those of bliss, and the heart voiced its glad exultation in the Psalmist's words:

[176]

IN THE HOME CLOISTER

Sing joyfully to God, all the earth:
Serve ye the Lord with gladness.
Come in before his presence with exceeding great joy.
Know ye that the Lord he is God:
He made us, and not we ourselves.
We are his people and the sheep of his pasture.
Go ye into his gates with praise, into his courts with hymns:
And give glory to him.
Praise ye his name.
For the Lord is sweet,
His mercy endureth for ever (Ps. 99).

Often I found myself regretting that outsiders could not
" listen in " at our retreats. Many a disbeliever in monasticism, many an anti-Catholic and heretic would be astonished
indeed to hear and see what goes on there. Such a person
would doubtless exclaim in his surprise: " Is *this* the way
things are with you? Why, I have known nothing about
you at all! Why do you keep your treasures so carefully
hidden? " To which we could only reply: " But all this is
nothing new at all, only something quite generally known
about, and practised, among Catholics. The trouble is, you
have been so entangled in silly delusions, thinking that we
were fanatics, visionaries, dunces, and the like, that you
would have nothing at all to do with us. Our glorious Faith
you considered a kind of collection of fairy tales; or at best,
a corrupt form of Christianity. So there was no way to help
you, just as with the Jews of Christ's own time, who had no
faith nor trust in Him because they wanted something dif-

ferent, something more in keeping with their own selfish ideas, than that which He chose to bring them."

Without doubt, the retreat master's task is one of no small sacrifice and self-restraint. It would be easy for him to give vent to his emotions and make things hot for the listener, in a torrent of noisy thundering and drastic accusation. But this seldom happens, and I scarcely remember a single instance wherein the speaker showed other than the greatest human sympathy and understanding in his task. The latter is certainly one of the highest and most beautiful services any priest can be summoned to perform: to give unstintingly of his most precious treasures to other priests and religious, rousing the drowsy, encouraging the faint-hearted, advising and soothing those who are in darkness or in pain. He is now more than ever in Christ's place, able to treat souls with that same kindness and love and devotion as the Master would. For all hearts are thrown open wide to him, all minds are full of readiness to receive his words. Souls pliable and plastic before him, ready for him to form them into other Christs. Although I can remember hardly one sentence from any of our retreats, I recall each of those who gave them: the man, his bearing, his eyes and voice, all so full of charity and zeal — and I thank them all from the bottom of my heart.

My feelings after the spiritual rejuvenation of a retreat made me often think of the broken-down cab-horse who finally is allowed to recuperate after long years of hard service. Once I saw one put out to pasture for a whole summer. It had become fat and rotund, and moved about easily and placidly, as though it knew there was no straining to do, no kicks and blows to fear. Its head was held erect again, and its hair had become glossy. There it stood in the middle of a fair meadow, alone, and lost in dreams; occasionally moving on to graze with its fellows in great content.

At other times I would be reminded of the sensations of a carrier-pigeon, who, on its safe return from a long and arduous journey, during which it has had a narrow escape from the claws of a swooping hawk, comes finally to rest in the home cote. It patters about cooing gleefully, bowing to right and left as if to salute its companions, thus showing both its respect for them and its own joy at being home again. Thus was I, too, back in my safe peaceful home-nest at Beuron, having escaped the dangers of lurid city-life, back among my dear brethren, whom none else could ever replace, even were they kindness itself.

And celebrating the glorious Easter Mystery in Beuron would always bring my soul new buoyancy, above all the one in 1908 which came after I had ended my stay in Munich. Now I was at rest again, and I recall doing several sketches in this mood. One was a view of the ancient wooden bridge uniting the two banks of the Danube near our monastery garden, which I did on Holy Saturday; and four or five were glimpses of the majestic surroundings of forest and crag seen from various points within our en-closure. It was so delightful to work outdoors, with no rattling of trams and confused bustle of human traffic, but only soft rural sounds, accentuated by the deep silence all around — shy songs of birds, a cock crowing in the distance,

[179]

a lay-brother ploughing in the field just below, calling *Ho!* and *Gee!* to his snorting horses, or a deer's sudden harsh cry of alarm from the woods nearby. Sometimes there would be melodious hymns and folk-songs from a group of pilgrims on their way to prayer — and always, each separate sound blending away and losing itself in the complete silence of God's wonderful creation. Painting, I would think of Verlaine's beautiful lines:

> *Mon Dieu, Mon Dieu, la vie est là*
> *Simple et tranquille.*
> *Cette paisible rumeur là*
> *Vient de la ville.*

With the coming of June that year, I had to give up painting in the garden, as I felt the need of doing more than simply copying nature. My need for rest had passed, and the new spiritual inspiration throbbing within my soul demanded some form of concrete expression. So the visible world had to give way to the invisible; not that I wanted to do without the former entirely, but only desired to make them both blend harmoniously. It is only in this way, I feel, that true creative art can come. I longed to decorate some wall again, and bethought myself of a mural of the Madonna with some angels which I had begun in Munich for the new music salon in our guest-house, but which I had left unfinished. I dragged it out, and set it up in the spot destined for it, which was a bare space about thirteen feet wide on the wall of the room. The latter was finished off on its four sides with high marble slabs; and I saw at once that my

[180]

canvas produced a crude and unfinished effect: my old impressionist manner could never achieve the desired result. So I set to work remodelling my Madonna project, resorting to water-colours instead of oil, the only method possible (outside mosaics, which were out of the question) to create a background which would harmonise with the exceedingly delicate marble coating of the hall.

Whatever technical methods are adopted in art, each one has its own peculiar effect and character. Thus, the use of oil, as a means of binding colour, has led to the very highest development from a purely artistic standpoint, but at the cost of line and delicacy. There is inevitably something heavy and greasy about oil, just as with water-colours there is always an effect of airy lightsomeness. These latter indeed have their restriction, but in spite of that, and perhaps because of it, they are the best for mural painting and are especially adapted for depicting religious subjects. But oil painting spoils one for this fresco work, as I was soon to discover.

While engaged in this project, I received an invitation to decorate the chapel of a Sisters' convent at Heiligenbronn, a small hamlet near Salzstetten in Württemberg. I was pleased with such a commission, and went as soon as possible to inspect the place, finding a large establishment which consisted of a school and orphanage for poor boys under the care of the good Sisters, together with an extensive farm. It was situated far away from everything, in the middle of a wind-swept plateau surrounded by dark pine forests. Nearby was an ancient pilgrims' shrine, while grouped about the institution were several homes occupied by the farmhands, and a small inn: a sort of little republic presided over by the energetic religious, whose labours, assisted by a small subvention from the state, provided for all the educational and other needs of these poor waifs.

The chapel was of the simplest kind, with a fairly roomy interior covered with a flat ceiling; the whole being 33 feet long, 23 feet wide, and 16 feet high, with two narrow windows in one wall. I made my plan, and started work in the beginning of August. By the middle of November I had finished, having painted an *Annunciation* on the right of the altar, and a *Nativity* scene on the left; and on each side-wall a procession of virgins dressed as nuns, with lighted lamps in their hands. Between the windows I put a *St. Francis Receiving the Stigmata,* this saint being the patron of the order to which the Sisters belonged. The architect Peter Behrens furnished appropriate ornamentations for the ceiling and walls, while my old colleague Herr Mayer once more helped me with the decorative backgrounds. At first I was quite satisfied with the work: but when I saw it ten years later I did not like it at all. The design seemed crude and clumsy, the colours too heavy and dark. Somehow, I had not succeeded with my fresco technique. I was aware of course, of the danger against which the Renaissance masters repeatedly warn us, that fresco painting has a tendency to become chalky with time; and perhaps my experience in Munich, where I had worked in oil only, had made me too partial to rich tints. But anyway, the good Sisters and

[182]

all their flock were delighted with what I had done, and on November 9, the eve of my patronal feast, they held a grand festivity in my honour, with speeches, games, and fireworks. On November 12, the patronal feast of the Archabbey, St. Martin's day, I was back in Beuron once more.

Before concluding this chapter, I want to say a word about my reading. It may seem a small matter, but for the monk, especially for the artist-monk, the choice of books by which he seeks to supplement the workings of God's grace in his soul, assumes a high importance. I don't know if I wholly agree with Ruskin's dictum, that it is safe to allow a young girl (*a fortiori* a monk!) to have the run of a complete classical library, leaving her to her own devices. " Let her loose in the library, I say, as you do a fawn in the field. It knows the bad weeds twenty times better than you; and the good ones too, and will eat some bitter and prickly ones, good for it, which you had not the slightest thought would have been so." Be that as it may, I *have* always seemed to possess a kind of sixth sense which told me what was good for me, or the reverse; though perhaps not with quite the unerring accuracy Ruskin's fawn possessed. But it is true that somehow, whenever I began to read a book or an article, I would know, after reading a paragraph or two, whether or not it was food adapted for my soul. Sometimes I even seemed to hear the mystic *Take and read* of St. Augustine, though of course not quite so clearly. On the whole, I was not an omnivorous reader, as I had not the time for it; but I did manage to read many books, and some of them several times. The Missal and Breviary of course were the normal staples of my mental diet, and each year I would find in them new treasures. Whenever worried with some problem, I would generally succeed in finding just the right book to help me in solving it.

For example, when I was recovering at Beuron from my harassing Munich experience, I came across a volume of *Hochland* which shed much light on the very problem I had been wrestling with. It contained an excerpt from Joergensen's *Our Lady of Denmark,* and an essay by Else Hasse: *Art, Beauty and the Spiritual Life.* Both of these were replete with valuable passages for me, especially Joergensen's quotations from Oscar Wilde, and Else Hasse's from Goethe, and their comments upon them. Wilde's weird effusions, turning truth upside-down, calling white black and black white, showed me clearly how far astray *beauty* may lead one, when it alone is taken for authority. In contrast with this, the excerpts from Goethe demonstrated how exhausting and surfeiting beauty is, when it alone is sought and enjoyed for a long time. I fully agreed with his

> *Diese Schönheit, wie sie blendet,*
> *Blendete mich Armen ganz.*
> *Ich vergass des Wächters Pflichten. . . .*

> All this beauty, how it dazzles,
> Dazzled me poor mortal wholly.
> I forgot the watcher's duties. . . .

(Faust II)

IN THE HOME CLOISTER

I had long known (for I had been warned enough by my spiritual preceptors!) how detrimental to spiritual progress any absorbing occupation may become, art especially. For art tends to possess you, thus making you forget the *essential* thing, the " one thing necessary," of the Gospels; and conscience becomes dull, character is harmed, a tendency develops to select means which are not sanctioned by one's final end. I had already deepened my knowledge of this truth by unhappy experience, the impulse toward beauty having so often proved stronger than my better judgment. But now I had come to the parting of the ways, the strain and exertion had been too severe, the experience too bitter.

CHAPTER ELEVEN

AN OCEAN VOYAGE

THERE is a pretty ceremony held in our monastery whenever a monk returns after a protracted absence. He prostrates himself in the middle of the choir, immediately before divine service, and the following prayers are recited by the community, led by the Abbot:

Let us beseech Almighty God, brethren, to grant that the return of this our brother may be unto his salvation.

(Verse) Save Thy servant.
(Response) My God, who hopeth in Thee.

V. Turn at length, O Lord;..
R. And be propitious to Thy servant.

V. The Lord be with thee;
R. And with thy spirit.

(Abbot) Let us pray. Almighty and eternal God, have mercy upon this Thy servant, and should the sights and sounds of his journey have caused him to retain images of evil happenings or vain talk, graciously regard them not, in Thine ineffable goodness. Through Christ our Lord. Amen.

These prayers represent the monastic attitude toward secular contacts, and during their recitation the monk concerned cannot but be made to feel remorseful if during his worldly intercourse he has somewhat besmirched his soul. But if on the contrary all has gone well with him, he experiences the greatest joy and thankfulness. My return from Heiligenbronn, unlike the previous one from Munich, gave me no cause for regret. All that I had seen and heard had been good, and I had been diligently and well employed each day. So I resumed my regular life with greater fervour than ever, perhaps because I anticipated being called away soon again, on an assignment to which I looked forward with no small pleasure.

Shortly before my departure from Munich, I had received a request from my old Franciscan friend in Fiesole, Don Giovanni Giani, to decorate the renovated chapel of San Francesco in the *Convento*. Though none too sanguine of my ability to do what was expected of me, I was allured by the prospect of seeing Italy and especially Fiesole again; and so, shortly after Easter 1908, I placed the proposal before my Archabbot. He urged me to go soon, but I begged to be allowed to remain in Beuron for a few months, to recuperate. Then came the Heiligenbronn assignment, during which Archabbot Placid died, and I had to take the matter up again with his successor, Ildephonse Schober (formerly Abbot of Seckau in Styria).

Not long after my return from Heiligenbronn, Archabbot Ildephonse received a letter from Don Giovanni repeating his request. He talked things over with me then, one day on a walk through the countryside; and when I assured him that my former Archabbot had given his consent, he replied:

[187]

"I surely will not go back on any promise made by my predecessor." But he would give me no definite decision; and when early in February of the following year I repeated my request, he only said: "Wait a bit, it is still too cold to travel." I appealed to him again at the beginning of Lent, but found him hesitant and thoughtful, as if unwilling to cause me disappointment. Finally he told me: "Your going to Fiesole depends on a number of other factors. For instance, there is some question of sending you to Jerusalem on another artistic assignment!" This was news to me, and in a flash, I saw all the advantages and disadvantages of such a proposal. It would be a wonderful experience, but would mean giving up my prospect of working in Fiesole, upon which my heart was set. But finally I decided: "Now it has become your turn to be made someone else's tool; so don't raise objections." So I simply told my superior in God: "The oriental heat will be hard on me, but *Deus providebit* (God will look out for that)."

So it was settled thus; and I wrote at once to Fiesole, telling them of the change in plan. Don Giovanni sent a characteristic reply: "*Non c'e da fare* [there is nothing to be done]; it is like lightning from a clear sky." I remained in Beuron all through Lent preparing for my journey, and on Passion Sunday set out from my monastic home once more, in company with my future collaborators in Palestine, Father Cyril Welter and Brother Simon Kebele. I was tired and depressed, as the last few days of preparation had been very fatiguing; but once on the way my spirits rose and I was all eagerness for the things in store.

AN OCEAN VOYAGE

We stopped first in Zurich, visiting with the family of Brother Simon, who resided there. We dined, visited a church which Fritz Kurz had designed, and then departed for our next stop, Ingenbohl, where we spent the night at the convent of the Holy Cross Sisters. Next morning we went on to Altdorf, calling upon the family of one of our monks who belonged to the community in Jerusalem. I recall my vivid impression of the surroundings in Altdorf, as I stood in the village cemetery high up on an eminence. The picturesque houses with their vari-coloured Swiss gables were massed together in shadow, and behind them lay a magnificent background of snowy mountains. The Alps with their soft, billowy tints are indeed most effective when seen towering above a scene of colour. At the monastery in Engleberg, where I went on a later occasion, I noticed precisely the same charming effect. From a vantage point just above the Abbey I looked down upon its interior precincts, as the early morning sun kissed its ancient walls and towers. The roof and windows were almost black, and over them, rising in majestic solitude to the heavens, stood a mighty snow-covered mountain.

That afternoon we entrained for Chiasso and the Italian frontier; and after passing through the customs late in the night, we arrived in Milan about eight o'clock next morning. It was Sunday, and we soon realised that we were no longer in staid Germany by the lively holiday atmosphere all about us. Clearly the Sabbath meant something quite different to these southerners than it does to us; instead of furnishing an occasion for quiet introspection and outward constraint, it allowed them to let loose a regular torrent of pent-up emotion, in a *laissez-aller* of nature that appeared almost savage at times. Whenever we showed ourselves in our black habits amid the merry-making, unmistakeable signs of dislike and even contempt showed themselves, especially on the faces of the younger men. Inconvenient and unwanted admonishers were we, for with the excitable Italian, everything black is a reminder of death. Why this intrusion then upon their Sunday pleasures? We should stay at home! The week has seven days.

That night we slept in a small hotel, or rather, tried to sleep; for owing to the continual hubbub in the streets, we — accustomed as we were to the absolute quiet of the cloister — could hardly close our eyes. In the early morning my two companions went on to Genoa, I remaining behind until three in the afternoon, in order to transact some business. After lunch I went to the Brera Gallery, where I devoted my attention this time to Tintoretto's *Finding of the Relics of St. Mark,* finding Veronese's paintings much less appealing than they were to me six years before.

In Genoa we found quarters at a hostel conducted by some German Sisters, and as it was pouring hard, we stayed indoors and got a good night's rest. In the morning we went to the station and had our baggage examined by the customs people, and then boarded the North German Lloyd steamer *Seydlitz,* which however was not to sail until the morrow, as the rain had held up the loading of its freight. But we were at once assigned our cabins, and got our meals without extra charge.

AN OCEAN VOYAGE

In the afternoon I took a turn about the city for an hour or so, but found it drab and uninteresting. It offered me nothing new, while the ship was a fascinating, unexplored world. So I went back to it, and discovered with delight a huge Dutch ship moored behind our vessel. It was an East India liner, the *Oranje;* and seemed to bring a greeting from my native land. Some troops bound for the colonies were on board, and when they perceived us monks standing on the deck of the *Seydlitz* a number of them saluted; then suddenly, a creaky gramophone gave forth the strains of *Silent Night, Holy Night.* Doubtless it was the only sacred number in their repertoire, but we were touched by the thoughtful gesture. Soon the port and city grew fairy-like, as thousands of lights struggled to replace the vanished day. Even the loading went on. It was mostly heavy marble blocks, and had to be all safely stowed away by morning. Despite the rattling of chains and rumbling of stevedores' trucks, I slept fairly well.

The next day, Wednesday, the rain had stopped, and by noon the weather was clear and fine. At three o'clock all is ready: the gang-plank is drawn up, the sailors hurry about obeying curt orders from an officer on the bridge — we are in motion! A puffing tugboat tows us at a snail's pace out of the roads. What a strange sensation, to see the shore apparently moving away from us! Handkerchiefs frantically waving from the pier, and being answered indiscriminately by everybody about me. This gives me a queer feeling about the throat, and I find myself wondering, " Will all go well with me? Am I to return to these shores again? " The harbour appears more lovely now, as we get a wider prospect. The sun, which has been hiding behind a cloud-bank, now suddenly bursts forth to set everything aglow in a perfect riot of colour, in which a glorious orange tint, more beautiful than I had ever seen, seemed to predominate. Even the blue waves sparkled with it, and the distant hillsides and villas were transformed in an aura of burnished gold that held me spellbound. Suddenly, little lacquer-coloured fishing smacks with white sails glide between us and the wharf, their tints in sharp relief upon a background furnished by the dun-coloured buildings and warehouses of the port. Such an orgy of colour, thought I, one hardly expected to find this side of the Orient! Still that frantic waving of handkerchiefs, reduced to one or two now, as though some forlorn bride had lost her groom, for whom the attractions of the boundless sea had proved too much.

The sea! I am wholly captured by it, and find myself envying those passengers who are travelling to far-off Australia, while I shall have to get off at Port Said. Now the screws of the *Seydlitz* begin to throb, and we dart ahead. Genoa gradually disappears beneath the waves, but from the port side we continue to enjoy a view of the paradise-like *Riviera di Levante*. The sea is smooth; no trace of sickness yet! So many sensations beset me that I must unburden myself, and go below to write letters to my mother, and to my friends Jawlensky and Prezzolini.

Next morning, which was Thursday, April 1, we passed Port Anzio, still in sight of the coast whose fine contours furnished new delights to the eye. Small silvery islands were continually rising up before us, and then sinking back into the waves behind, as in some magic game. At about four in the afternoon we entered the Bay of Naples, but as we faced the sun heading into the city, our arrival was not so thrillingly beautiful as had been our departure from Genoa. And old Mount Vesuvius had lost its tapering peaks, in the great eruption three years before.

But there was plenty of commotion as we drew near the landing stage. A boat filled with musicians came to meet us, emitting the catching strains of *Santa Lucia* to the accompaniment of mandolin and guitar. On the dock, there was great pushing and screaming over the luggage of departing passengers, and I decided to remain on board. But a Russian fellow passenger begged me to accompany him to the Turkish Consulate to see about his Palestine visa, and help him with his Italian. So off we went, and got a taste of colourful, tuneful, seething Naples.

Back to the ship late at night, and away in the morning again under a leaden sky. Now we were soon out of sight of land, bound for Egypt and Port Said. So I settled myself in my cabin, and spent delightful hours with Goethe and his *Letters,* and Bethge's *German Lyrics.* (I had recently been suffering from an addiction to poetry-writing, but had speedily recovered!) Toward six in the evening we passed the Straits of Messina, and smoking Stomboli: the district which but a few months earlier (December 28, 1908) had been laid waste by a terrible earthquake. We searched the shore with glasses. Reggio in the distance was almost completely destroyed; nearer to us lay Messina, abandoned by its populace, who were occupying tents on the outskirts of the town. Suddenly the scene was shrouded in darkness and we could see no more. We went below, much sobered by this terrible sight.

Saturday was uneventful, but on Sunday there was a High Mass on the main deck, at which I was celebrant and Father Cyril the preacher. But the ceremony did not seem to have a general appeal; many passengers continued to converse and smoke, and some kept their hats on. What a void there must be in life, to those who have not faith! We approached the island of Crete, and from that point on we went through a rather agitated sea. I was not seasick, nor were many of the passengers; but all seemed to be affected with a kind of sluggishness and ennui. The exhilaration of the first day or two had passed; and now to me the ocean seemed a vast desert where man can have no fixed abode, and human civilisation is barred. Perhaps our sluggishness was due in part to overeating and too much lolling-about. At least, that was all there was to do, it seemed; although I did not succumb totally to it, and kept on with my reading.

On the following day, which was Monday of Holy Week, we made Port Said. The African heat reached us as we neared the harbour, and we all suffered intensely from it. As we entered port, and the mouth of the Suez Canal, our ship's band struck up a sprightly air, and soon we were surrounded by swarms of small boats filled with blackamoors. Some coaling barges also drew alongside, each manned by fifty or more carriers of similar hue, who laughed and shouted like so many children at play. In each boat there stood a ferocious looking Turk, armed with a stick.

We prepared to debark, as here we had to catch the Austrian steamer that was to take us up to Jaffa. I was expecting a money-order by wire from Holland, but with the arrival of the mail, there was nothing for me. Somewhat perturbed, we made inquiries in the town, and after being sent " from Peter to Paul " through the hot, dusty streets, we finally found the letter at the main Turkish post office. I could not help thinking of a scene from some comic opera, as we passed through those rickety, dilapidated streets. But at the post office, the official refused to hand out my money unless someone would vouch for me. So I hastened back again to the Lloyd agency, where a clerk, on hearing me begin my tale of woe, suddenly spoke up: " What, *Willibrord Verkade?* Surely I saw some paintings by an artist of that name in Munich! Are you the man? Yes? Well! How small the world is! " So, jotting down a few mystic words on my telegram, and adding a seal or two, he said: " There! That ought to do the trick. It may be stretching the rules a bit, but it's a pleasure to be of some service to you." Thanking him heartily I was off, and had no more trouble with the hard-headed post-office officials.

On the Austrian steamer all the cabins were taken and we three were assigned a room belonging to one of the crew. It reeked with the smell of stale tobacco smoke; and next morning we were glad to find ourselves anchored outside the town of Jaffa. Small boats came to take us off, and we were thankful to a beneficent Providence for the calm sea. If it is rough, landing is impossible, and the voyage must be continued up to Haifa. Our boatman bore the picturesque name of Roubine Abd-el-Wahab, and as he was vouched for by the friars at the Franciscan hospice, we felt safe in entrusting everything to his care. And lucky for us, as otherwise it would have been a terrible ordeal getting through the customs and on our way up to Jerusalem. Aided by lusty shouting and swearing on the part of our guide, we were at last on our way, and delicious perfumes coming from the orange groves, through which we passed, soothed our frayed nerves. Toward evening we reached the Holy City, and found our way finally to Mount Sion Abbey, where our Beuron brethren gave us a hearty and touching welcome.

CHAPTER. TWELVE

IN THE HOLY LAND

PALESTINE, the 'Promised Land . . . . flowing with milk and honey " hard by the arid desert, what scenes of tremendous historic moment it has witnessed! Thrice-sacred soil, whereon God's plan of Redemption was accomplished, after long years of preparation: " The Word was made Flesh, and dwelt among us . . . . He came unto His own, but His own received Him not . . . . But as many as received Him, He gave them power to be made the sons of God, to them that believe in His name " (John, I). In the course of time the Promised Land has expanded into the whole Christian world, and the Chosen People become the Church Universal. God is adored everywhere now " in spirit and in truth," being as truly present in the Blessed Sacrament as He was when preaching in Jerusalem's fair Temple. Bethlehem and Golgotha are daily renewed in the Mystery of the Christian altar, and every Catholic Church is a true Cenacle, a banquet-chamber where Christ nourishes His faithful members with His very Flesh and Blood. So all this makes a visit to Jerusalem seem somewhat superfluous, above all for the artist who has in addition seen its historic glories so wonderfully depicted on canvas, as in some of Rembrandt's masterpieces. These often convey the essential impressions, far better than does a mere visit to the Holy Places. Yet, going there is valuable in clarifying one's knowledge of biblical events, in giving an insight into Oriental psychology and modes of thought, so different from our own.

In my own particular case, Palestine influenced me deeply, though in an unusual way, and one which I was not conscious of at the time. I can describe it best perhaps by saying that here, far off from the activity and turbulence of Europe, I *matured*. On entering the monastery I had become a *child* again; and then the next ten years or so were spent in developing as a youth. Then came a period of storm and stress represented by my Munich experience, as with a young man who first begins to " feel his oats," and on the threshold of manhood oscillates between independence and submission to law. Thanks to a wise Providence, I now had a period of nearly four years, under ideal surroundings, in which to pass through this crisis, and settle myself once and for all.

The artist finds much stimulation in the scenic beauty of Palestine. Though barren and scorched most of the year, the landscape is truly sublime. The mountains have something dignified and imposing about them, as though they realised the greatness of the events they had been privileged to behold. And everywhere there are little touches of detail which mysteriously yet unmistakably tell us of the distant past.

My most enduring memory of Judea is this: an intense blue sky, across which an occasional large fleecy cloud is floating. An undulating plain broken by rocky hills and deep ravines, its colour suggesting an over-ripe apricot, or that of a copper kettle blackened by the fire. Here and there are visible a clump of dusky trees, or the soft green of olive branches. More rarely, one sees the fresh light green of vines growing on a hill. Red cattle reduced to skeletons, wandering aimlessly about; a herd of black goats clambering up a hill after a few mules meandering along the white-hot, dusty road. A village on the mountain yonder, lonely and isolated, dark and sombre-looking, as though it might be a fortress — and then, " down to Jericho " and the Dead Sea, which is another scene entirely. The tropics, in very sooth: luxuriant vegetation and flowers everywhere; magnificent gardens and farms with towering palm trees, and orange groves whose blossoms in the spring emit a perfume so heavy and exotic that some tourists are made ill. The Jordan river flowing down the valley, through a thicket of trees so dense that one is reminded of a primeval forest.

And the Arab population! What a study in ethnology! Judging these sons of the desert by European standards, they constitute at best a hopeless puzzle; but I am far from believing our standards to be infallible. The Arab puts a totally different value upon the things of life than we do, so that if we are to understand him we must adjust our methods of reasoning. Thus, he has no patriotism in the sense that we have; allegiance to the native land, or to a political grouping. He loves indeed the country of his birth, but still more his family, and numerous kinsfolk. He takes it as a matter of course that if a man has sufficient means to live on, he does no work; and his respect for such " gentry " is great. He prefers poverty with liberty to a more comfortable existence under the restraint of law and custom. Yet he does not necessarily despise those who exercise authority and power: he would do the same if he were in their place. And there are always means of circumventing government. He knows the adage: "You can't squeeze blood from a stone"; and so he will cut down his last olive tree, or sell it stock and branch, rather than pay taxes. He has many good qualities. He is content with little, and gets along well on the most elementary necessities of life. He is most hospitable, and never looks down upon a pauper. When it is cold, or wet and rainy, he is depressed; but as soon as the sun shines again he will sing. And always when you ask: "How are you?" he answers: "I am content." As indeed he is, needing so little. And yet on the other hand, he is often miserly and grasping.

These and many other details which might be cited show how widely divergent are the European and Asiatic points of view. Perhaps they can never be reconciled, and a gap will always remain between the two races. Personally I never felt at home in Palestine, in spite of my admiration for the natural beauty of the country and my sympathy for its inhabitants. Doubtless, the rather difficult climate had something to do with this, for my vitality never seemed to rise, and I never felt so well there as I did at home. From May 3 to September 14, the two feasts of the Holy Cross, rain is a rare event; and the temperature hovers between 90° and 108° in the shade. Yet even this would be bearable, were it not for the continuous parching drought, due to the prevailing east winds from the arid desert. At other seasons the west winds from the nearby sea are cool and refreshing.

IN THE HOLY LAND

November and April are the most agreeable months, as they bring welcome rain which makes everything sprout; and the sun, reflecting through the clear washed air, bestows an iridescence upon the landscape that is beautiful beyond words. The winter is mild, but somewhat enervating because it does not offer sufficient contrast to the heat of summer.

The site of our monastery on the Mount of Sion had been originally acquired by Emperor William II, through his friendship with the Sultan Abd-el-Hamid. In 1898 he purchased a large section of ground upon which had stood a grand basilica in Byzantine times, the *Hagia Sion,* built in honour of the original Cenacle or Upper Room in which the Last Supper had been held, and which ancient tradition had located at this spot. It was therefore regarded as the " Mother of all Christian Churches," and in addition, was supposed to have been the place where the Blessed Virgin spent her last days on earth, hence its name *Dormitio* or " falling asleep " of our Lady, designating the place of her death and miraculous Assumption into heaven.

The former Kaiser turned the site over to the Catholics of Germany, and the *Deutsche Verein vom Heiligen Land* or " German Holy Land Society " was formed, which collected money and built the church and monastery. The architect was Herr Renard of Cologne, who made a masterly disposition of the uneven and rather confined space available. His plan was executed under the architect Sandel and the builder Gohl, and the resultant edifice attained a standard of beauty that would be difficult to excel, in the opinion of many European experts who have viewed the building. Sandel used Arab workmen throughout, training them himself; and the work of his stone-cutters is especially excellent. The Arab is not original at all, but is a very good imitator. On March 21, 1906, the *Dormitio* was formally turned over to the Beuron Congregation, and four years later the church was completed, being consecrated April 10, 1910 — a year after my arrival.

On Wednesday of Holy Week, 1909, the morning after we reached our destination at the Dormition Abbey, I was taken on a tour of inspection about the premises. Due to the limits of space, there was room for only twelve Fathers, so I suppose this community must remain only a small one for a long time. The beautiful bell tower, 164 feet high, commands a wide view over the city and surrounding country: the Cedron Valley, Mount of Olivet, and the Garden of Gethsemane in one direction, and in another the old city with its close-huddled roofs and minarets, with the cupola of the Church of the Holy Sepulchre in the centre; and on the outskirts, the Temple site. Further on one could clearly see the road to Bethany, Mount Herodius which overlooks Bethlehem, and the distant mountains of Moab.

Holy Thursday was a most important festival at the *Dormitio,* owing to its relation with the Last Supper; consequently throngs of pilgrims assisted at our liturgical function. In the afternoon I ventured out into the old town for the first time. Rarely have I felt such a flood of vivid impressions as in that short space of an hour or so. The commercial quarter, or *Suk,* with its threadlike passages and

[202]

tiny shops stuffed with articles of every description, the teeming, noisy throng of marketers with their picturesque costumes and strange ways, the eerie colour-effects of the sun struggling through some narrow aperture and falling upon the kaleidoscopic scene, filled me with an indescribable emotion. "Surely it is Rembrandt who has painted this *chiaroscuro* scene, somewhere," I mused.

On Good Friday I went into the town again to take part in the Way of the Cross devotions. Each Station is marked by a slab of some kind on the exact spot where our Lord passed through the streets on His way up to the hill of Calvary. We knelt and prayed before each one, oblivious to the noise and bustle of the traffic. At the seventh station there was a dispute between the police guarding it, and some Arabs who were leading a train of heavily laden mules through the narrow passage. Finally they got through the praying multitude, their wild shouts contrasting strangely with the low murmur of our prayers, and the voice of the good Franciscan father who was our leader. Finally we reached the summit, and the Church of the Holy Sepulchre, which was filled with a polyglot crowd of worshippers each conducting their own ritual: Greeks, Armenians, Russians, Copts, and ourselves the Latins. But we did not mind this sort of confusion so much, as it was more devotional, and full of sincere faith in Christ.

During the Easter festivities our Arab neighbours came to the monastery to present their greetings to Father Prior. We newcomers were duly presented to them; and a swarthy turbaned individual said to me: "I am pleased indeed that you have become my neighbour. For a good neighbour is better than a good friend." A deep bit of Arab philosophy! Later we paid visits to several of our religious colleagues: the French Dominicans, the German Lazarists, and the Fathers of St. Pierre, a foundation recently made by the famous Jewish convert, Marie-Alphonse Ratisbonne. From now on, we three newcomers were accepted representatives of our order in the Holy City.

My cell looked out upon a large Christian cemetery, which was shared by both Orthodox and Uniate Catholics: the former being Greeks and Russians, and the latter Armenians, Copts, Abyssinians and Greek Uniates. Many varying and strange funeral customs was I privileged to witness, the most interesting one being the " wailing ceremony " of the Arabs who belonged to one or other of these rites. (There are quite a number of these Mohammedan converts in Palestine). This usually took place the day following the burial. Several women would appear dressed in flowing white draperies, followed by a servant carrying a huge barley cake coated with sugar. This was placed carefully on the grave, and a small lighted candle stuck into it. Then the wailing began, the nearest kin of the deceased sitting at the head of the grave, the others around it. Rocking back and forth, the women gave way to paroxysms of weeping, such as one sees sometimes with little children. Now and then they would pause, and converse with mournful gestures, or sing a funeral dirge; and then suddenly resume their loud lamenting again.

Such grief of course could not always have been genuine,

but as a rule it was, I think. These Orientals are much more spontaneous and uncontrolled emotionally than we are. Especially their womenfolk, whose love for husband and children sometimes approximates adoration. I cannot help but think that such a custom is a sane and healthy one, for it affords a natural outlet to those forces of the soul which clamour for expression in great human crises. When this outlet is denied, serious harm may result.

The wailing ceremony always ended with the coming of a priest, who recited some short prayers and incensed the grave with his swinging censer. Then he was handed a glass of wine, from which he took a sip and poured the remainder about the grave. Sometimes he accepted a piece of the barley cake as well. Then all withdrew.

Sometimes a number of Russian paupers would gather in their section of the cemetery directly beneath my window, to be fed by a group of ladies who went among them distributing food in a most kindly and cheerful way. Always they began and ended with prayers said in common. At the end, the ragged fellows would slouch wearily away, the women remaining behind to collect the spoons and dishes, and have a social chat.

One day I heard a strange singing just outside my window, and, looking out, saw a black Abyssinian priest sitting on a stone near the open-air altar of the cemetery. In one hand he held a book, in the other a fly-chaser which he brandished slowly, keeping time with his chant. His cloak lay in the sun some distance away, probably as a counter attraction for certain insects that can become most obnoxious in the Orient. He was chanting his office, beginning on a very high note and then sliding down the scale by means of half and quarter notes in a most curious way. But it was truly beautiful, the song of that solitary negro priest. It seemed to breathe of heaven in its quiet joyousness, its absolute freedom from care and trouble, its forthright simplicity. Perhaps he was singing that beautiful hymn to Mary in the ancient Ethiopian Liturgy:

Thou radiant, pure, and holy One: no song thy praise can sing,
Who once upon thy tender hands, the Lord of Life didst bring!

From my window I could also see, in the distance, the battlements of the Citadel with its ancient " Tower of David." Every evening the Turkish military band would play a martial air, in which the bass drum took a predominant part. Then all at once they would stop in the middle of a measure, pause a second or two, and then, in three descending intervals, produce such a terrific discord as would turn the stomach of the most modernistic musician. Then a loud rolling of drums, terminating with a resounding bang on the big drum, and a loud *hurrah* for the Sultan.

I had not been in Jerusalem long when I witnessed one afternoon an interesting festal procession of a hundred or so Mohammedan Arabs. First came the children, mostly girls, who proceeded along in a graceful dance-step. So effortless was it that they seemed to float on air, their expressive arms

[206]

giving the impression of wings in flight. Then came the men, whose part consisted in the somewhat less æsthetic performance of firing their long rifles into the air as fast as they could load them, all the while grinning and shouting with delight. Next came the older women in their best finery; after them, on a fine white Arab steed, two boys of four or five years, each with a *tarboushe* and a garland of flowers on his head. As I learned later, the lads had just been received into the Mohammedan community by a ceremony equivalent to our baptism. They clearly felt their importance and behaved with solemn dignity. Behind them walked the maidens, closely herded together like sheep, and singing an Arab air which never changed, except in intensity with each repetition. This easygoing, carefree demonstration impressed me as comparing well with some of the festive processions we have in Europe, which except for a few features might very well serve as funeral processions. With all our seriousness and " good manners," we have, I am afraid, forgotten how to rejoice naturally and spontaneously. Either we show an exaggerated dignity and self-consciousness in our celebrations, or we go to the other extreme and throw away every vestige of restraint and order.

For most tourists, the sacred sites in Palestine constitute the main attraction. But strangely, this was not the case with me. Some places I loved, such as the Mount of Olives and Bethany. The unkempt hills where once the City of David had been, and the dark Valley of Josaphat below them, attracted me very much; as also did old Jericho, the

Jordan and the Dead Sea. Bethlehem, above all, with its charming surroundings, captured my heart. But for the hundred-and-one other traditional sites, even those of Golgotha and the Sepulchre and the Place of the Ascension, I could not for the life of me summon up any real devotion. After all, one cannot worship a *site;* and then, what difference is made by a few metres more or less, if the whole place has been sanctified by the presence of the Son of God? Surely the whole of Mount Olivet is holy, by the fact that our Lord spent that terrible night of agony there — and the pretty flower-garden of the Franciscans at its foot recalls nothing of death, nor treason. And in the Church of the Holy Sepulchre, there is too great a cacophony of various rites, too much noise and confusion.

The artistic work that I was called upon to do at the *Dormitio,* was, I regret to say, a dismal failure. I was assigned to decorate the new " chapter-house " or hall where conventual meetings, such as conferences and elections are held; and though I put in nearly a whole year at this, and took great pains, the result was a disappointment to all the community, myself included. I prefer not to discuss here what factors lay behind my failure. I shall only say that it assisted wonderfully in that slow purification of my soul which I needed so much, and which Palestine finally brought to me after four years. My Prior was a most broadminded man, and gave me much freedom to develop myself artistically as I wanted, in a country where an atmosphere of steady, quiet *constancy* predominates: the spirit of

IN THE HOLY LAND

Eastern mysticism and contemplation, in contrast with the *activism,* the ephemeral and hectic turbulence of our European world of art. Step by step came a purification of my artistic self. At first, only a few minor signs of " fermentation " showed themselves, such as my tendency to gush and "boil over " in my notes and letters of that period. This showed that a real change was taking place; although they manifested some self-conceit, too. But when artists boast, it is not too bad a sign: they show thereby their realisation of some incapacity, an unconscious reaction against frustration of effort. The true artist is never really proud, but on the contrary, humble and worshipful.

What force within me was behind that slow ferment, that inexorable inward metabolism of purification? It was, I doubt not, my own deep longing (in spite of my imperfections) for *beauty* high and pure, yet full of life's warm glow; a longing too, to *express* myself, to communicate what treasures I had, in chaste abundance. And my naturally lively fancy kept this urge always fanned into a flame. Taking imperious command of my subconscious self, it was forever conjuring up before my mind pictures of entrancing beauty in which virgin nature and opulent blossoming united in flawless grandeur. Adding fuel to this was the constant quickening influence of the picturesque country and people about me, the many sublime examples of Egyptian and Greek art (which I grasped more intimately here, under the perpetually blue and peaceful skies of Palestine), and my constant reading of classical literature, especially Aeschylus and Goethe. And of course, my daily companionship with the inspired Scriptures, and the writings of the Saints.

And yet I was far from living in a continual state of ecstasy. The fires of ardent longing never went out, but often remained submerged and unknown to me. Due, I suppose, to my native limitations, my very impotence to nourish and express them, as well as to my aenemic constitution, which underwent the rigours of the Oriental climate only at the cost of loss of energy and perseverance. I always had to husband my strength most carefully, and paid dearly for any extra exertion such as walking or riding. And the frequent visitors were a constant strain.

But I suppose my own faulty artistic habits were really my greatest obstacle, and they were terribly hard to shake off. I would not learn that working in haste gave small chance for my modest natural ability to develop, and that I was one of those who can accomplish good things only when allowed to concentrate on one single project for a long time. And merely synthetic work was not enough to satisfy my creative urge, though now I realise it is what I can do best of all: painting together ready-made details mosaic-wise, so that taste and imagination produce a symmetric whole. This is true creative art, which pleases not for a few moments only but in which the beholder can make constantly new discoveries. But living as I was in an era where spontaneity ranked supreme, and where a sketch was preferred to a finished work, I suffered untold harm.

In spite of all this, my quest for beauty drove me into constant effort. I would not allow barren longings to consume my soul, and was always trying my hand at something. Two or three larger paintings and a great number of sketches done in oil, water-colours and aquatints were the fruit of this interior struggle, and tell faithfully the story of my purification during that four-year period in Jerusalem. All done too hastily, they show, especially those I painted towards the last, unmistakable signs of refinement and chastening in my taste.

My friendships too, gave me much stimulation. My associations with my monastic brethren were pleasant, of course; though I am afraid my temperament got the best of me sometimes, under the strain of the excessive heat. We were a small community, and lived so close together that little oddities in character became easily magnified. But my Dutch calm and natural cheerfulness helped wonderfully; while the daily Office and High Mass were a continual solace to us all, the grand dimensions of our church made our little choir of seven sound like a heavenly chorus and our humble harmonium echo like a great organ. I made many friends outside among the clergy, such as Father Lagrange, the renowned exegete, and biblical scholars like Fathers Abel, Vincent, Dhorme, Jaussen. Intercourse with great lights like these was always stimulating; and then there were plenty of other congenial people, like Fathers Van der Vliet and Burtin, two White Fathers, who helped me greatly in a similar, if more informal way.

Father Van der Vliet was a fellow countryman of mine, but together with his companion had been schooled entirely in the French manner. I never could quite swallow this, and used to have great fun mimicking their "*on ne fait pas cela,*" or their "*soyez convenable.*" Then they would try their theological skill on me, with often amusing results; but it was good for me: good-humoured correction I have always appreciated. In fact, my many French contacts in Jerusalem proved a great advantage, helping especially in my correspondence with Denis and others which I always kept up. I owe much indeed to the French language, for it has vitalized and developed my sense of clarity and precision.

At this period too I began my literary career, contributing a series of ten articles on Palestine to the Dutch journal *Maasbode,* and two *Art Letters* to the *Munich Zeitschrift fuer Christliche Kunst.* These were only gossipy bits, of no great literary value; but they procured for me the pleasure of seeing myself in print: "*la plaisir de se voir imprime,*" which is not by any means always an indication of vanity. Every intelligent man, the artist especially, feels the need of creating something and communicating it to others. The *logos* or "word" thus engendered is the medium of this self-giving. It is not easy to write well, just as it is difficult to speak well; and those who succeed in their literary attempts confer a boon upon humanity. It is a blessing that in the kingdom of letters there are so many mansions; and writing, even that which reaches only the level of polite and clever conversation, has its own real value, and is a labour of love.

Another interesting experience was my association with a young Dutch artist, Piet Gerrits, who had been living

[212]

for a long time in the Holy Land and spoke fluent Arabic. He was held in high esteem among some of the local Bedouins, as he was conversant with many of their customs, was shrewder than they were, and could ride a horse supremely well. We spent many delightful hours together, and I was able to assist in several of his projects, in Jaffa, es-Salt, and other places. Once we were working together at a polychrome altar in the parish church of Bir-ez-Zet, where, in the rectory, during our three days' stay, we came to know an exquisite old Arabian woman. She was the pastor's housekeeper, a widow of the *fellah* class; and the truest, most charming type of Oriental that I ever came across. She always wore her veil, a coarse linen cloth of white which hung loosely over her plain blue dress and woolen girdle. But the veil evidently was not enough, as whenever she appeared before us she would hide her long face, that looked like a piece of wood-carving, in the folds of a huge shawl which she carried in addition. Only her aquiline nose and piercing black eyes were visible as she solemnly paced in carrying the dishes for our supper, which she had cooked before an open fire in her sooty chimney-less kitchen. It took courage to eat her viands, too; as she was most unkempt and dirty. But we knew that it was a matter of principle with her to wash but rarely: she must show, by her neglected appearance, that she was a faithful widow who sought to please no man. She claimed never to have looked at a man since her husband's death.

At table, the good pastor, Don Psgara Abd' Rabbo, would sometimes tease her. " Oh, the things I have had to

put up with during the sixteen years you have been here! "
he would complain with a sigh. " How can you say that?
she would reply sharply. " Nobody on earth fares as well
as you do. I have cared for you as if you were my own
son; cooking for you always the choicest meats, giving you
the very best of everything. And you do nothing the whole
blessed day. And you are an *Effendi,* a gentleman: and yet
you complain! " Whereupon she would sweep out of the
room, carrying herself like a Byzantine Empress. She evidently considered herself a paragon of Arab virtue, and
would never touch eggs or fish. Had she not seen in Jaffa
once, the carcass of a horse washed ashore? Well, fish feed
on such filth! And the hens who lay eggs after scratching
in a dump-heap, how about *their* food? No thank you: the
master could have them if he wished, together with those
cucumbers stuffed with meat which had been killed God
knows how long ago. Arabs are sensible people, eating only
freshly-killed meat. Thus one race jeers at the other, whilst
the angels in heaven shake their heads in wonderment.

An interesting experience was our trip together to es-
Salt, a town of 20,000 inhabitants (largely Christian) in
Transjordania; where we collaborated in decorating the
parish church. It took us nearly two days and nights to
travel there on mule-back; and we started working the
morning after our arrival, March 24, 1911. Piet Gerrits had
charge of the general line of the work; my principal task
being to paint a *Christ appearing to His Disciples* on the
wall to the left of the high altar. I made my design, transferred it to the wall on the fourth day, and started to paint.

[214]

IN THE HOLY LAND

There was no time to lose, as I was due back in Jerusalem on April 12. But what joy to work again without any criticisms to fear! Nobody ever came to es-Salt. It is different now, for with an auto the place is reached in four hours from the Holy City.

On April 11, at 10 A.M. I put the last touches to my work, and an hour later was in the saddle. Piet Gerrits remained behind to finish up, so I had only a young Mohammedan to escort me. We reached Jericho at about six in the evening, but as the inn was full and we were not overtired, I decided to press on to Jerusalem by night. We rested until about eleven, then started our long upward climb towards "the City on a Hill." It was much cooler than travelling by day, and I began to understand the Arab preference for night journeys. The mystic grandeur of the landscape was profoundly impressive; the dark shadowy hills kissed here and there by the soft rays of the Paschal moon, the brilliant starlit sky, the whisper of a damp nocturnal breeze, all formed a picture that was beautiful beyond words, and mysterious. Often we passed Arab wayfarers: farmers taking grain and charcoal to the market; a group of men and women going to celebrate the feast of Nebi Mousa; three daughters of Mohamet on a pilgrimage, riding in a palanquin slung between two mules; a squad of evil-looking Bedouins — and in every one of these nomads, a regal dignity, albeit couched in rags. It all reminded me strangely of Daumier's *The Fugitives*.

We rested and had a cup of coffee at the " Good Samaritan " house, half way up to Jerusalem. The proprietor invited us to take some rest, but I refused, saying we had to push on at once. Though by now much fatigued, I could not stomach the sight of the dirty divan he offered us, with its smell of vermin. Near Bethlehem we were caught in a rainstorm, which disgusted my guide so much that he wanted to stop, and spend the rest of the night in a nearby cave. I would not hear of it, as we were so close to home; and when he still objected I yelled *Female!* in Arabic to him, which was the unpardonable insult. This expedient, to which I added the magic *Baksheesh!* (" a tip! ") overcame all his scruples, and soon we were knocking at the door of the *Dormitio*.

This was the longest trip I took in Palestine. I never got up as far as Galilee, as I was always afraid of catching fever, of which my companion Father Cyril had died during the second year of our stay in Palestine. Usually I was too tired to think of travel, especially during my final year there. I wanted now more and more to get back to Europe, but put away this thought until finally the opportunity came.

The Benedictine monk, by his vow of " Stability " attaches himself not only to the monastic state which he embraces, but also to the particular community which he has joined. Though he may be sent away for special reasons, as for instance to do work such as mine, or to make other foundations, he always is considered a member of his original community or *Familia* and has the right to return to it. In keeping with this vow, each group of monks always settles in a place where nature affords both beauty and fertility of surroundings, so that the human side of monastic life will receive proper stimulation and nourishment. Thus a true *home* is created, and the monks always have an attachment to it that is hard to break. This explains how monasteries can continue to exist under the most trying conditions, and why some Abbeys have endured for many hundreds of years. So it was natural for me to feel homesick for my " Mother Beuron," and the graceful curves of the young Danube by its side, the dark pine forests around it; in spite of the charms and valuable associations of Palestine.

Though our Beuron Fathers are generally expected to remain at least five years when sent to the *Dormitio,* I felt in conscience bound to ask for an earlier return, as my old friend Plecnik in Vienna (with whom I had been corresponding regularly) was urging me to undertake some decoration in the new Carmelite church in Vienna-Doebling. I wrote him in February, 1912, that my Abbot's permission would have to be obtained. This he eventually succeeded in getting for me, so that in November I finally left Palestine, spending much time in the intervening months making my designs and cartoons; yet not without great effort, for I was listless, tired.

What had the Orient done for me? As I have already said, it allowed a blessed ferment of purification to take place within my soul. But this was only accidentally the work of the Orient; basically, it was a complex of forces proper to Christianity; forces that had been driving me onward and upward despite my weakness, ever since (and

[217]

perhaps before) I had embraced the true Faith. And the Orient added little to my cultural formation in comparison with countries like France, Germany, or Italy. At best, it gave me some new artistic impressions, and a more detailed knowledge of things already learned. So it was in Europe after all that I was to find a new acceleration, a more fruitful stimulus to my soul.

Chapter Thirteen

RETURN TO EUROPE

WHEN I left Jerusalem the country was displaying its best aspect: that soft variegated beauty that I had learned to love so well. I found myself almost regretting my departure; yet, thought I, it was far better to live in a harsher climate and amid less lovely surroundings and be able to do real work, than to live half-crippled in an Arcady.

I entrained for Jaffa, where I was to take the coastal steamer for Port Said, and from there a "Khedive" liner for Alexandria and Naples. But difficulties beset me. I arrived in Jaffa at noon, and found that my ship had been delayed by storms, and would not arrive until the morrow. I waited impatiently, and as soon as it came in I went on board. Free at last! The sun was casting its last slanting rays over the heaving tide and a flock of tiny craft in the harbour. A magic glow suffused all things, just as when I had left Genoa. A dolphin was frolicking in the gentle swell, its glistening, graceful body ofttimes being fully visible. In a rowboat just below us, two married couples sat — evidently Germans; they were doing well in Jaffa, it seemed, from their well-groomed appearance. A peculiar quiet brooded over the whole scene, as if a storm were coming. But the sky was clear: perhaps it was only my imagination, this growing tenseness in the atmosphere that I seemed to notice now more frequently, here in the mysterious East. But of late there had been much talk of war.

Next morning we docked on schedule in Port Said, but were not allowed to leave the ship for several hours, as there was a cholera scare, and everyone had to undergo a medical inspection. This delay, coupled with the day we had lost before leaving Jaffa, made me miss my connection for Naples. At first I was downhearted, but when I learned that the next ship would not arrive before ten days, and I could fulfil a lifelong ambition by visiting Cairo and its ancient treasures, I was overjoyed. So I set off for the southern capital without more ado. Here was the chance of a lifetime, and Egypt was now to take the place of Italy in my itinerary, as my ship would stop at Marseilles instead of Naples.

Night had set in when my train arrived in Cairo. Most of the way we had followed the course of the Suez Canal, and it presented a lively, picturesque scene, with its many boats, both great and small, crawling slowly along, often seeming to be moving over the flat desert landscape itself. One was a great ocean liner, a regular Colossus among the rest, with its sides towering high above the banks. Ablaze with lights at every point, it seemed a true *deus ex machina,* the last word in modern technique and in effete luxury. " What right has this devilish monster to intrude itself upon so chaste, so sublimely peaceful a landscape? " I thought to myself. " And all these myriad electric lights: what wanton desecration of the starlit night! "

I put up at the Hotel Bristol, where I got a cheap rate

and special attention through the kind offices of a North German Lloyd agent who met me at the station. Next day I spent in looking around the city and its Arab quarter; and the following morning went out to Gizeh and the Pyramids. The Great Pyramid of Cheops impressed me most profoundly, with its enormous mass rising up to a great height, the whole built of such huge, ponderous blocks of stone. Great heavens, what a herculean labour! I stood amazed, but soon began to feel great compassion for the poor wretches who had been forced to build it, and a rising aversion for a system which could reduce a whole people to so abject a slavery. Despotism is abhorrent to us moderns, but above all to the liberty-loving Hollander, who loses his phlegmatic calm and turns to rage at the first sign of any encroachment upon his personal freedom. But doubtless the ancient Egyptians had a different psychology altogether, and were really servile at bottom. A trace of this is found in the writings of the early Egyptian monks; and certainly, if the facial expressions on some of the *bas-reliefs* in the Pyramids are trustworthy evidence, these people went about their servile tasks with joy rather than grumbling and complaint. Undoubtedly too, they shared their rulers' taste for grandeur.

Today I look upon these monuments in a somewhat different light, having acquired a greater respect for work done in common, under the direction of a superior will, which uses even force when necessary. The Great Pyramid is a symbol of this kind of thing: an enduring, grand monument, happily uniting intelligent purpose, artistic sense, religious faith. A powerful monarch builds his " House of Eternity " to defy time and change. His mausoleum is no utilitarian structure, like a lighthouse, or a railway bridge, but primarily an edifice of the spirit, whose end and aim is accomplished in its own self, and is of deep intrinsic value.

In contrast, buildings whose form is based solely upon the structural requirements of the ends they are to serve, bear always a stamp of incompleteness. A *totality* of purpose is lacking. True, this totality alone could create only an empty frame: it must be aided by a form deriving from the purpose of the building, but the latter should be made to harmonise with it and, if possible, be kept subdued and unemphasised. It is this effect of *concealed assertion* that we observe in all God's creatures. The bear, for instance, has a skeleton; but there is scarcely any visible evidence of it in his powerful body. The sheep's daintily shaped head and legs cause the bones to stand out more prominently, but this is overcome by the effect of its body, covered with fleecy wool. The tiger attracts our attention to his striped skin, and we scarcely notice the bony structure so prominent in several parts of his body. Two protruding humps set off the bone-structure of the camel; while the rooster's shape seems to be based upon his gaily coloured plumage, especially that of his tail! *Obvious* structures like the Eiffel Tower are merely skeletons, while a peasant's cottage in the Black Forest, with its low-hanging shingled roof, bears the stamp of completeness.

Modern architecture follows utilitarian ends too exclusively, and therein lies its weakness. Poverty and cheapness

[222]

of exterior aspect are the inevitable result, no matter how much is lavished on construction. For the same reason, much that we see in modern churches is hideous, as for instance pulpits which seem stuck into a wall, instead of growing organically out of it. How infinitely more suggestive is a mushroom growing out of an old tree-trunk!

From the Pyramids of Cheops I walked through the crisp desert sand over to the Sphinx. It was an old friend of mine, its photograph having for long stood upon my desk at home. I found precisely what I had expected: a primitive, half-savage embodiment of exultant strength so characteristic of Egyptian art. It is a clearly conceived model, enlarged to colossal dimensions; and though hardly a new creation, it certainly is the work of a great master. It represents a ruler, whose face, turned towards the Nile which is the backbone of his kingdom, gazes directly at the rising sun. Each day its light surrounds him with an effulgence appropriate to his regal state, as crouching in an attitude of invincible power, he defies his enemies and strikes terror into the hearts of evildoers. With one blow of his symbolic lions' paws he can annihilate an army; and yet his features betray no semblance of harshness, but rather cheerfulness and clemency. Probably the Sphinx (*Neb* or "Master" in Egyptian) was for the people of the Nile what Phidias' Jupiter was for the ancient Greeks: a source of strength and encouragement in all life's troubles.

On returning from the Sphinx I had a magnificent view of the surrounding country, whose entire expanse is dominated by the elevated site of the ancient burying-ground.

[223]

The Nile was just completing its annual task of beneficence in the vast plain, and a few palm-groves were still inundated. Far away to the horizon in all directions, except to the southwest where the great desert began, a carpet of green was spread. And the charms of that distant horizon, bathed in purple haze! I thought of my dear Holland, which is a delta too. . . .

How are we to account for the interest manifested by this primitive race in applied geometry, and their bent for clothing its rules in enduring form? I once asked a scholarly philosopher this question, and was told that primitive peoples, cleaving as closely as they did to *nature,* had a heightened awareness and comprehension of rudimentary intellectual forms, such as numerical relations and fundamental spatial dimensions. More explicitly, this meant that a primitive race by its intimate association with nature would be more able to grasp geometrical principles than a race living further away from nature. It is fundamental to man not only to live within space, but to *sense* it, and to guide himself by it. This already constitutes a rudimentary basis for distinction and construction, from whence it is but a step to the determining of dimension and dimensional relationships such as point, line, plane, body.

I was greatly pleased with this explanation; and desirous of getting something more out of my preceptor, mentioned the theories of Maspero and Speigelberg, who claimed the Egyptians had a totally different concept of reality and its representation than we have. With them, the " image " or outward appearance of a living being was in essential relation to the latter, so that even death did not separate the two: they remained conjoined and bound together in some way forever, just as they were in life. And it was this concept that had induced the early Egyptian artists to desire great durability of material, to prefer *bas-relief* to painting, and so on. My philosopher friend said this theory did not cover everything, for a people so deeply immersed in fable as were the Egyptians of the early dynasties, would make absolutely no distinction between being and appearance, reality and concept, imaged and image. For them, any representative portrayal of an object would be regarded as identical with the object, in a reality of relationship far transcending our metaphorical way of saying: " The picture *is* the man." Then, he said, their art would naturally reflect their belief in a continuous existence which death can only modify slightly. The modern idea of death as *destruction* more or less complete would be so utterly strange to them that they would demand conclusive proofs of it rather than of immortality, as we do.

Next, the National Museum of Antiquities opened to me its treasures, and for three whole days I wandered about from room to room fascinated by everything. Only a few of my impressions can be set down here. For instance, the effect of the colossal *Amen-Hetep II and Queen Teje* on the grand staircase was truly overwhelming, although its details do not show that delicacy of workmanship possessed by similar works of less tremendous proportions. But the faces of the royal pair are exceedingly well done, and express such good-nature and cheeriness that one feels they must be very happy, sitting there side by side. The smaller female figure standing between them is on the other hand, a remarkably fine piece of delicate symmetry. The statues of kings belonging to the earlier dynasties, which I came upon in an upper hall, held me spellbound. I knew them all, of course, from reproductions I had seen; but now to stand before them face to face and almost to see them live and breathe, what an experience! For the lifelike effect was uncanny. There was old Re-Hetep and his wife Princess Nefret, and King Chrephren with his falcon (in black granite), and the so-called Village Magistrate. The Pharaoh's noble head and finely-cut mouth expressed a world of clemency. He appeared indeed the *Good God,* as his subjects called him in distinction to the *Great Gods.* And what a marvellously shaped ear, what a perfect torso! Strange, that the harder the stone, the more perfect is the product coming from the really great sculptor's hands. Seemingly altogether different qualities are evoked from this than from softer stone. Perhaps it is because the artist is forced to work very slowly, in spite of those powerful impulses urging him to go fast.

And what a captivating couple, Nefret and her husband! The colours of the painted statues are still quite fresh, the chaste white folds of the princess' clinging garment setting off delicately the softer shading of her body, an effect which is heightened by the dazzling whiteness of the high-backed chair. But more effective still is the tenseness and suppressed animation of the figures, reflected differently in the entire bearing of each. What a contrast, and yet what harmony of

[226]

detail! One feels that here indeed is a well-matched pair, each mysteriously supplementing the other. Seeing them is like listening to the exquisite harmony of two musical chords blending perfectly together.

The statue of the Magistrate originally was painted too, but now there remains only the wooden nucleus. Yet even this reflects a marvellous fidelity to nature, in spite of the unfinished effect, and the severity of the erect figure. Primitive plastic art, and yet how filled with life! Passing into the mummy exhibition room, I stood for some minutes before the remains of Setos I and Rameses II, musing on our debt to them for the erection of such grand temples. Why could not these mighty kings be left in some more worthy resting-place, close by the monuments which tell so enduringly the story of their grandeur?

No ancient art has come down to us with such completeness as the early Egyptian, preserved as it has been so carefully in those " Eternal Dwellings " of the silent dead. But now that it has been exposed to profane light, how long will it survive? Night and darkness are by nature preservative, while daylight consumes. There should be no more excavations: something at least should be left intact for posterity. It is terrible to think how in a few moments fire or an outbreak of wild vandalism can utterly demolish what has survived for thousands of years. But man's curiosity is insatiable: always there are people who must fill the gaps in their knowledge by means of new discoveries. But will a few more added details really supply a key to the whole? New developments mean swift changes in our attitudes

[227]

towards what has gone before. Will minds be able to keep step with them? We have all watched the growth of young people during their later adolescence with utter amazement — and where there are jumps, there are also gaps left behind, to be overcome only by leaping too.

The key to a true appreciation of Egyptian art is to be found I think, in understanding clearly *what* it aimed primarily to express. An artistic representation may stress one of two forms: that of *reality,* and that of *appearance.* The latter has been followed by the pure impressionists, for instance: their main concern is rather the surface-light on the object than the object itself. But the Egyptians, on the contrary, in keeping with their tendency to unite object and image as already indicated, aimed at depicting the very reality, the form of being itself as they knew it, rather than its mere appearance. Thus, a standing figure is portrayed with head and feet in profile, shoulders seen from the front, body in semi-profile. There is no fore-shortening; the arms are generally full-length. At first sight this seems grotesque; but when viewed from the proper angle, every detail is seen to be extremely well done. The whole figure fits perfectly into its allotted space, and the contours are of exquisite beauty. It is high art, and this is decisive; even though it reminds us at times, possessed as we are of our modern fancies, of children's drawings.

The Egyptians were certainly part-masters in the dividing of surface, as is shown in their reliefs and hieroglyphics. Their ornamental inscriptions such as those on the thrones of Nefret and Re-Hetep are most charming. The Greeks with all their dexterity in treating flat space, as seen in their vases, never reached the high perfection of the Egyptians in this regard. In fine, the artist who takes pains to study the latter will certainly improve his eye as to the division and distribution of surface.

Unfortunately, I could not visit the great temples at Luxor, not having enough money to get there. But with my knowledge of the Pyramids and Sphinx, I could muster some idea of their grandeur. In this connection, I quote an opinion of Father Desiderius Lenz, which I recently found jotted down upon a sheet containing some ground-plans of temples he had sketched: " The art reflected in the Egyptian temples creates an impression of fear and horror. It is articulate force, power, strength, unrelieved and unrelenting, in majestic repose. Its truthfulness and solidity of character make it melodious, but with a melody for which even trombones would be too weak." I do not agree wholly with this, believing that the impression of overpowering strength must often have been softened and relieved by the outward embellishment of the structures.

This seems to be borne out by a famous passage in St. Clement of Alexandria (d. *circa* 217) in which he compares the female weakness for exterior finery with the Egyptian manner of decorating their temples so lavishly when all is empty and barren within. He then says of the latter: " They take the utmost care of their temple-rooms, vestibules, sacred groves and meadows. The courtyards are adorned with rows of columns, and the walls within glitter with precious gems and artistic paintings (probably colored reliefs) so that nothing seems lacking anywhere. All sparkles with gold and silver, and rare stones from India and Ethiopia. Curtains of gold fabric conceal the innermost parts, but if you penetrate thither expecting to find something still more sublime in the figure of the temple-god, you are forced to break out laughing. For when the heathen priest, with serious mien, and perhaps chanting a sacred hymn in Egyptian, lifts the veil a little, you see not what you expected at all, but only some ridiculous animal: a weasel, a crocodile, a local serpent or some other beast wholly out of place in a sacred edifice, belonging rather to the regions underground, or to some dirty puddle. So the god of the Egyptians is but a beast, lolling on a purple bed."

So the great St. Clement had certainly received a deep impression of the exterior beauty of these temples, despite his loathing of the pagan rites performed in them. He even speaks in another place of a " still more sublime impression." Indeed, there probably has never existed a people with so high a regard for the sanctity of divine things, in spite of their erroneous conceptions of God. They often chose things more fitting to Divine Majesty than did some worshippers of the true God in later ages. Perhaps some day there will be a renaissance of the Egyptian conception of religious art. Our Father Desiderius long cherished a dream in which he hoped to execute a mighty church dedicated to the Sacred Heart, inspired by these concepts. Had it even been realised, there would certainly have been something *compelling* about it, something that moved the worshipper to bend his knee.

RETURN TO EUROPE

Egyptian art has deeply influenced my own work; hence I have dwelt upon it at some length. When I left the country, I was more resolved than ever to give close attention to contours in my art.

On Wednesday, November 27, I sailed from Alexandria on board the North German Lloyd steamer *Prinzregent Leopold*. It was not an agreeable voyage. The ship rolled heavily, and the weather grew colder every day. There were only a few passengers on board. I remember particularly a congenial Englishman who was quite a character. He told me he had already seen most of the world, liking nothing better than to be on a ship. The longer the voyage the better, for he could always read undisturbed. He had made a list of over three thousand books, all of which he felt called upon to read. He lent me a volume of Keats, and on handing it over to me, raised it sentimentally to his lips, saying with much tenderness: " A lovely book! " I was particularly struck with Keats' famous lines: *" A thing of beauty is a joy forever . . . "*; and copied them out for future inspiration.

On the following Sunday we sighted the coast of France. Fighting a contrary wind and choppy sea, we had some difficulty in negotiating the harbour. I recall the first mate, a veritable old salt, looking defiantly out from the bridge upon the turbulent waves as if to say: " It's no use, old Neptune. We're going in, in spite of you." And so we did, all the passengers breathing sighs of relief as we finally berthed. On the quay, I was handed a letter from my brother Erich containing one hundred francs, a most welcome surprise, as my expenses in Cairo had been higher than I anticipated. Then I went over to the Cathedral, where the first Sunday of Advent was being celebrated with a High Mass and solemn procession. It was most edifying, but I nearly froze in the dank edifice, with the temperature around 28° Fahrenheit. In the afternoon I visited an ancient church formerly a part of the famous Benedictine Abbey of St. Victor, and was harangued by an Italian priest I met there, on the recent " providential " collapse of Turkey. Italy had just taken possession of Tripoli.

I wanted to leave early next morning for Lyons, but the hotel-keeper failed to wake me, despite all his solemn promises of the night before. So I missed my train, and had to wait until noon for the next one, a most happy misadventure for me, as the sequel proved. On boarding the train, a distinguished-looking French gentleman helped me in, and got me a seat next to his. When I explained, in answer to his question, that I belonged to the Order of St. Benedict, he told me he was on most intimate terms with the Benedictines of Marseilles, now living as temporary exiles in Italy; and that he was interested in collecting rare ecclesiastical vestments.

We got on famously together, and as we neared Tarascon, he prepared to get off. I casually inquired if Montauban was very far from there, as I was interested in Ingres' paintings which the master had bequeathed to its museum. " No, it is not far at all," he told me. " By all means go. You can get a good connection in Tarascon. Now is your chance! " I looked into my purse somewhat dubiously. Yes, I had just enough money left. " Let us go," I said, as the train stopped. But my friend's kindliness had only just begun to show itself; before we parted, he had bought my ticket for Montauban, and given me fifteen francs as stipends for two Masses to be said for his intention. But I had some remorse of conscience when, on boarding the train, I discovered how late the hour would be before I should arrive in Montauban. It was quite a long side-trip, for which I had gotten no permission. Luckily I could not reflect much, as after passing through a ravishingly beautiful countryside on the Nimes — Cette — Nar — bonnie route, it grew suddenly dark and I fell fast asleep. We arrived in Montauban at one in the morning, and I spent the remainder of the night in the station, as it cost nothing.

At daybreak I went out for a walk through the town. How sweet, this wandering about wherever luck would take me! A little rain fell, and the air was soft as in Holland. Many old recollections and sensations crowded in upon me. I wanted to offer Mass, and finally met a workman who directed me to the nearest church belonging to a religious order, the chapel of some Carmelite nuns. It was half-past five, yet I saw no light in the place. I rang the bell; but for a long time nobody answered. Finally I saw a light gleam through a window in the upper story of the convent, and then one above the entrance. " Ah, Monsieur l'Abbé! " came a whisper behind the door. I moved closer, and discovered a nun's kind face peering through a small grating. " May I say Mass in your chapel? " I inquired. " Ah, certainly," came the reply. " Only you must wait until the

[233]

church is open at six o'clock. Then, *ces messieurs* will come."

I waited patiently till six, when I discovered the identity of *ces messieurs:* two local priests who appeared punctually on the hour to celebrate their Mass. I had to show them my papers, as evidently they did not trust strangers, and was allowed to celebrate when they had finished. It was cold inside the church, and by the time I had finished I was trembling all over. But the good Sister-Portress made a fire in the sacristy, and brought me a huge cup of coffee and some bread. I returned to life.

Came the hour when the museum was opened, and I could realise my ambition for an intimate acquaintanceship with Ingres. I spent four engrossing hours there, to the great disgust of the attendant who finally asked politely: " Monsieur l'Abbé, when do you wish to dine? " When I told him how far I had come just to visit this museum, he replied patronisingly: " Yes, this is the place to learn something, more than in Toulouse," and left me in peace. But at last I had enough, and departed. The remaining hours before train-time I spent in another ramble, purchasing on the way some provisions for my journey to Lyons during the night: sausages, bread, figs and apples. I was highly satisfied with my trip to Montauban.

In the last century France became undoubtedly the leading nation in the world of painting. Good artists there were elsewhere, but aside from Constable and Bonnington, their influence remained confined to their own country. Leadership comes only through universality of appeal, which quality in French art procured it a general validity. Perhaps this came about through the state of mind which prevailed in France in the early nineteenth century, that she was *la grande nation* and destined to march at the head of European civilisation. Poets, sculptors and painters were regarded as representatives of that vocation, and respected as such; while modern technique had not yet usurped the center of interest, nor had photography and coloured prints become the dangerous rivals of art.

Two great personalities, Ingres (1780–1867) and Delacroix (1799–1863) brought French painting to heights that equalled, without surpassing, those attained by the art of past ages. The great merits of the French character, clarity combined with ardour and buoyancy, were embodied in these two masters; though in such different proportions that each seems to disown the other. Ingres went back to the Greeks and Raphael; Delacroix, to Rubens. Nor was this a mere accident, as both tendencies represent the French spirit which has successfully fused both Classic and Northern culture into an organic whole, whose most lofty expression is *contained abundance*. Thus, it is significant that Ingres did not exhaust himself in line, nor Delacroix in colour. King Louis of Bavaria could never have said: " A painter should also be able to paint," i.e. not only to draw, on viewing Ingres' pictures, as for instance his portrait of *Madame Riviere* or his *Nude Back* in the Louvre. The elasticity of Delacroix's talent is fully demonstrated by his ability to paint surpassingly well such divergent subjects as his *Barque de Dante* and his *Harem Scene.* So my study of Ingres' drawings in Montauban confirmed my opinion of how deeply he has influenced French art in the last century. Indeed, I see this influence even in the *motifs* of some French postage stamps issued in the last decade.

Towards evening my train started for Lyons, and as I settled down comfortably for the long ride, my feelings of good cheer were by no means dampened on my discovery of an uncorked bottle of wine and a gigantic slice of cheese, carefully wrapped, which someone had left behind in the compartment. Now I could dine *à la Lucullus:* first course: sausage-meat and bread; second course: bread and cheese; dessert: choice fruits; and the whole washed down with *vin du pays.* After finishing the bottle I stretched out and was soon in deep slumber which lasted nearly the whole night. Shortly after dawn I stepped off the train in Lyons, feeling fit as a fiddle.

It had been twenty years since Ballin and I first visited the capital of southern France. Its museum was, of course, known to me, but I was glad to visit it again; and its atmosphere of venerable ecclesiastical tradition thrilled me now as before.

Boarding another train I reached Zurich the same evening, stopping overnight and leaving for Beuron in the morning. On arriving home again, I handed over with a wicked glee the remainder of my funds, amounting to the sum of exactly one mark in German money. But I was pleased with my economy, having made my pittance go a long way.

My brethren accosted me with the question: " How long

will you stay with us *this* time?" I did not blame them, as I had become somewhat of a traveller, in spite of my deep desire to remain at home all the time. So I had to tell them that there was an interesting piece of work calling for me in Vienna. But my Abbot hesitated in granting me permission; and not without good reason, as up till now I had never really succeeded in producing a finished work all by myself. But I finally won the day with my plea that an important task like this one should bring out the very best in me, and the interest many people were taking in it would be an added stimulus. But I experienced anew the truth that no one is a prophet in his own country. Those near and dear to us look for the ideal person in our mortal frame, and when we fail to meet their expectations, love is disappointed. Often outsiders judge us more correctly, being further removed from the sight of our human deficiencies.

I had now entered upon the period of maturity in my monastic life. The hard years of transition were over, and my striving for form and expression was to be crowned with success at last. When that success came I grasped it greedily, hungrily; not quite realising that it was due more to the arrangements of Providence than to any efforts of my own. Not that I overestimated my own powers; I always knew, I think, that I was not and never could be a great master. But there was always the *drive* to produce a few works of real beauty with the help of the gifts (however meagre) with which I had been endowed. He who adds but one to the single talent he possesses shall be praised

[237]

as a faithful servant. And is it not enough to be able to record at least one or two real successes in a lifetime, at least some approach nearer to the very Best, the Most Beautiful? Or even, to have recognized the most sublime possibilities, to have glimpsed the secret of immortal creations? Is not honest effort sufficiently rewarded when one has learned humbly to admire?

CHAPTER FOURTEEN

VIENNA AGAIN

I LEFT Beuron for Vienna on Saturday February 22, 1913; and as the train halted several hours in Munich, I had the chance to see a few old friends again. In the streets of the pretty capital I felt my old feelings of unrest and pain bearing in upon me again, but in the homes of Jawlensky and Dr. W. which I visited, I was quite at ease once more. In the latter, the excellent Denis collection did not look well in new surroundings, for easel-pictures depend much on their environment, although each constitutes a small world in its own right; while in the former, a number of extremely odd paintings showed that Jawlensky had become definitely an expressionist. He was as affectionate as ever, and brought in to see me Her Excellency von Werefkin (who showed me some very good paintings of hers), and the artist Bechtejeff. But we could not talk long together, as I had to catch the night express. We never met again. The war put a cruel end to Jawlensky's promising career, and Bechtejeff too was killed in action.

On arriving in Vienna next morning, I went straight out to Doebling to inspect the Carmelite Church, whose new side-chapel I was to decorate. The stained-glass window had already been executed according to the coloured cartoon I had sent on from Jerusalem; and everybody was much pleased with it, especially the donor, a wealthy and generous Viennese business man whom I shall call Herr Z. In keeping with the latter's suggestion I had used a Carmelite saint as my subject, St. John of the Cross, who appears beholding the *Ecce Homo* scene, with angels on either side looking on in great distress.

I was full of enthusiasm, and decided to hurry on at once to Prague where friend Plecnik was staying, in order to settle the details for the rest of the chapel. I first held a long consultation with Herr Z., whom I found to have sound artistic taste, besides being a most charming host. He was a typical Austrian, and I never realised before how much that type of German differs from the one found within the borders of Germany. Like the Hollanders, who differ too because of the peculiarities of their country and their subjection to French influence, the Austrian character had been deeply influenced by contact with a variety of other nations, so that while remaining German it nevertheless has a certain added *plus* which makes it *sui generis:* a species in itself.

Then I went on to Prague, where Plecnik greeted me joyfully at the station, and took me immediately to his studio in the School of Applied Art where he was a professor. Over a cup of coffee we had a long chat in the delightful carefree manner of two bosom friends whom long separation and community of interest has made hungry for each other's company. Since our last meeting we had both learned many things, suffered and experienced much; and all this must be told, poured forth in a spontaneous babble of words which probably made the angels smile.

VIENNA AGAIN

Next day, my architect friend called for me at the Abbey of Emmaus where I was stopping, and we went over to St. Gabriel, the church of the Benedictine nuns which I had helped to decorate sixteen years before, in my Oblate days. The daring piece of work still pleased me, and in spite of a few imperfections does great credit I think to Father Desiderius, under whose direction it was accomplished by us raw beginners.

After remaining for the Vesper service, we returned to Plecnik's studio; and there carefully examined several sketches the latter had made for the proposed altar of St. John of the Cross. I was not quite satisfied with them, as the space above and around the altar seemed inadequate for what I wanted to do. But next day he submitted a design which solved all my problems. The chapel was to be re-formed entirely, with a barrel-vault terminating half a meter below the stained-glass window; and this would allow me an ideal semi-circular surface for my picture. By thus dividing the chapel into an upper and lower compartment, the whole appeared as having gained in depth. In addition, a low marble railing extending out into the nave gave an air of seclusion to the new chapel.

Our next step was to go out to the church and take the exact dimensions of the chapel. Then Plecnik made a pasteboard model, on to which I drew a *Descent from the Cross,* with St. John about to grasp the limp arm of our Lord. It was a success, and after I had made a few corrections suggested by my friend, our general plan of grouping and measurement had been settled, and inside of a week we had finished the nucleus of our composition. Then I commenced to work on my figures, as meanwhile the work of reconstructing the chapel was being carried out under Plecnik's direction. I progressed very slowly, as I was bent on creating something perfect in its own right, with the aid of all that I had now learned, and shutting out every outside influence. I had quarters at the Carmelites', but Herr Z. gave me a small studio in his factory where I did my coloured sketches. Weeks and months passed by, until finally when spring came I was ready to draw the coloured cartoon for the niche. For this an additional room was assigned to me, as I needed to work from living models.

No artist can do without models. If he attempts to, he will become subjective and barren. Perhaps if his early training has been especially good, he may be able to make some shift without them, or perhaps get along with anybody that happens to be around him. The bodily structure presents hidden difficulties, and must be faithfully depicted before its actual *beauty* is thought of. Neck, shoulders and arm offer special traps for the unwary; and if the head and feet are not placed correctly, all is lost. Beginning and end are always important, in preaching sermons as well as in painting pictures, and in our life's story, too. But the very best results are obtained if the artist can work from models he knows and reveres. Thus not only is imagination stimulated, but also heart and mind. Or at least, if he is able to recall as he wields his brush, the memory of some ideal person, whose intelligence, piety, beauty are made to live clearly before him. Such qualities are, of course, rarely found in any single model, at least in the proper proportions; but by combining several, good results can be gained. So often handsome people are dull, intelligent people are ugly, pious people stiff and affected.

Then, there is conceit: how often have I had to sketch two or three children before I could get *one* face that looked natural! One had always to show the utmost indifference, lest the thought of being admired brought out tell-tale signs of vanity. But for my *Descent from the Cross* figures, I found what I needed with no trouble at all, and in a manner both delightful to me, and full of rare understanding on the part of my subjects. It turned out that Herr Z. had cherished a dream of perpetuating somehow in the chapel the memory of his numerous family; and when I discovered this, and saw that with his several children ranging from little boys and girls to grown-up men and women I had all that I wanted, I offered to use them in my picture. He agreed quite naturally, and thus was my big problem happily solved.

Speaking of the value living models have in awakening both intellectual and imaginative forces in the artist, I am reminded of the modern trend to emphasise the former at the expense of the latter. That is to say, we place less value upon the feelings of the heart than our ancestors did, and frown upon such things as the display of tender emotion, and the shedding of tears. Instead, we aim to produce results chiefly by means of cold, calculating thought. Now, I believe this to be a sad mistake, which, if allowed to carry through to its logical conclusions, will mean the death of high art. True, all extremes in sentimentality are to be frowned upon,

[243]

but less because they are signs of weakness than because they are *untrue* to human nature at its best. On the other hand, we are *not* avoiding the extremes of unleashed brain-power: intellectual pride and frivolous vanity, scepticism, heartless destructive criticism, and other manifestations which so easily blight creative effort and ideal passion.

Personally, I believe sentiment or artistic feeling has been overrated in the past; and for a time I tried to cast from me everything savoring of it. I succeeded so well that a friend once remarked to me that he failed to see how I could be an artist, since I had no sentiment! But now I see differently, and realise how precious a thing it can be in art, if properly ordered and balanced with the other forces of the soul. Here, for instance, are some of the valuable services it can render the artist:

It is an efficient " scout," advancing upon objects too far away for the intellect to comprehend; it finds out much useful information about them simply through the reactions of pleasure or dislike they cause. It is a reliable barometer of the soul's condition, indicating whenever anything is essentially wrong, by clear signs, and vice-versa. It is a faithful sentinel, crying, " *Who goes there?* " at the slightest unlooked-for disturbance. In difficulties and problems, it is always a wise counsellor, giving advice without which the intellect would often find no solution. It is a *gourmet* of the first order, and its critical palate may be trusted in many circumstances. It is ofttimes a prophet too, sensing what is to come with an uncanny accuracy and warning us in time. It often finds true *beauty* more quickly than the intellect, by that mysterious spontaneity of recognition which defies and transcends the powers of reasoning.

All these activities of artistic feeling and emotional passion must, of course, not be allowed to develop at random. No one of them should become an end in itself or for itself, not isolated from the control of the other spiritual powers. When this happens, true feeling dies or loses itself, transforms itself into an enemy which sucks the life-blood of the soul. Scouts, reporters, and sentinels never lead an army; nor is a prophet but rarely made a king. His task is rather to encourage, to lift his hands to God during the shock of battle, and to sing thrilling songs of praise when victory comes.

True sentiment shows itself in a multitude of ways, and garbed in different raiment; the red robe of charity and love, the white of innocence, the purple of modesty, the gold of piety, the violet of sorrow and regret, the black of mourning. False sentiment dons false robes, like the soiled one of lust and impurity, or the tattered one of rage, despair. True, the impulsive force of sentiment is strong, and therefore dangerous:

Das maechtige Gefuehl sich im Gesang ergoss.
"Mighty sentiment found vent in song" (Wieland's *Oberon.*)

For it is essentially *unseeing,* so that unless its blindness is guided by intellect, its dynamism checked by will, it can lead only to disaster. Of course, it can never be the *final* motive power in creative art, but only a stimulator, a mediator, a complementing and sifting factor in the mind's final vision and the will's final choice. Its origin and precise nature must in the last analysis remain an enigma; but we must not forget that it belongs to the make-up of the human soul, a simple substance, whose native powers are therefore all basically one and the same. So the *soul* is acting, no matter which of its several powers may seem to be leading it.

Sentimental characters like those in classic drama, or in Goethe's *Werner* seem no longer to exist in life; though in Vienna I discovered traces of the ideal passion which inspired the latter masterpiece. The buoyant intensity and dynamism of Viennese life aroused the dormant emotional faculty in me, and again I could feel and touch and taste and hear, receiving valuable impressions of every kind that a short while before would have left me unmoved. The spirit of Mozart and Grillparzer, of Waldmueller, Froelich and Schwind was still a tangible thing in 1913, living on in little romanticist circles that scarcely knew of one another's existence. Music was still the familiar property of the masses, and remained, tenderly fostered as it was, the best expression of the Austrian character. Classical music was nowhere appreciated so universally as in Vienna, largely I believe on account of the interest in choral work. Scarcely a Sunday passed without some famous Mass being sung in one or other of the churches, to the accompaniment of a full orchestra.

When listening to a quartet by Haydn (1732–1809) or Mozart (1756–1791), I marvel at the heights of pure sentimental expression these masters have attained. How is it possible for mere mortals to clothe terrestrial joy in robes of such heavenly beauty, simply by means of happy rhythm and soft, tender sound? During the unfolding of the constantly variegated theme, my soul seems transported into an idyllic landscape of springtime, where apple-trees blossom, finches warble, and the cuckoo calls. Red-cheeked children dance joyously beneath green branches: *allegro!* Their parents, seated on rustic benches nearby, and clad in flowing *rococo* garments, are dreaming of their own carefree childhood, and a smile of wistfulness steals over their toil-marked faces: *andante!* But the joy of the little ones is contagious; soon the parents rise and greatly astonish their offspring by doing a graceful *minuet* together. Then the *finale:* all dance in unison, blissfully forgetting care and trouble. The red sun moves down on the horizon, so they break off and go home. But all are refreshed, revived.

Beethoven (1770–1827), too, belongs with Haydn and Mozart, though he was not an Austrian, by birth or character. Perhaps he embodied to a high degree that resemblance the Rhinelanders have always borne to their cousins of the Danube region; for he certainly showed that he was at home in Vienna as soon as he arrived there at the age of twenty-two. His earlier teacher Neefe had prophesied that he would become another Mozart; and he himself seemed to have had still greater aspirations, judging by the brimming confidence he showed in himself. He became a pupil of Haydn, and at once asserted himself so strongly that his master jokingly called him " Our Grand Mogul."

Arnold Schmitz thus describes this peculiarity in his character: " His early successes confirmed him in the opinion that because of his superlative talent and intellect, he ought to be treated as a *grand seigneur*. He considered himself a kind of superman, and wanted society both high and low to recognise him as such." But at bottom he was warmly affectionate, and stood in need of affection in return. His first *Will,* which he wrote in the so-called Beethoven House not far from the Carmelite Church in Doebling, shows this clearly. Its opening cry of anguish reminds one strangely of some of Michelangelo's lamentations; and indeed, he had much in common with the latter. Perhaps his growing deafness heightened his feelings of loneliness; and certainly it was a great humiliation to him.

When finally he could no longer hear a single sound, the unfortunate man became ever more reserved and suspicious, a solitary in the midst of that whirl of social life he had once loved so well. But for all that, he is deeply indebted to Vienna for the inspiration he found in its warm hospitality, indulgence, ready affection — and abundant life. In turn Vienna is indebted to him. Though the depth and intensity of his works are perhaps more typically German, the works themselves grew on Austrian soil, and in them the spirit of the vibrant capital stands immortalised. The tragedy of his life has endowed Vienna with an unusual dignity. Beethoven has crowned the work of Haydn and Mozart in his own peculiar way, so that the three comprise a trio of incomparable harmony, whose noble heights of perfection were scaled in Austria's fair metropolis, to its undying glory.

How to account for the peculiar seductiveness of the Viennese atmosphere? Why is it that there one becomes more cordial, affectionate, carefree, than is one's wont? The climate certainly has little to do with it. Possibly it is due to the attitude towards *life* that has developed there since time immemorial. Your true Viennese demands a life that is always tolerable, flecked with a bit of sunshine and of joy. He cannot stomach the bore, the slow-poke, the gloomy pessimist; and expects everyone to be like himself, pleasant and happy-go-lucky; to call you " *Lumperl* " (" dear old rascal ") is the greatest compliment he can think of, and shows perhaps best of all the peculiar quality in Viennese temperament.

All nations have some such method of designating their standard of preference in people. Thus, the man who reaches the highest popular esteem is called, in North Germany, *a competent man;* in Holland, *an alert man;* in the United States, *a successful man;* in France, *a most intelligent man;* in Suabia, *a reliable man;* in England, *a gentleman;* in Spain, *a dignified man (un señor formal)*; in Italy, *a good chap (un buon tipo)*. And in Austria, a *lumperl!* — Thus are the various human qualities variously preferred. In North Germany, Holland, America: will-power; in France: intellect; in England, Spain, Suabia: the moral forces; in Italy and Vienna: sentiment. Of course, all these designations imply a great number of other qualities besides the one actually expressed, showing only which one is most highly prized.

So in the long run, no stranger can resist the Viennese influence. If he is a weak man, he will possibly come to grief; but if he is strong, he will be mellowed, enriched, made to radiate the warm glow of human sympathy, for fire enkindled in the heart will eventually penetrate the frostiest exterior. Thus was I too softened *suaviter et fortiter* (" sweetly but strongly ") in Vienna, and the hard shell under which I had long hid my affectionate nature was broken. This was a great spiritual boon to me, as I became more sensitive to the in-pourings of Divine Grace, and newer, broader channels were opened between my soul and God. Perhaps this was due partly to my concentration on a religious subject, aided by the fact that my exemption from choir-duties left me more dependant on my private prayers. For the religious, these two kinds of prayer should help and complete each other, just as in everything that has its objective and subjective side. But if it is impossible to keep a proper balance between the two, it is wise to allow predominance to whichever one is most needful, at particular times.

In the beginning of April 1913, the re-shaping of the chapel-niche was completed, but the walls were yet too damp for painting. Otherwise I could have begun work immediately, as my main cartoon, thanks to the help accorded me in every way, was about finished. Not only had I been able to make many sketches from life, but capable hands had furnished me with photographs of heads and draperies which helped me greatly in getting the proper distribution of light and shade. About the middle of May I could begin in the church; and after first tracing my cartoon on the wall, I had an expert gilder raise the haloes on my nine saints' figures by means of stucco, so that they stood out plastically. But now the contractor who had to set up the altar and marble balustrade appeared, and I was forced to retire until he had finished. This made me nervous and depressed — branches hang low when they are heavy with fruit, as though longing to have their burden removed. I amused myself as best I could with various diversions, but as soon as I could paint once more, I would brook no further interruption. Patiently and completely absorbed, I worked at my picture day after day, though at times I was hard put to discourage the attentions of my many friends in Vienna. It is especially cruel to disturb a painter on a day when the light is favorable. He should admit callers only on dark days when there is not much chance for work.

After painting diligently all day, I would finish my Breviary in the evening, and recite Matins and Lauds for the morrow. I went out but seldom, and made it a rule never to look at a newspaper. Indeed I have never taken much interest in the latter creation of modernity, nor have I ever had cause to regret it. On the contrary, I advise everybody to do the same, especially members of religious orders; for I believe that it helps to preserve a balanced judgment on questions of moment, and clarity of mind. One always finds out somehow all he should know about important events; and for the priest and monk, it is essential that his heart hold room for all the world. This is most difficult, if each day a newspaper fills him with a thousand distractions and, by its commonplace reporting of crime and tragedy, dulls his finer feelings. There must be thousands of men today who are able to read the most distressing news without being in the least affected by it, drinking their glass of beer in comfort, or smoking placidly. Fortunately women are less addicted to newspaper reading, or there would be little compassion left in the world.

On one occasion I did leave my retirement, to make a pilgrimage to nearby Maria Zell, a famous Austrian shrine to our Lady. Again I was touched with the many scenes of pious fervour, such as I had witnessed in Monte Vergine, and so often in Beuron. Shrines like these are true oases in the desert of the indifferent world, especially if in them the Liturgy is celebrated in all its grandeur, as in monastic churches. True, the pious family is an oasis too, but it is more exposed to the blinding sandstorms of the world. Doubtless there are many souls who, after passing from the body unto the vision of God, marvel how it was possible for them ever to have forgotten or become indifferent to Him in life, amid the empty pleasures of our large modern cities.

What an insidious, blighting disease is spiritual indifference! It atrophies the soul, which under its influence gradually becomes a total stranger to the finer emotions such as love, sincerity and selfless zeal. Any sort of change-for-the-better is countered by its motto: "It is all the same anyway; nothing really matters much." Its roots are manifold and hidden, and therefore difficult to get at. The true indifferentist leaves you alone, and offers nothing but the blandest and most innocuous exterior as he passes by, so there is apparently nothing you can accuse him of. Of course, herein lies his deepest sin: in minding his own business only, he has forgotten the business of God.

VIENNA AGAIN

The city of Vienna has had its plagues of religious indifference; and perhaps more than its share, because of its gay, carefree attitude towards life. But it has also had great awakenings, usually brought about by some terrible event, or the fiery words of some extraordinary preacher. Two of the latter whose names are written with letters of gold in Vienna's history are the Augustinian, Abraham of Santa Clara (born near Beuron) and St. Clement Hofbauer.

During my stay in Vienna, the famous Father Abel was carrying on an apostolate of extraordinary fruitfulness that reminded everyone of his great predecessors. I heard him preach a number of times, and noted with much interest his special fitness for the task before him. For no preacher can get a hearing in Vienna unless he has a big and warm heart, indomitable courage, and a boundless sense of humor. He must be absolutely frank, and able at the same time to express the bitterest truths both sweetly and wittily. Above all, he will succeed if he is something of a woman-hater, for the female Viennese are past-mistresses in the art of completely subjugating their male consorts by spoiling them; and the latter have therefore the highest respect for anyone who has known how to preserve his own freedom. If the preacher can address himself in such a way that his audience feels he is speaking " for men only " he is immensely popular.

Father Abel had all these gifts, and thus followed nobly in the footsteps of flaming orators like Abraham of Santa Clara, whose books, containing his addresses to the Viennese after the great plague of 1679, are still regarded as classics in their own way. First came his *Vienna, remember it!*:

a fiery arraignment of the various classes in society, and yet couched in terms with which no true Viennese could take offense; and then his *Vienna, listen!* an exhortation to do the works of penance, written in the same inimitable style.

Towards midsummer of this year, another interruption came to me, in the shape of a visit from my twin-brother Erich. We had lately been corresponding much more regularly, and found ourselves drawing closer together in thought than ever before. For nearly seven years now he had held an important executive position as manager of the Netherlands Yeast and Alcohol Manufacturing Company, a large concern. His character had thus been able to shape itself on firmer lines than mine, as each day he was called upon to make quick and precise decisions, or write letters that were sagacious, yet brief and to the point. So I found him sure of himself, and free from anything savoring of irresolution; which was more than my own work had done for me. His horizons were perhaps less extensive but more clearly outlined than mine.

It was delightful to have my twin-brother all to myself, away from his business and family, and in a foreign country. In Vienna we were on more equal footing than we could have been, say, in Beuron, or even in Holland. But I won an advantage over him when I introduced him into the family circle of Herr Z., my zealous Catholic patron. It was a world totally unknown to him, and yet he was most favourably impressed, everyone treating him with such genuine kindness and sincerity. Afterwards he set down the impressions of his visit in a letter, which read: " I owe deep thanks to the Z. family. . . . They enabled me to see you in natural surroundings, and yet I could see that your religious views were more precious than bread to them. It was something far beyond the merely *ecclesiastical*. . . . For the first time in my life I beheld — paradoxical as it may seem — the reality of unreality. I remained as I was before, but gained enough knowledge to understand a man like yourself, and your religious views. I think I know better now what piety means. . . . Your work too interested me greatly. Not only the versatility that it showed, but above all, the evolution in you that it represents. . . . I think the creative artist is worth more than ten industrial men like myself, for he is master of his own work, whereas we can only lead the work of others, or propose things which others put into practice. I think I now know more than before, but I am not sure just how much."

Later in the summer I received alarming news of my mother's health. As I had not seen her for six years, and she was now past the age of seventy-two, I got permission from my Archabbot to pay her a visit. Towards the end of November I was able to leave my work in the Carmelite Church, as the cold and short hours of daylight made progress difficult. So I again went up to Holland.

It is a blessing I think, that women so generally survive their husbands. They remain sprightly much longer, and can attend to their usual duties in the household even at an advanced age; whereas men become a burden to themselves and others when obliged to give up their profession. Sometimes a bereaved wife seems to revive wonderfully after burying her husband, in spite of the genuine tears of sorrow she shed at his passing. Perhaps he was a grumbling and exacting partner, especially towards the last; and though she never faltered in love for him, now she is free to care for herself, with peace and leisure to think of God, and the needs of her own soul. But there are women whom the passing of their husbands affects in quite the opposite way. He who was their chief solicitude through long years, the focus and inspiration of all their activity, is gone. There is a void, something indispensable is wanting, and they are alone, and lonely. And thus they too gradually decline, as though they had no longer a right to live.

Something like this was often seen in the lives of monks, during the last century. Wholesale suppression of monasteries had severed many a one from the central interest in his life, the regular duties and routine which had become part and parcel of his being. And even without actual severance from his monastery, the monk who is approaching old age must be watchful and circumspect, lest he fall into the slough of laxity when in the very sight of his coveted goal. Leniencies and exemptions are afforded which endanger his faithful perseverance unto the end. Perhaps the Psalmist had this in mind when he prayed:

" *Cast me not off in the time of old age:*
When my strength shall fail, do not Thou forsake me "
(Ps. 70).

Long visits fatigued my failing mother, so I took up quarters with my twin brother in Delft. It was a beautiful old eighteenth-century mansion, well-restored, yet fitted up with antique furniture throughout. Erich was always happy when he could save some beautiful old object from destruction and restore it to a good use. In such tasteful, dignified surroundings, I became conscious of the fine depth and universality of old Dutch bourgeois culture. Here, modern pieces of furniture were made to look grotesque and crude, and had to be kept out of sight as much as possible.

I had many happy visits with my relatives and friends, during which everything always came off so well that my brother, in a subsequent letter, was pleased to describe my home-coming as " a veritable triumphal procession." There is no doubt that I acted more *humanely* and naturally than during my last visit, perhaps because my soul had mellowed, my character become more rounded and settled through my previous experiences. I had finally succeeded in blending the old and new in me, so that a new and more harmonious being emerged.

The last two days of my holiday were spent at home with my mother. She was as sprightly and charming as ever, though greatly aged. She still corresponded to the description someone had once given of her, that she possessed the consistency of point-lace, together with its grace and delicacy. Her mind was as keen as ever, and her amiable conversation continued to show both the limpid simplicity of her soul and the high quality of her intellect. She possessed indeed real literary and artistic talents, but had always kept them subservient to her wifely and maternal duties. It must have been hard to repress those aesthetic inclinations of hers during so long a life; and yet on the other hand she was to be considered lucky in having married a manufacturer instead of some penurious professor or artist, for she was no person to work miracles on a small income. In fine, she was a *mother* in the true sense of the word, than which there can be no higher praise.

Her joy at having me with her was so great that she seemed to forget her age, and sometimes would repeat, as we sat together, some lines of Heine's poem *To My Mother,* saying that some of my letters from Vienna had reminded her of them. The Hollander cannot stand unhappiness, and usually knows how to chase it away. Rarely giving in to tender effusions, he sometimes grows crusty and severe. He will become sentimental only when alone with the object of his affections, but if there is anything standing in the way of his need for unfettered love and companionship, he can renounce, without being too unhappy.

As I had to be in Beuron again for Christmas, I was obliged to set my departure for the evening of December 20. The hour of separation arrived. A mother will always remain a mother, and as for me, I felt again those painful emotions of eighteen years before, when I first left my home to enter the novitiate. We could hardly swallow the food of our last meal together. Why must people always eat before going away? In order to " brace up," we talked of inconsequential matters, never referring to what was in our hearts. Came the maid, announcing that my carriage was ready at the door. Again my mother anxiously inquiring: " Have you everything, my Jan? " " Yes, mother." A last embrace

VIENNA AGAIN

— I jump into the carriage and am driven to the station, staring vacantly, miserable, almost in despair. When love's bonds are torn and broken, a shadow of death passes over the soul, as though life itself were approaching its end.

Towards midnight my train arrived at Cologne, and I was a little less miserable. What I had left behind now seemed very distant, and I was again in a land where my life had become rooted, and where those roots had never been disturbed, nor would likely ever be, as they had been in my old home. On the platform were many soldiers bustling about, their arms full of Christmas packages. They were going home on furlough; my furlough was over, but yet I was going home — home to Beuron, where I could celebrate Christmas with such joy and fervour.

Next day, after attending High Mass in Cologne Cathedral, I went on as far as Bingen, where I got out and ferried across the Rhine to visit the Abbey of St. Hildegarde, just above the town of Eibigen. This ancient cloister had been occupied since 1904 by Benedictine nuns from St. Gabriel's, in Prague; its church had been recently decorated in the best Beuronese manner by Father Paul Krebs and his assistants. They had been working for nearly six years, and the whole edifice shone from top to bottom with grand mosaics and frescoes, which remind one strangely of the ancient basilicas of Rome or Ravenna. Over the door leading into the convent is painted an impressive *Orante* figure and underneath it the words *SOLI DEO* (*To God Alone*). An impressive motto indeed; it filled me with awe. Sister Antonia opened

[259]

the door for me. I had known her well in Prague; but she hardly recognised me at first. Soon the nuns were chanting Vespers. How lovely their true, clear voices sounded, in that fine old church! Yes, it was just as in Prague: the same absorbed, close unison, without any loss of vitality in tone. Evidently, these people loved their work — the Work of God. Afterwards I strolled out around the garden wall, whence one has a commanding view of the Rhine valley, with its lovely contours and striking contrasts. I love it best when the sun, struggling with the mist, reveals only the main grand outlines of the scene, and hides the mass of detail.

On the day after my arrival in Beuron, I received a sweet little missive from my mother, which I quote in full:

"My dear boy! You cannot imagine how much I miss you today. As long as you were in Delft or Zaandam, I always could say to myself: 'Oh, he will run over tomorrow.' But now that you have left for good, you are constantly in my mind, and I am sad whenever I think: 'When shall I see him again? Perhaps it was the last time I shall ever hold him in my arms!' However, I am grateful for your visit. I never before knew you to be so affectionate, so congenial, so interesting. You have found your balance, and have acquired a character that will not bow to new influences. This is for you specially necessary, since you are striving in so many ways to do good, and continually seek *harmony,* whether consciously or not. I am with you in thought on your journey. A train was wrecked near Dortmund today. How lucky that you went by way of Cleve! I feel quite well,

but just a little lonely. . . . Margaret is coming over this evening. . . . Your mother embraces you."
Villa Tromp, Dec. 21, 1913.

My mother's premonition proved correct. I did not see her again. She died March 8, 1917, in her seventy-sixth year.

But " Mother Beuron " took me in her arms, and led me always closer to sweet union with God. Opportunities for the contemplation of divine things were many there, and precious. To approach His Kingdom, and even sometimes to catch a ravishing glimpse of it and Him, what a blessing! Unhappy is the man who remains a total stranger in the land of spiritual reality lying beyond his senses, during his whole life. For it is not hard to find, if he does not consume himself entirely in material concerns, and turns his thoughts quietly to God at stated intervals. Like the afflicted ones who waited beside the Pool of Bethsaida for the stirring of the waters by God's angel, so we too must wait and watch, for the opening of the clouds when we can look into Heaven, albeit only momentarily and at a great distance. Daily tasks, humdrum life in the world, are not necessarily incompatible with this, if they are always sanctified by good intentions, and if some leisure be devoted to quiet peaceful intercourse with God, whether in prayer, holy thoughts, or pious reading. Sunday has been given us for this purpose.

> " *If thou turn away from doing thy own will in my*
> *holy day,*
> *And call the Sabbath delightful,*

IN QUEST OF BEAUTY

Thou shalt be delighted in the Lord,
And I will lift thee above the high places of the earth "
(Isaias, c. 58).

Sometimes too, God approaches close to us by means of extraordinary events, which as it were transport us out of ourselves, and lift us up to Him. A sudden, terrible blow, or an unexpected stroke of marvellous good fortune comes to us, and we are either paralysed with the fear and woe of this new revelation, or enraptured, carried away by the grandeur of its magnificent promise. In either case we are swept away from our poor mortal trappings into close contact with the Eternal, the Absolute, the Incomprehensible: our soul has felt God. Blessed is he who has experienced this sometime in his life, witnessing the truth of the Psalmist's words:

" Oh taste, and see that the Lord is sweet! "
(Ps. 33).

More blessed still is he who has been able to spend long weeks in an almost uninterrupted communion with his Lord.

Christmas had come, and it was truly a " delightful Sabbath " for me in Beuron. A season of special graces abundant and strengthening. Just as the body gains new strength when allowed to rest in nature's healing embrace, so the soul recovers itself when enjoying close union with God, peacefully and naturally. Christmas Eve seemed to bring me a new and deeper understanding of the words in the Gospel of the Feast: *" He was the True Light, which en-*

[262]

lighteneth every man that cometh into this world." All was light and warmth within my soul; and I even succeeded in prolonging this blessed Christmas spirit for many days, by concentration, reading, and prayer. To him who knows how to retain, more will be given.

St. Gregory the Great says in one of his Homilies, that carnal desires lead to satiety, and satiety brings disgust; whereas spiritual desires and longings satisfy in themselves, and yet are ever creating new desire. Again, the foretaste and expectation is sweet, with carnal desires; but their consummation creates loathing; while with spiritual desires the expectation counts for little, the experience pleases more and more.

Sublime thoughts like these, culled during Office or my own private reading, impressed me profoundly during these days. I could not get enough of St. Bernard, St. Gertrude, St. Francis de Sales. The latter's *Treatise on the Love of God,* together with his *Letters,* I found particularly fascinating. This noble saint is a marvellous work of nature and of divine grace, uniting in his character both French and Italian traits. The resultant product is a living work of art wherein the *Splendor Ordinis:* the beauty of good order, reveals itself in quiet gleaming. His fiery will is kept always so well in hand that he appears to gain his results only through kindness and meek persuasion. His *ego* intrudes not at all, so that he can be flawlessly objective, honest, natural at all times, and in all things.

But what strikes me as being his finest quality is, that his undoubted virility is laid over with noble traits usually asso-

[263]

ciated with the weaker sex, like tender feeling, sweetness, emotional appeal. A similar phenomenon one can note in many feminine saints, as for instance St. Teresa of Avila: masculine strength and courage, mixed with true womanliness. St. Francis de Sales is powerful, and yet with a captivating quality that wins the heart, and at the same time forbids familiarity. There is a glamour about him which attracts and yet keeps one at a proper distance. Perhaps in this he resembles Jesus Himself, who said to His mother: " *Woman, what is that to me and to thee?* " or to Mary Magdalene, " *Noli me tangere* (Touch not thou Me)." And of course, a man of such eminent, well-rounded sanctity and prudent discretion could love others without detriment to his own soul, as we see in St. Francis' great affection for persons like St. Jane of Chantal.

But with the beginning of Lent, I had to descend somewhat from my heights of contemplation, and enter active life once more. My superiors sent me to help in a number of parishes, and when Easter came I heard hundreds of confessions. But perhaps it was fitting, for Lent is a time when we should be glad to give up consolations. After all, why should I keep all that our Lord had taught me, just for myself? So I tried to have an encouraging word for every penitent, and to show tenderness and sympathy that came from the bottom of my heart.

A fortnight after Easter the time had come for me to resume my work in Vienna, so again I bade farewell to my brethren, and set out on April 25, 1914, in company with Brother Fidelis Failer, one of our sculptors, who had been

[264]

assigned to help me. At the same time he was to further his knowledge by visiting the museums at Munich and Vienna. I shall never forget our journey. The train seemed to be rushing through a blossoming landscape all the time, where peace reigned and prosperity was evident everywhere. The horrors of war were as yet not even dreamed of. At Salzburg a group of four youths got in and sat in our compartment. They were strapping young fellows, out for a day's frolic. They seemed to fit into the cloudless, beautiful day, and to emanate refinement, good sense, peacefulness. What became of them, I wonder, only a few months later? And why is it that this fleeting contact with them impressed me so? Did I live more intensely in that hour?

We arrived in Vienna, and were cordially received by the good Carmelites. Next morning we took up our work again, and slowly, laboriously, we brought it to completion. One stroke of the brush, carefully, then another. There were many hundreds of thousands of them. Finally the head of St. John of the Cross was finished, and fully satisfactory. But I had given it of my very best, and it was hard to repeat what the inspiration of a lucky moment had brought about, in all the rest. But at last all the other figures seemed to have attained the same satisfactory standard, but it took several more months.

It is nearly impossible to carry out a large project like my *Descent from the Cross* without some mishap. But there is generally an amount of good luck, too, for compensation. He who is always unlucky had better examine his conscience. Now, my bad luck was in being unable to get the painted

[265]

wall-surface to dry. I would thus have to put off the gilding of some parts of my picture, which made it impossible to gauge the effect of the whole until toward the end. But luck aided me, for one day, when our work was far advanced, I discovered that the blue on the upper part of our Lady's mantle appeared far too light in contrast with the lower part (having dried more slowly); and I resolved upon a desperate expedient. Grasping a sponge in my hands, I gave the too-dark section a good rubbing; then, covering it over again with a thin glue, I added a soft white tint, and shaded the folds of the garment with cobalt-blue. Result: perfect matching of colour throughout, and nothing left to do! Herr Z., who happened along just as I was conducting my dangerous experiment, was frightened; but said only: "You are a brave man."

This noble patron of mine had qualities of character so rare that I think they should be acknowledged here. Though of fiery temperament, his innate honesty of soul had made it possible for him to become an ardent believer after many years of scepticism. He was a logical thinker, and always sought for the *essential,* whether in facts or events; and no amount of sophistry or drawing-of-red-herrings could swerve him off the track. So finally he came to Truth; and his surrender was complete when he discovered Goodness and Beauty too, with the help of his native idealism, his contempt for all that is mean and base.

Noble characters like his always wish to see fulfilled in others, what has been denied them either through early carelessness, or by their lack of proper equipment. Thus, for instance, the true parent. Thus too with patrons who hope by fostering talent in other persons to realise ideals they themselves could never accomplish. And the parental instinct, or its extension in the patron, is the only one able to bear the strains and crosses bound to accompany this fostering task. For like children, so also do the beneficiaries of patronage often show ingratitude, forgetfulness, and fickleness. But great is the joy of the fatherly patron if, in spite of all, the work of his protégé is crowned with final success. This could never have come about, he knows, without his aid, and, therefore, is, in a sense, his own work. Thus he has found some completion to his nature, some worthy expression of himself, and he rejoices, and feels free.

So Herr Z. gave rein to his desire for *creating,* accomplishing true and lasting things by patronising promising artists. He was also interested in studying the problem of artistic intuition, having a theory that the true genius is inspired with " the spirit of eternal order," and that greatness will come provided genius is subjected to God's sway, in heart and mind. For only God knows the final laws of Beauty, Truth, Goodness; and only obedience to these laws can produce a true artistic masterpiece. My patron also was fond of comparing artistic instinct with the instinct in animals, claiming that unless it was as *active* in man as it is in inferior forms of life, it will not produce anything of perfect, pristine beauty. Man must become the blind, plastic slave of this mystic force, this Platonic " frenzy," creating only under its compulsion. The more he can bring himself under its domination in his art, the less dependent will he be on his

[267]

own thought and will, so that he acts unconscious of himself, like a true prophet.

Herr Z. also tried his hand at literature, writing two books: *Das Weltantlitz* (*The Face of the World*) and *Die Glaubensfrage* (*The Problem of Belief*), using the pseudonym of "Joannes Aquila." In the latter he ably defends the thesis that Wagner had composed in his *Lohengrin* a poetic synthesis of the Catholic Faith, albeit unconsciously, and under some mystic spiritual compulsion. For the poem from beginning to end (as the author shows) represents Catholic dogma, which because of its logic and soundness overcomes the severest and keenest criticism.

On November 26, 1914, Cardinal Piffl, Archbishop of Vienna came to consecrate the new Carmelite chapel, and next morning I celebrated a Mass of thanksgiving before the completed picture. Shall I attempt to describe the latter here? It will be better perhaps if I allow one of my friends to speak for me.

"*The Descent from the Cross* is a powerfully moving picture. The sombre Cross stands upon a background of gold, and just behind it, Joseph of Arimathea is seen standing on a ladder which touches the left cross-beam, having just released our Lord's hands from their terrible pinions. Nicodemus holds the precious Body from below, while the Blessed Virgin is in the act of taking Jesus to her bosom in a last embrace. Her blue-white mantle glows as with a celestial hue, and every line of her form expresses the tenderest devotion. She is the picture of grief, and yet maintains a regal, an almost priestly dignity. The corpse seems light and transparent, as though already having assumed its state of glory. Mary Magdalene kneels in the left background, bending low to kiss the foot of our Lord. Her blond hair hangs unbound, her lips tremble with suppressed grief. Opposite her is St. John of the Cross, clad in the white Carmelite choirhabit. As he kneels and grasps one of our Lord's hands with loving reverence, his typical southern countenance glows with emotion; while his profile stands out sharply relieved upon the golden halo which he wears. Two other female figures portray the same deep yet well-controlled sorrow, and one of them bears a family resemblance to both Mary and the Saviour. St. John the Apostle stands aloof and somewhat preoccupied, seemingly not sharing in the general grief. His eyes seem to reflect already some Apocalyptic vision. . . . The whole work is tremendously impressive and uplifting, seeming to resolve terrestrial misery in a flood of heavenly brightness. . . . One feels the artist has truly been through the school of St. Benedict, for if his ability is not of the greatest, he at least shows fidelity to objective truth, and a profound discipline of soul. There are some signs of an imperfect technique, but none of hackneyed routine or slavishness. The whole is naïve, simple, honest, and truly touching."

My old friend Herman Bahr wrote from Salzburg three years later, to tell me he had finally been able to see my picture. "It is wonderfully beautiful," he wrote, "so full of peace, power, purity. In the very centre of the Imperial City, I felt as though I was in the depths of some virgin forest. It is a pity that the chapel could not have been made more secluded . . . I shall never forget it. . . ." Hans Preuss, in his book *Das Bild Christi im Wandel der Zeit,* has this to say : " No one can look at this picture without imbibing some of its heavenly calm. The noise of the work-a-day world seems hushed, as if in fear to disturb the sacred stillness of this death-scene by the slightest sound. With what infinite tenderness do the four saintly personages receive the Body of Jesus, hardly daring to touch it, as if it were the Eucharistic Host! . . . An unforgettable contrast is that between our Lord's pallid countenance, and our Lady's suffering one. The former is so divine and noble that the latter, despite its fine delicacy, would appear almost coarse beside it, were it not for the artist's perfect distribution of light and shade."

I give these opinions not in any spirit of pride (for you will have noted the first opinion's reflection on my " greatness "!) but simply to note how my ideal, my *quest for beauty* came to be realised, however humbly and obscurely. For that has been the theme of these rambling pages.

One Sunday afternoon in August, I came home from an excursion to find the populace in a tumult. Archduke Ferdinand had been assassinated! A shudder seemed to shake all Vienna, for he had been Austria's fairest hope, and now the future held only blackness and anxiety. He who alone could have restored stability and order in the land, and have instilled life and activity again, was now snatched from them. What would happen next — *war?* Four weeks later the World War burst upon the world, like a terrible, fateful explosion. It was only the echo, tremendously magnified, of the bomb of Sarajevo.

CHAPTER FIFTEEN

THE WAR AND AFTER

BY a singular coincidence, the period of distress and turmoil, ushered in by the World War, marked also the end of my spiritual strugglings. My quest was over: peace reigned in my soul at last, and artistically I had matured. It was high time, as I had reached my forty-seventh year. When a man attains that age, he has a right to expect the seeds he has planted and nurtured with such anxious care, such patient toiling, to bear some fruit. How did I know that my strivings were happily ended? Simply by my conviction, as certain as it was sweet, that I had at last created something that was both a true and a worthy expression of myself, and a source of joy and holy inspiration to others. Thus had I in some measure justified my existence, both as a monk and an artist.

Little remains to be recorded of my life. Since the end of the year 1914 to the present date (1931) I have left my beloved Beuron only once for any length of time, and then only because of a weakness in my lungs, which made me take a rest-cure from November, 1916, until Easter, 1917. My brush was completely idle for a period of nearly ten years, during which (1915–1924) the universal distress made it impossible for me to fulfill any commissions, and I devoted myself instead to the task of writing my memoirs, at the insistence of many friends. It was completed in 1917;

and the following year I translated Ruysbroeck's *Das Reich der Geliebten* (*The Kingdom of God's Lovers*) from the Flemish into German, as a festal gift for our new Arch-abbot, Dom Raphael Walzer. He had just been elected to succeed Archabbot Ildephonse Schober, who had been forced to resign because of ill health. This translation was not published however until 1924, along with two other of Ruysbroeck's works which I had revised: *Die Zierde der Geistlichen Hochzeit* (*The Adornment of the Spiritual Marriage*), and *Das Buch von den Zwoelf Beguinen* (*The Book of the Twelve Beguines*). During this period also I acted as Guest-Master in the monastery, which, along with my literary efforts, kept me exceedingly busy. But I did not mind, as I was thus able to keep up contact with many of my friends, and at the same time, exercise my priestly ministry in a thousand fruitful ways. As the story of my conversion was gradually becoming known, people began to visit me or write letters asking for advice, with increasing frequency. In 1924 I was allowed to visit Vienna again to undertake the decoration of a second chapel in the Carmel-ite Church, but was recalled to Beuron before I could finish, to assist in some important administrative tasks in the mon-astery. I was then given the office of Cellarer, or Treasurer and Business Manager. I held this until 1928, when my health broke down completely, shortly after I received word of the death of my dear twin brother Erich. My release from all responsibilities gave me leisure to write this long promised second volume of my memoirs, insofar as my physical condition would allow.

[272]

THE WAR AND AFTER

The war went on much longer than we had expected. Yet Beuron remained an abode of peace. Only once did we hear the roar of cannon, when the fighting took place at Hartmannsweilerkopf. Over a hundred of our community had been conscripted, twenty-one were killed. It was always a great sorrow when our funeral-bell would toll, telling us that one or other of our *Familia* had fallen in battle, or succumbed to his wounds. Then the word would be whispered from mouth to mouth, that Brother Jordan, or Frater Willigis, or Father So-and-so, had been killed; and soon we would gather in the church, to recite the *Prayers for the Dead*.

The war made our hearts heavy, as its consequences do still. Nature continued to display its glorious beauty, inviting us to be joyful and happy, but we no longer knew how, it seemed. We suffered little physical privation, as Southern Germany was not affected by the scarcity of food which prevailed in the more densely populated regions of the North. This brought many northerners down to us, and many of them admitted that in the more Catholic regions especially, we had preserved portions of German culture that were no longer to be found in their section.

But the war brought about an unmistakable quickening of religious life. More pilgrims than ever came to Beuron, and we were continually taxed to care for their demands on us, in the confessional and in the parlor. Many were the heart-breaking tales we heard. " Father, we had but one son, our only child," some poor mother would say. " He

[273]

was killed in battle. Our whole life was lived for him; now he is dead, and there is nothing more to live for. What shall we do? " Or this: " Father, now our third son has been killed in battle. The last one is still in the army, at the front. I am completely broken; and cannot even pray any more."

How infinitely sad it was for these poor people, trying to solve such tragic situations! Their grief alone was bad enough, but when in addition one had to try to make intelligible what to them was only a mad puzzle, it was terrible. Some even thought themselves guilty of rebellion in God's sight, by their inability to resign themselves to His Will as revealed in their fate. To these, I would try to explain the difference between manifestations of merely human feeling and those of our higher will. Almost always I could get them to see that their higher spiritual faculties still remained in obedience to Him and that their deep sorrow had only made them less conscious of this. Even our Lord's heart had seemed to rebel against His Father's dispensation of suffering, there in the Garden of Gethsemane; until at long last His higher Will triumphed, and He could say: *Thy Will be done.* So they too could triumph, but it would take some time. Thus often they would take hope, and go away consoled in some measure.

When I was finishing up my chapel in Vienna-Doebling, I used often to say Mass on Sunday in a neighbouring hospital, the *Rudolfinum.* As soon as war was declared, the good Sisters awaited anxiously the coming of the wounded.

[274]

THE WAR AND AFTER

For a long time, none came; but then all at once the hospital was flooded with them. One soldier who had had both legs amputated told me his tragic story. He had been wounded, and had taken refuge under a bridge, where the ambulance people had missed him; and so he had lain there for sixty-four hours. Thus his legs had been frozen. But the terrible ordeal seemed to have transfigured his soul. His face shone with a mysterious beauty, and in his voice there was no semblance of complaint, but only a soft, sweet echo of humble patience and restraint. He seemed to be most grateful for his warm clean bed, in exchange for that of the frozen soil.

One morning after Mass I was called to anoint two dying men, who had been brought in during the night. Both were in the last throes. One was gasping terribly; he had been shot in the chest, and was restless, and very sullen. The other lay motionless and apparently unconscious; and so, after the surgeon had done all he could for him, I began to give him the Sacrament of Extreme Unction. After reciting some short prayers slowly and distinctly, in case he should be able to hear them after all, I then proceeded with the sacred rite, making little crosses with my thumb, dipped in the holy oil, upon his eyes, ears, nostrils, mouth, hands, and feet. His fine face however remained oblivious to what was going on. Then all of a sudden, when I had finished, and two nuns were reciting the *Prayers for the Dying,* we saw his right hand lift slowly up, and touching his forehead, move down to touch his shoulders and breast, in a solemn *sign of the cross!* We were astounded, and looked at one

[275]

another aghast, as though we had seen a miracle, a dead man come to life. The dying man fell back again into the coma from which he was never to rouse again; but he had made that holy sign, telling us that he knew, and was prepared for what was to come. When I returned again three days later he had passed away; but his companion still lingered, and to my astonishment had also become sweetly and submissively resigned to his fate. The passing of his comrade, and the near approach of his own death, had made him humble.

Towards the end of the first year of the war, I began writing the story of my conversion. I did not have much leisure, but made it a point to write at least one paragraph each day. Monastic life is by no means a succession of peaceful quiet hours, for with the exacting choir-duties, the daily administrative or manual work, the monk has comparatively little free time. Still less has he who must attend to the parish work, or to the guests. But during the winter months, when Beuron is bedded in snow, fewer people come; and as it grows dark quite early, many are the blissful hours the monk can spend in his cell. It seems as though the peace of heaven itself has descended there, so quiet and hushed everything is. It is as though the world had receded to a very great distance, and that one was hidden in the middle of a deep forest, where all is dark and mysterious.

The objects in the room seem each to have its own personality, as they gleam softly in the light of the reading lamp on my desk. The wardrobe, the plain bed, the prie-dieu, and the huge cockle-stove; the statue of Madonna and Child with its wreath of dried flowers, and over it the Crucifix, with our Lord's arms extended towards me. The table with its portfolios, books, and letters, and several excellent picture-postcards representing some grand *chef-d'oeuvre* of the Creator, or of some inspired artist. These cards must be changed from time to time, so that the eye does not become weary, but experiences ever new joys on seeing these pretty reminders. Such evenings often brought new inspiration, as when one delved into a choice book, noting the patient dexterity with which the author carved out his euphonious sentences and paragraphs. One would then give a final touch to what had been written before, experiencing sweet feelings of relief at this clear and complete expression of one's inmost thoughts.

In writing, I aimed only at simplicity of style, trying at the same time to observe the laws of logic, rhythm, and sound. With an almost painful exactitude and frankness, I related the events of my life, avoiding all frills of speech. I always tried to complete what I wanted to say at once, having found out by my experience in painting that it is better to finish what one can on the spot, than to make rough sketches which must be filled in later. My decision to write in German kept me from falling into routine methods and hackneyed terms, which could not have been avoided so easily had I written in my mother tongue. By degrees I acquired a more limpid style, which showed itself towards the end of my book.

I am indebted to Hermann Bahr for the title: *Die Un-*

ruhe zu Gott.[1] He had read the early portion of my manuscript, and made the following entry into his journal which he later published in the *Neue Wiener Journal:*

"*Beuron, Oct. 13, 1917.* Father Willibrord Verkade, who painted the beautiful fresco in the Carmelite Church at Doebling, has given me the story of his conversion to read. It ranks far above the usual run of these accounts, which generally seem based on some disappointment, or feelings of disgust and frustration. But here we see a hale and hearty youth who at no time turns to bitterness, but is always enamoured of life, abounding with enthusiasm for it. A tall easy-going Hollander, towering head above ordinary mortals, his eyes sparkling with animation, he attacks the problems of art with a vigour and a surety that befits both his youth, and his exceptional talent. But to this man, solidly rooted in the world as he was, and possessed of all that life could give, came at long last a mysterious restlessness. He was not dissatisfied with himself, for failure had not yet come to him, nor had disillusionment spoiled the beauty of his fair ideals; and yet vague feelings of unrest, strange longings that he could as yet but dimly fathom, began to possess his soul. Gradually, imperceptibly, they led him into the Catholic Church, and the monastic cloister. . . . His is a case where no one can say patronisingly: ' After all, there was nothing left for him to do; whereas with me, things are far from that.' Even the most worldly-minded will be made to reflect on reading these pages, for they

[1] Literally: "The Unrest for God." English title: "Yesterdays of an Artist-Monk." (New York: P. J. Kenedy & Sons.)

show strikingly how true it is that there is real happiness to be found in life, above the merely human and sensual. Perhaps they will cause others too, to experience the felicity of the *Unrest for God!* . . . No other modern book has made me so clearly conscious of the profound happiness and consoling atmosphere of the Catholic Faith. . . . It is like a Mass by Haydn."

In contrast to this encomium, a certain Herr Molert wrote the following appreciation of my conversion in the *Theologische Literaturzeitung* (1922): " Verkade, the son of a Dutch Mennonite merchant, had during his youth never troubled himself about religious questions, and had never been baptised. Having qualified as an artist in his native country, he went to Paris and mingled with the circle of the Symbolists there. Then he went to Brittany where he became a Catholic, and ended up by joining the Benedictine Order where he still remains, after wanting at first to be a Franciscan (*sic*). A convert friend of mine considers this account the best of its kind in recent years; but for my part, I see nothing of special interest in it. For Verkade had never learned sufficiently what Protestantism consists in. Catholicism has a strong appeal to people who arrive at faith after a life of religious indifference, and to artists above all; but Verkade scarcely touched upon the rational difficulties inherent in the Catholic system, and hence his story will have no persuasion for those of a less naïve cast of mind. At best, the book is an interesting description of life in many countries, written by a candid and congenial observer, who is however hardly an outstand-

[279]

ing personality (outside his art, of which I am unable to judge, save that it seems to afford little in the way of instruction for the ordinary layman)."

I quote this review because it emphasises what does seem to me to have been an unusual feature in my conversion, *viz.* my lack of acquaintance with Protestant beliefs, and my failure to delve deeply into the " difficulties " presented by the Catholic system. But why complain? Is it not true that many others who did know Protestantism thoroughly, and investigated the " difficulties " of Catholicism just as thoroughly, ultimately became Catholics? Why should it not have been the same with me, had I taken the trouble? I certainly had to come across those same " difficulties " eventually, and yet I remained a convinced Catholic in spite of them.

No; the decisive step must be taken in the darkness of faith, not in the light of cold calculating reason; whatever the road may be that leads us to the Church. We say *yes* always because we love, however aware we may be of the possibilities of disillusionment. In the process of conversion it is of course not always clear just when this *yes* has been pronounced.

I have never regretted becoming a Catholic: I have been very happy in the Church, and in my order. True, I had a talent for being happy, with my carefree Dutch nature, and my easy-going, rough-and-ready ways. My spiritual digestion had never been spoiled by exotic sectarian diets, so that its natural powers of assimilating what is generally true and beautiful have always been able to function normally. Perhaps I owe an additional debt of gratitude to my Protestant ancestry, as Protestantism engenders a spirit of greater liberty, in a sense, than does Catholicism. But liberty alone does not make one happy: only the right use of it.

To what must the success of my *Unruhe zu Gott* be attributed? Including the translations into foreign languages, more than fifty thousand copies have now (1931) been sold, and it is still in great demand. I believe this is due to two factors: its publication at a time when people were more interested in serious reading than ever before, due to the horrors of the war, and had an especial liking for books about conversion; and then, it was an account written when I was in the prime of life, and could look back upon my early years with a true perspective that carried an especial appeal. Certainly my book would have been a failure had it appeared ten years or so earlier.

And so it came to pass that a writer with nothing outstanding to recommend him at all met with success just because he happened to profit by the psychological moment. When I finished the book I felt immensely relieved; for besides being able to look upon a hard task completed, I was now as it were *released* from the past. It is always detrimental to the soul's progress to live so exclusively in the past, as becomes necessary when writing a book of memoirs. I have experienced the same feeling while writing this second volume. But love demands self-sacrifice when the çause is just, so I am not apprehensive over what the cost may be.

My editions of Ruysbroeck's writings during this period

were, on the other hand, of the greatest personal benefit to me, although they were far from becoming best sellers. Translating deep mystical treatises like these is a task most beneficial to the monk; it goes well with his prayers. He need not step down from his contemplation of God's presence, and can be interrupted at odd times during the day, without serious detriment. Happy the monk to whom such a task is a labour of love, to which he hastily returns whenever other duties no longer call him away.

I had first come across Ruysbroeck's works in 1891, when I was staying in Brittany. Mogens Ballin had with him a translation of *The Adornment of the Spiritual Marriage,* (which is Ruysbroeck's best work, in my opinion), made by Maeterlinck. I dipped into it only occasionally however, and without great comprehension; and yet sometimes it thrilled and uplifted me. But I made little of my failure to understand it, as Maeterlinck's *Preface* had already warned me to expect something outlandish, if at times sublime. The author, he said, united in himself the ignorance of an infant and the wisdom of a soul risen from the dead, mixing childish nonsense with pages that reminded one of Plato. He was like a wild eagle, soaring crazily over snow-clad mountains, and so on. I never became really interested in the great Flemish mystic, until the year 1917, when, on a visit to Holland in connection with a peace mission, I came across a new edition being brought out in modern Dutch. I read the *Adornment* with greater penetration, and, at the same time, felt the same mysterious *uplifting* that I had experienced twenty-six years before. I thus became a devoted disciple of Blessed Jan Ruysbroeck, and have so remained.

And I now see clearly how erroneous was Maeterlinck's appraisal. A wild eagle, a stammering child, a theatrical performer, forsooth! An eagle, perhaps, if by that is meant one who can gaze unflinchingly into the dazzling splendour of the sun; but a foolish, vain, illogical child, never. I have never met a work more beautifully and harmoniously constructed than the *Adornment;* and I well agree with Lambert's comparison of it to a majestic Gothic cathedral. True, many of the topics treated are deep and abstruse, but they are handled with such lucidity and conciseness that they cannot fail to enlighten all who truly seek spiritual perfection.

Ruysbroeck gives one a deeper insight into the mystical life than many other writers, by this emphasis upon objective realities rather than subjective states. He is not inclined to record many personal experiences, nor to become effusive and to digress, as does for instance, St. Teresa of Avila. Thus he is a valuable preceptor for all who aspire to the heights of mystical union with God; and though there may be few indeed who actually attain those heights, it is none the less a joy to learn from him, what blessings await them, be it in this world or in the next.

My term as Guest-Master in Beuron brought with it many opportunities for self-advancement, both spiritually and intellectually. The proverbial hospitality to all comers, which the Rule enjoins, has to be carried out in practice chiefly by this official; so it devolved upon me to see that

" all the guests that come were welcomed as Christ Himself " (Ch. 53). No one could be turned away; the poorest
beggar always received his bowl of soup and slice of bread
at the Porter's office, and if he wished, a place to sleep for
the night; while the continual stream of pilgrims and
strangers who desired lodgings with us, or at least an opportunity to view the cloisters, kept one busy constantly.
And then there were the special cases of people who wanted
a closer insight into our life with a view to conversion, or
to joining us, or perhaps to understanding better the *Opus
Dei:* the Liturgy of the Church, which it is our privilege
to perform each day with full solemnity.

Each guest (and we often had over eighty at once) must
be welcomed, assigned a room and place at table, given
books to read if he desires, escorted to the various functions
in church, shown around the monastery; and in addition,
one must evince a readiness to help him in any particular
problems he may wish to talk about. All this demands a
great amount of self-sacrifice in the Guest-Master, if he is
to fulfill his task adequately and with success; but it brings
on the other hand a constant enrichment of his own character. And there are always interesting personages coming
to Beuron: writers, philosophers, great pulpit-orators, musicians, famous converts, and other notable characters, who
never fail to stimulate the mind and broaden the outlook
of him whose duty it is to look after their wants.

And then, there are the swindlers! Even the sacred precincts of the monastery are not proof against their artful
devices; and the Guest-Master usually can count on having

at least one per annum to deal with. I do not refer to the ordinary man with a " hard luck story " who comes begging for assistance. Usually we prefer to treat them as genuine cases of distress, as it saves time and trouble, and avoids the possibility of turning away some really deserving case. But now and then we did have people who got themselves admitted as guests on one pretext or another, and then at the opportune moment commenced their fraudulent operations. But with a little experience and watchfulness, one can usually detect them before much damage has been done; and then it becomes necessary to turn them out, firmly and uncompromisingly, though with charity.

What an abode of peace and light is the Benedictine monastery for all kinds of souls! Rich and poor, intelligent and illiterate, strong and weak, all meet there in a brotherhood of faith and charity, to drink together from the Well-spring of Eternal Life. An institution, indeed, whose origins reach back into a hoary antiquity; but for all that, one that seems still able to meet the most pressing needs of modern life. At no period in Christian history have we witnessed more spiritual suffering than we do today, and I can think of no more apposite remedy for the morbidity, the doubt, the mental anguish afflicting the minds of so many thousands than that found within the monastic *milieu*. The mysteries of God daily celebrated with a decorum and an ardent uncompromising faith that cannot fail to impress the most hardened onlooker, the spectacle of divers characters living and working together in an harmonious fellowship which yet leaves room for the development of individual talents, the example of an unremitting devotion to God's concerns in preference to those of the world and of the flesh, what a lesson for the people of our day!

My enforced neglect of painting from 1915 to 1924 caused me some pangs at times, but I was able to suppress them; and when at last the opportunity came for me to create again, I seized it with an even greater joy. It came none too soon, for I had come to a kind of deadlock again in my spiritual life. It was as though a part of me had fallen ill, due to lack of exercise; and no other sort of labour could galvanise me into proper action any more. The Carmelite Fathers in Vienna asked me to do another chapel in their church, dedicated this time to their spiritual mother, St. Teresa of Avila. Father John of the Cross, one of their number, had finally collected enough money to erect it, and the architect Kathrein had agreed to superintend the construction.

So I went to work, choosing this time a *Transfiguration* scene as my motif. In the centre I placed the glorified Saviour, and on either side of Him the prophets Elias (whom the Carmelites venerate as their father) and Moses. Next to them I put three great Carmelite women-saints, all named Teresa; the one of Avila, the "Little Flower" of Lisieux, and another who was martyred during the French Revolution. I knew quite well that I could not hope to equal the dramatic power of my *Descent from the Cross* in this picture, but I did my level best, and in the end, the result seemed to please everyone. The golden background and subdued colours are especially effective in the soft light of early evening, or at dawn when the candles are lighted on the marble altar.

My recall to Beuron forced me to leave the work unfinished, as I have mentioned already; but in 1927 I was able to return to Vienna, where I spent two more months putting on the finishing touches. All told, I had spent about two years with the good Carmelite Fathers, and although their patience must have been sorely tried at times with my demands, they always showed the utmost courtesy and willingness to coöperate, for which I am sincerely grateful. Their monastery is a true oasis in that tumultuous city, and a popular rendezvous for many tired souls; who find in the lovely church, peace and solace in prayerful communion with our Lord and His blessed Mother.

I am nearly finished, and only wish to devote a few lines before closing to what may interest many readers, namely the business side of monastic life. As I have stated, the office of Cellarer was given to me for some years, and I had therefore much to do with the administration of material affairs in our large Archabbey. I had several assistant functionaries, all of whom are provided for in the Rule. The Procurator is the bookkeeper, and does all the ordering. The Father Depositary has charge of distributing such articles of general use as paper, ink, pens, glue, soap, and so forth. The Vestiarius looks after the clothing of the monks; the Kitchen-Master is responsible for the preparation and serving of the meals; the Econome superintends the farm and live-stock. The Brother-Gardener attends to

[287]

the flowers and shrubs, the House-Master to the assignment of cells, and the general cleanliness and upkeep of the house, while the Father Infirmarian is in charge of the sick and aged, and the Almoner looks after the poor and the distribution of alms.

Each of these officials has his subordinates, usually lay-brothers, whose work he is responsible for. This well-defined organization simplifies the Cellarer's task, but in the end he is responsible for everything, as all the various branches are united in him. No official is allowed in Beuron to have any cash of his own, no more than the Fathers or lay-brethren. Even the smallest sum has to be issued by the Cellarer, after permission from the Abbot has been obtained; and if a monk goes away on a journey, he is required to turn in whatever money he has remaining, immediately after his return. Thus the Cellarer is able to keep a constant check upon his accounts, and balances the cost and yield of each separate department at the end of every month.

This leads to the question: " Are monasteries rich? " If our large and flourishing Archabbey of Beuron can be taken as any criterion, I can answer with an unhesitating and emphatic "No." Most such large institutions are incumbered with heavy debts, usually secured by their real estate, which scarcely ever can be maintained at a profit. Whatever comes in from the various works of the monks enables them to live; and the monastery can probably save a little towards paying off debts or for future expansion, if all is carefully administered. The most rigid economy and simplicity of life is of course observed, since each monk works for the love of God only, and is satisfied with the mere necessities of life. Sometimes a monk on entering the monastery brings a considerable fortune with him; but these cases are few and far between. In fine, there is no "profit" in running a monastic foundation; and even if the income would so far exceed overhead and other expense as to create a profit, this would soon be dissipated in other projects and activities. For there can be no profit without the "profit-motive"; and there is no room for the latter in an institution which exists solely *Ut in omnius glorificetur Deus* ("To glorify God in all things").

And now, I am growing old. Most of my friends who appear in the *Yesterdays* have passed away. But beautiful memories of them still console my heart. Especially edifying is the account I received from Mogens Ballin of his wife's death. She bore him five children, and as her end approached each one was brought in, one after the other, to say good-bye. The eldest, who had been named *Jan* after me, said to his mother: "Mamma, when you see God, give Him my love." Ballin was plunged into a deep dejection for a long time afterwards, and when I wrote him a letter of gentle remonstrance, he replied in part: "Do not try to lead me from my path of sorrow, for it is *my* path. You and I are of very different dispositions, and what applies to you does not necessarily apply to me. . . . I will find serenity and resignation in time, do not fear. Meanwhile, let me bear my cross. . . ."

IN QUEST OF BEAUTY

It seemed that my well-intentioned interference in his mourning was as unwelcome as if I had disturbed a happy celebration. The terrible shock of separation from his noble wife had changed his whole attitude toward life. Giving up his studio, he devoted his entire energies thenceforth to the education of his children, and to the interests of the Catholic Church in Denmark. He was especially instrumental in the founding of a large Catholic public school. He died after a short illness in January, 1914, fully resigned and prepared. His aged mother was at his bedside, together with a Jesuit Father; and while the latter recited the Psalms in Latin, his mother said them in Hebrew.

Old age does not seem to have impaired my mental strength, though physically I am weakening. Consequently the desire and impulse to live is less strong. The days come more frequently now when one is inclined to reflect: " What a good thing it is not to live to be a hundred years old." And yet there are moments still when one feels as sprightly as a young colt, and is moved to make far-reaching plans, in spite of snow-white hair, falling teeth, gradual diminution of sight and hearing. More impressive than ever are the words of the Gospel: " Let your loins be girt, and lamps burning in your hands. Be you then also ready, for at what hour you think not, the Son of Man will come." But the fear of Judgment is tempered by an eager expectation to see what mortal eye has never beheld, to hear what ear has never heard . . . and one rejoices at being old. . . .

THE WAR AND AFTER

Like all old men, whose weakness requires the careful husbanding of energy, I have become resigned to a life of comparative inaction, restricting myself to the most indispensable forms of physical effort. I still delight in watching the lively actions of others: children waxing vigorous by means of sport and games, older people doing hard work such as digging, hammering, carrying heavy loads. Proximity to them brings a pleasurable feeling of participation still in life, and one is content with the privilege of being just an onlooker.

To grow old happily means learning how to disappear and withdraw oneself gradually from the scene of life, and at the same time, consciously and resolutely surrendering oneself to the designs of a higher Power. It is as though the soul steals away softly, carrying with it the treasures of knowledge dearly purchased, into a solitude where only God and Self are, where only the Essential, the Absolute, have meaning, and all that is empty and vain are refused admittance — a safe harbour with one's Lord and Creator, after a perilous voyage.

I have written this book because I was moved by an imperious urging to depict the experiences of my inner and outer life in a series of clear-cut descriptions, in the hope that hearts and minds similar to my own might thereby find sustenance and comfort. At the same time, I wanted to improve myself by expressing regret for my faults and failures, thankfulness for God's graces and mercies to me; and thus perchance to induce others to repent and give thanks with me.

IN QUEST OF BEAUTY

I wanted finally my advanced age to light up clearly once more before its end, just as a candle will often do, giving out one last bright blaze while the wick is burning low.

The Feast of St. Jerome, September 30, 1931.